CETA: *Politics and Policy, 1973–1982*

C·E·T·A
Politics and Policy
1973–1982

GRACE A. FRANKLIN
RANDALL B. RIPLEY

The University of Tennessee Press

KNOXVILLE

Library of Congress Cataloging in Publication Data

Franklin, Grace A.
CETA : politics and policy, 1973–1982.
Bibliography: p.
Includes index.
1. Manpower policy—United States.   I. Ripley, Randall B.
II. Title.
HD5724.F725   1984   331.11'0973   84-5145
ISBN 0-87049-437-6

Contents

207073

Tables and Figures

Tables

Appendix Tables

Figures

Preface

THIS BOOK IS A POLICY ANALYSIS of a major public program in the United States that operated between July 1, 1974, and September 30, 1983. The analysis reflects the concerns of a pair of political scientists, as well as their participation in a great deal of original research on that program during its entire life. The literature of politics and policy contains few program analyses that follow a major program from its inception to its termination. This book represents one of the few exceptions to that generalization.

The Comprehensive Employment and Training Act (CETA) was signed into law near the end of 1973 and replaced previous employment and training programs on July 1, 1974. CETA was really multiple programs since the Act had many titles and because it was amended frequently both legislatively and administratively. CETA vanished as a concept on October 1, 1983, when the Job Training Partnership Act (JTPA) was formally implemented. The period from 1973 through 1982 provides us with the program data that we discuss in this book.

In this analysis of CETA we were able to undertake a series of tasks simultaneously:

★ We examine CETA in and of itself as a major program that existed for over nine years. Such an opportunity for political scientists who are interested in policy analysis is rare.

* CETA, although complete in a formal sense, also had programmatic roots in the decade preceding it and has been replaced by a program that changes some of its major features but still resembles it. Thus our analysis of CETA from 1974 through 1982 is set in the context of its predecessors since 1962 and its successor in the 1980s. Consequently the analysis is not of a single dead and forgotten federal effort but of one major federal effort that was both preceded and succeeded by related major federal efforts.

* CETA was one of five major domestic programs loosely labeled "block grants" that emerged between 1966 and 1975. We compare CETA to the other four programs to see what important common patterns were observed.

* We analyze CETA in light of what is known generally about the politics surrounding virtually all domestic policies in the United States.

CETA was a major public program. About $55 billion from the federal treasury was spent on it from its inception to its replacement by JTPA. Millions of people were served as "clients" (or "participants" or "beneficiaries") each year by CETA programs.

Modern employment and training policies and programs from the federal government were initiated by the Manpower Development and Training Act (MDTA) in 1962. CETA succeeded MDTA in 1974. And CETA was in turn succeeded by JTPA in 1983. CETA occupied a critical middle position both chronologically and administratively between efforts that were managed primarily from the federal level (MDTA) and those under JTPA that have been delegated basically to states, localities, and the private sector with minimal federal participation (except, of course, through the presumably benign function of providing the cash).

CETA was, in many ways, a dream come true for social scientists, including those of us who study politics, because it set up a long-term program, created a natural comparative framework between different localities, mandated an extensive central bank of quantitative data, provided research money, and was overseen by a Department of Labor (DOL) that, from 1974 until early 1981, actively funded a rich variety of research. DOL wanted to hear about results of research and at least ponder incorporating some of the implications of those results in subsequent legislative and administrative actions.

CETA gave economists the opportunity to learn a great deal about the function of specialized, targeted training in the labor market. It was also an opportunity for political scientists who wanted to explore empirically a number of major themes with data that were comparable both over time (longitudinal, as the jargon would have it) and between different geographical areas responsible for implementing and administering the program. These themes included implementation itself as the overarching concern and the more specific themes of the nature of the impact of federalism on programs, "citizen participation" in the form of mandated advisory councils or councils with the power of concurrence, the functioning of local political and governmental systems to produce decisions about organization as well as allocations, and the meaning of public-private "partnership" in concrete terms. Inevitably and properly both economists and political scientists joined in asking questions about a final theme: results for participants. Also inevitably and properly the two different groups of social scientists pursued partially different goals. Political scientists were eager to explain why services looked the way they did and why the body of clients was constituted as it was. In short, they explained results largely in political terms. Economists often ignored political factors in decision-making. They treated them as happening in a "black box" in which they had no particular professional interest. They were, instead, intent on explaining (in a statistical sense) placement rates and wage gains (economic features of results) in terms of type of training offered, while controlling for type of client in terms of gender, previous work history, race, and other demographic and labor force variables.

The natural attractiveness of CETA as a subject for extensive study and the simultaneous availability of money to support research helped scholars produce a burgeoning empirical literature during the 1970s and up to 1981, when both money and the desire to learn from research dried up in DOL. Naturally, the quality of the outpouring of research results is mixed. A fair amount of even the best work does not address political aspects of the functioning of the program and so is of little immediate use in this volume. In what follows we mine a considerable portion—but not all—of the diverse literature on CETA produced during its lifetime. Centrally, we rely on a good deal of original research that we conducted over the period. Our focus in assembling these varied data is primarily on the portions of CETA dealing with training and employability development. We address public service employment only occasionally.

In five instances from 1974 through 1981 we served as Director and Associate Director of major projects evaluating different aspects of CETA implementation. In all cases the major funding was provided by the Employment and Training Administration of the U.S. Department of Labor. Less funding, but major support, was provided in all five cases by the Mershon Center of the Ohio State University. In one of the five cases additional funding for the research was provided by the State of Ohio. A few relevant details on those five projects will appear in appropriate places as our analysis proceeds. When we report results from this original work we focus on the themes outlined above. Our concern in this book is to look at the original research both as a cluster of work covering central aspects of a major program throughout its life and in the context of research done by others. In short, we want to extract the broadest meaning from our unique opportunity to study all principal aspects of a program for many years. Thus, we will frame general arguments and make general assertions in the pages that follow. But those arguments and assertions will be firmly based on the analysis of a very large data base, much of it original with the projects we directed.

In addition to the five core projects for which we led a group of colleagues in major data-collection and analytical efforts we also served as research associates ourselves in nine additional projects during the same period (we both served in two projects and the others were unique to one or the other of us). In addition to providing us with enormous first-hand analytical experience in looking at the politics of employment and training, work on these fourteen different projects over a nine-year period also provided us with an immense amount of field experience. We personally conducted a few thousand interviews with knowledgeable people in Washington (DOL and interest groups), five of the ten federal regional offices, and 33 different localities (with three of those localities being state operations). Some sites we covered together; more we covered separately. A few interviews we conducted together; many more we conducted separately.

Our data base for the analysis that follows is large and complex. In our original work we have had access to thousands of interviews, both those conducted personally and those conducted by our colleagues in the five projects we directed. We also collected and analyzed reams of documents at all territorial levels in those projects. We have had general and generous access to the major data bank maintained by DOL in timely and conscientious fashion through Fiscal Year 1981 (September 30, 1981). And we sat in and observed many meetings dealing with employment and training all over the country.

Numerous other studies on CETA we have used base their conclusions on similar kinds of data (although our interview data base is unique in the entire area of employment and training) and on additional information on more strictly economic variables such as wage gain for individuals receiving services. We use this literature selectively by employing the criteria of both quality and relevance to our central, political concerns.

Political scientists undertaking this kind of policy research are still not numerous. Pioneers in looking at the rich politics of the employment and training arena were Roger Davidson, now of the Congressional Research Service, Peter Kobrak of Western Michigan University, and Erwin Hargrove of Vanderbilt University. A number of our colleagues in the projects centered at Ohio State have moved elsewhere and made major marks of their own in the area. These include, so far, Carl Van Horn of the Eagleton Institute of Rutgers University, Donald Baumer of Smith College, Mary Marvel of the School of Public Administration at Ohio State, and Lance deHaven-Smith of Florida Atlantic University. Other colleagues such as Charles Jones at the

University of Virginia have worked in analogous ways in other policy areas (air pollution in his case, with a splendid book as the major result). A few economists have also made major assessments of political factors in their work on employment and training. Central among these are Sar Levitan of George Washington University and Garth Mangum of the University of Utah. The references attest to our various intellectual debts to others in addition to these key figures.

We wish the literature contained more comparable comprehensive studies of other programs. We have used comparison where we thought it provided insight. Unfortunately, there are not many genuinely comparable studies. We suspect that is both because this kind of comprehensive program analysis is a fairly new form of inquiry in the social sciences and because the financial resources are rarely available to social scientists to undertake this type of research, which is very costly.

In the book that follows we have organized the chapters as follows. Chapter 1 deals with the background, emergence, and evolution of CETA and provides framework for our analysis. Although the book is not intended to be a comprehensive history of CETA, we offer enough history to make the analysis of selected topics comprehensible. Chapter 2 explores in some detail the first few years of the transition to CETA at the local level.

Chapter 3 focuses on local program management and Chapter 4 extends that analysis by concentrating on planning, used in a broad sense, as one critical local variable that helps determine the nature and results of programs. Chapter 5 examines the relationship between CETA and the private sector, particularly in the case of a separate title (VII) aimed at enlisting participation of the private sector. In Chapter 6 we assess the politics of federalism throughout the whole CETA period, concentrating especially on the role of the federal government, both through DOL at the national and regional levels, and through the almost constant intervention of Congress.

Finally, in Chapter 7, we assess the importance of CETA. First, we summarize the broadest general observations from the preceding chapters. Second, we present a summary of what we learned about CETA's accomplishments, broadly conceived. Third, we relate the patterns found in the analysis of CETA to the broad features of domestic politics and programs in the United States.

The theme of *implementation* pervades all chapters. We deal with some aspects of *federalism* in Chapter 2 and focus exclusively on federalism in Chapter 6. The role of mandated *councils* receives considerable attention in Chapter 2, Chapter 3, and especially Chapter 5. The *politics of local decision-making*—both organizational and allocative—occupy us throughout Chapters 2, 3, 4, and 5. We concentrate on the *public-private relationship* in Chapter 5. Treatments of several layers of *program results* appear in Chapters 2, 3, 4, and 5 and, in somewhat different form, in Chapter 6. And Chapter 7 gives us the opportunity to treat all of the major substantive and analytical themes in the book one final time.

Although there have been many studies of different aspects of CETA, ours were the only ones that both continued throughout the period and systematically tried to explain the changes and variations that were observed. Virtually all other studies were primarily descriptive rather than analytic, and most dealt with only a short period of time. The few other longitudinal studies offered primarily elaborate description and some insights. Our original research provides the major empirical material in Chapters 2 through 5. Observations from other studies are summarized where appropriate. But the central point of this book, as well as of our research from the beginning, is to analyze the relationships of variables in order to explain changing policy results. We also seek, however, to go beyond the data to comment on broader patterns, and we select data only on the points we consider most important. Not wanting technical matters of methodology to intrude on our presentation of the substantive analysis, we have relegated those we thought essential to include to footnotes and, more often, to the appendices.

We make no apology for presenting considerable data and careful analysis of those data because we are not just guessing about reality but have solid information to support our conclusions. However, we want the reader to remember the substantive parts of our analysis—especially the broader meaning of what we have observed—rather than the details of the data themselves.

Acknowledgments

We owe several intellectual debts beside the ones we have already acknowledged. These are to the reviewers of both the prospectus and especially the manuscript for the University of Tennessee Press: Erwin Hargrove, Vanderbilt University; Donald F. Kettl, University of Virginia; Marian Lief Palley, University of Delaware; Paul Schulman, Mills College; and Anne Hopkins and Tom Ungs, University of Tennessee at Knoxville; to Howard Rosen, retired from the U.S. Employment and Training Administration; and to Seymour Brandwein of the Employment and Training Administration. Rosen and Brandwein were thoughtful critics of our work as well as heads of the units in ETA that provided the major financial support for it. We are also grateful to two successive Directors of the Mershon Center at Ohio State University, Richard Snyder and Charles Hermann, for their unwavering and substantial support of and interest in our work.

The acquisitions editor at the University of Tennessee Press, Mavis Bryant, was consistently helpful and supportive, as was Katherine Holloway, the senior editor at Tennessee who worked with us on this book. Bettie Mason provided a thorough and much appreciated editing of the manuscript.

Our numerous colleagues on the various research projects mentioned above both helped with data collection and provided a number of analytical insights over the years. Finally, we are especially indebted and grateful to the thousands of men and women who took time out of their busy and often hectic schedules to talk with us and our colleagues about what they were doing as they struggled to make CETA work.

CETA: *Politics and Policy, 1973–1982*

CHAPTER ONE

★

CETA: *Programmatic Overview and Analytic Preview*

 MODERN WESTERN SOCIETIES HAVE APPROACHED THE CHALLENGE of preparing their populations for the needs of the labor market in different ways. Some have not dealt with the issue at all. Others have attempted to achieve a rational allocation of resources to meet future labor needs and to prevent the growth of large numbers of unemployed and unemployable people. These societies have generally used centralized planning and implementation involving some combination of the government, business, and organized labor. Other societies, including our own, have consciously avoided a centralized approach, and have allowed manpower or employment and training[1] policies to emerge in piecemeal fashion. Particularly in matters affecting the functioning of privately owned businesses, the reigning ideology in the United States about the importance of "free enterprise" and of limiting governmental interference with business has inhibited comprehensive and consistent government manpower programs or employment and training efforts.

1. We use the terms "manpower" and "employment and training" interchangeably throughout this volume. "Manpower" was the standard term from the Manpower Development and Training Act of 1962 to the mid-1970s, when it was replaced by the less sexist term "employment and training."

The Comprehensive Employment and Training Act (CETA) block grant created at the end of 1973 marked the beginning of a potentially new era in manpower programs. CETA consolidated a number of previously categorical programs and transferred responsibility for planning and operating them to local elected officials.

Ten years later, on September 30, 1983, CETA ended, replaced legislatively a year earlier. During the more than nine years of CETA's life it generated a complex set of political relationships. Presidents, Secretaries of Labor, bureaucrats throughout the Department of Labor (DOL) both in Washington and in ten regional offices, mayors, county commissioners, governors, state legislatures, city councils, national interest groups, local interest groups, local agencies responsible for program delivery, and all kinds of state and local bureaucrats were involved in varying degrees and ways. Accordingly, a great deal can be learned about American politics in general by a close analysis of the functioning of this one large, complex program. Many patterns in American politics are generic, crossing the boundaries of what is at stake substantively. And, of course, every major program also generates some unique patterns and questions.

This chapter provides an introduction to and an overview of CETA. After describing the historical context from which CETA emerged, we summarize the legislative gestation of CETA and the major issues and compromises in the legislative debate over CETA. Then we briefly sketch CETA's development between 1973 and 1983, describing major new programs and funding levels. Finally, we present the analytic framework used in the remainder of the book.

CETA's Predecessors

THE NEW DEAL

Federal attention to programs for employing and training the nation's work force was negligible prior to the Great Depression of the 1930s (Clague and Kramer, 1976:1). Military manpower planning existed, of course, and a program of federal grants to states for vocational education and training had been available since 1917. But it was not until the economic collapse of the 1930s that the federal government became involved in any large-scale employment and training programs.

The principal purpose of the government's Depression-era manpower efforts was to provide work for some of the millions of unemployed. One of the Roosevelt Administration's first acts in 1933 was to set up the Civilian Conservation Corps (CCC), which recruited unemployed young men, stationed them in residential camps, and put them to work on construction and conservation projects devised by the Departments of Agriculture and the Interior. The public employment service (federally funded state agencies with local offices), also created in 1933, administered the new unemployment insurance program and provided a labor market exchange function for employers and potential employees. The Works Progress Administration (WPA), created in 1935, increased the number and size of publicly subsidized jobs and service projects. The WPA drew up and implemented plans for public service activities, such as building and repairing roads, schools, libraries, parks, or writing guidebooks, and filled these jobs with unemployed workers.

During the Depression the government only dabbled in the training portion of manpower policy. In 1937 DOL was authorized to promote the training of journeymen workers in skilled trades, but this apprenticeship program was miniscule compared to the jobs programs of the CCC and WPA.

The manpower programs of the 1930s represented significant new responsibilities for the federal government. This active economic role for government was controversial, but it won enough acceptance to be reinforced in a formal statement of policy. The 1946 Employment Act declared that government should promote maximum employment and employment opportunities using "all practicable means." President Truman hailed this Act as a signal of the federal government's commitment to "take any and all" steps needed to promote a healthy economy *(Congressional Quarterly,* 1965:348). In practice, however, the Employment Act failed to stimulate additional federal attention to employment and training policies in the next 16 years. Its provisions were not mandatory, and the political and economic conditions necessary for the creation of federal programs were not present.

PROLIFERATING PROGRAMS 1962-1973

In sharp contrast to the lack of federal attention to manpower after the Depression, the 1960s were marked by a proliferation of programs. Two major laws, the Manpower Development and Training Act (MDTA) of 1962 and the Equal Opportunity Act (EOA) of 1964 spawned a myriad of categorical programs in almost frantic succession. These programs paid a living allowance to participants while providing a variety of services— vocational training, work experience, subsidized employment in both the public and private sectors, remedial education, supportive services, and placement assistance. The various programs of the 1960s embodied two fundamentally different philosophies about how the government should attack unemployment and poverty. Some programs sought to change the individual so that he or she could fit into the social and economic system; others sought to change institutions to better accommodate the needs of individuals.

Thirteen of the principal manpower programs generated prior to CETA are described in Table 1-1. These programs—Neighborhood Youth Corps, MDTA institutional training and on-the-job training, Job Corps, Work Incentive Program, and others— had overlapping purposes, served similar client groups, and usually had separate administrative structures. The federal government was responsible for reviewing and rewarding grant applications and for monitoring performance of local program operators. Even excluding the vocational educational skills training program that operated in public schools for all students, the pre-CETA manpower programs embodied about 10,000 separate contracts between the federal government and local program operators.

Table 1-1 indicates the complexity present among just the principal pre-CETA programs. The actual degree of complexity was heightened by a number of additional programs, some small and some large that also operated in the same period. These included skills training for adults unemployed due to automation (Area Redevelopment Act, 1961), skills training for adults unemployed due to imports (Trade Expansion Act, 1962), recruiting and assistance to place minorities in apprenticeship positions (Labor Education Advancement Program), manpower projects run by the Model Cities program after 1965, and work experience and training programs for welfare recipients (prior to the Work Incentive Program). These were relatively small programs, but the Vocational Rehabilitation program run by HEW served hundreds of thousands of persons, and the remedial education program for adults authorized by EOA in 1964 assisted millions during the MDTA era.

The need for coordination among manpower programs and agencies serving the poor became increasingly apparent during the 1960s. A fearsome degree of fragmentation and rococco complexity resulted from the large number of separate programs, each with its own target groups, application procedures, funding cycles, and delivery mechanisms (Levitan and Zickler, 1974). Programs overlapped and provided redundant services. Except through trial, error, and perseverance, an applicant looking for assistance has no way of knowing what manpower resources existed in his or her community. Bureaucratic rivalry and hostility among DOL, HEW, and the Office of Economic Opportunity hampered effective provision of services to clients. There were many attempts to improve coordination during the 1960s—a presidential commission in 1964, congressional hearings in 1966, congressional amendments to the EOA in 1967, the addition of the Comprehensive Employment Program in 1968, the Cooperative Area Manpower Planning System, and a pilot demonstration Comprehensive Manpower Program that took shape in 1972–1973. But meaningful coordination required sharing and compromise among local operating agencies, and they successfully resisted giving up what they perceived to be "their" power, even after agreements had been arduously negotiated at the national level.

Why did manpower programs expand so dramatically in the 1960s after a relatively long period of federal inactivity? Several factors drew governmental attention to the area: a concern with education and manpower planning emerged after the Soviets

TABLE 1-1: *Major pre-CETA manpower programs, 1960s and 1970s*

PROGRAM NAME AND AUTHORIZING LEGISLATION	DATES OF OPERATION	GENERAL PURPOSE	ADMINISTRATIVE AGENCIES
Institutional Training (MDTA, 1962 and amendments	FY 1963–74	Vocational skills training in a classroom setting	*National:* HEW, DOL *Local:* ES, school districts, Skills Centers
On–the–job training (MDTA, 1962 and amendments)	FY 1963–74	Subsidized training in the private sector	*National:* DOL *Local:* ES
Vocational education (1917 Smith Hughes Act and Vocational Education Act amendments)	FY 1964–74[a]	Occupational skills training in the public school system	*National:* HEW *Local:* School districts
Neighborhood Youth Corps (EOA, 1964 and amendments)			
In–school	FY 1965–74	Subsidized work experience in public and nonprofit agencies	*National:* DOL *Local:* CAAs, local governments, schools, ES
Summer	same	same	same
Out–of–school	same	same	same
Job Corps (EOA, 1964 and amendments)	FY 1965–74[b]	Vocational training and basic education in a residential setting	*National:* OEO; DOL after FY 1969 *Local:* Job Corps Centers (71 in FY 1972)

Client groups targeted	Number of people served by the program	
	Average annual enrollment	Enrollment in peak fiscal year
Initially, adults unemployed because of automation; emphasis shifted to economically disadvantaged and youth by mid-1960s	126,200	177,500 (FY 1966)
In principle, same as institutional training; in practice, fewer disadvantaged and youth were served	83,700	151,000 (FY 1972)
Youth and adults in the general population; amended to include handicapped	8,674,000	13,556,000 (FY 1974)
Disadvantaged youth attending school	129,400	186,000 (FY 1972)
Disadvantaged youth during school vacation	362,500	759,900 (FY 1972)
Disadvantaged youth who dropped out of school; later included some adults	84,300	166,900 (FY 1966)
Disadvantaged youth	42,100	84,000 (FY 1967)

Abbreviations: HEW - Department of Health, Education, and Welfare; ES employment service; CAAs - community action agencies; OEO - Office of Economic Opportunity.

TABLE 1-1: *Major pre-CETA manpower programs, 1960s and 1970s*

PROGRAM NAME AND AUTHORIZING LEGISLATION	DATES OF OPERATION	GENERAL PURPOSE	ADMINISTRATIVE AGENCIES
Operation Mainstream	FY 1967–74	Subsidized employment in public and nonprofit sector jobs, especially in conservation	*National:* OEO; DOL after 1967 *Local:* CAAs
New Careers (EOA, 1966 amendments)	FY 1967–74	Subsidized employment in paraprofessional jobs in public and nonprofit agencies	*National:* OEO; DOL after 1967 *Local:* CAAs and public agencies
Job Opportunities in the Business Sector (Presidential initiative, 1968)	FY 1968–74	Subsidized training in the private for profit sector	*National:* DOL and National Alliance of Business *Local:* NAB offices
Work Incentive Program (Social Security Act amendments)	FY 1967–74	Training, work experience, support services, placement	*National:* DOL *Local:* Welfare, ES, and WIN offices
Comprehensive Employment Program (EOA, 1967 amendments)	FY 1968–74	Assembled existing local manpower programs and made them available in a single location	*National:* DOL *Local:* CAAs, local governments, program vendors (82 CEPs operated in FY 1972)
Public Employment Program (Emergency Employment Act, 1971)	FY 1972–74	Subsidized employment in public sector jobs	*National:* DOL *Local:* Elected officials in areas of high unemployment

Client Groups Targeted	Number of People Served by the Program	
	Average Annual Enrollment	Enrollment in Peak Fiscal Year
Unemployed older adults	22,500	41,900 (FY 1974)
Disadvantaged adults	20,000	65,900 (FY 1972)
Disadvantaged and unemployed adults	49,300	92,600 (FY 1971)
Recipients of AFDC (mainly minority females)	124,700	353,100 (FY 1974)
Disadvantaged adults and youth	92,900	127,000 (FY 1969)
Unemployed adults generally	224,300	268,900 (FY 1974)

[a]Vocational education programs operated before FY 1964; we are limiting our examination of enrollment to 1964–74 in order to compare to the MDTA era.
[b]Figures for FY 1965 –67 are estimates.
Sources: *Manpower Report of the President*, 1969:253; 1974:358; 1975:317 & 332; 1970:321. Ruttenberg and Gutchess, 1970; Levitan, 1973; Clague and Kramer, 1976; Levitan, Mangum, and Marshall, 1976; Mangum and Walsh, 1973; Van Horn, 1979; Levitan and Mangum, 1981; Levitan and Zickler, 1974; *Congress and the Nation*, I:1220; II:734.

launched their Sputnik satellite; increasing reliance on automation and technology led to a concern about their effects on employment; and the level of unemployment crept persistently higher after the Korean War. In addition, the poverty problem in America was discovered, as well as the link between poverty and lack of education and job skills. Finally, the civil rights movement, a national concern for equal opportunity in employment, and urban riots in the 1960s all helped to push manpower programs onto the government's agenda as part of a broad set of domestic policy concerns.

These factors served as external stimuli to turn the government's attention to job training legislation to relieve unemployment, urban unrest, and social inequality. But features inherent in the policy-making process also contributed to the proliferation of programs. Since individual members of Congress and the bureaucracy perceived problems in different ways, they advanced different solutions. Legislation and appropriations emerged from separate committees with different jurisdictions. Ardent lobbying groups pushed for programs serving their own special needs. There was no time to research or carefully evaluate alternative proposals; pilot and demonstration programs were rejected in favor of large-scale, visible programs to show that the government was attending to the problems. In short, the policy process itself promoted a piecemeal, distributive approach and impeded a comprehensive, coordinated one.

Shaping CETA: *Issues, Actors, Compromises*

THE ISSUES

Beginning in the early 1960s, Congress had adopted numerous individual manpower programs, but the possibility of comprehensive manpower legislation did not emerge until the end of the decade.[2] In 1969 and 1970 Congress devoted intense attention to manpower reform in terms of both the substance of

2. This discussion of the legislative evolution of CETA reflects three main sources: Davidson, 1972; Van Horn, 1979; and *Congressional Quarterly Almanac*, 1973.

services and programs offered and the methods by which these were organized and provided to clients. The focus on delivery of services was new, reflecting a growing concern with the effectiveness of programs added during the Great Society initiative (Davidson, 1972:70).

The legislative chronology culminating in the passage of CETA is summarized in Table 1-2. The struggle to adopt a manpower reform bill was lengthy. Although everyone involved could agree that something needed to be done to simplify programs and improve coordination, they quickly disagreed over how to simplify and coordinate. During the more than four years that manpower reform was before Congress, the principal issues that divided participants were decentralization, decategorization, special revenue sharing, and public service employment.

Decentralization involved shifting responsibility for decision-making, planning, and administration of manpower programs from the federal level to the state and local levels. The sub-issues were how much responsibility to delegate, what the federal role would be if the states and local governments received a larger role, and what the balance among states, cities, and counties would be. Decentralization raised serious questions about the ability and motivations of state and local governments to carry out programs that primarily served the disadvantaged.

Decategorization meant an end to earmarked funds for specific programs and eliminated guarantees that specific "categorical" programs would be continued. The decision to let the marketplace and local manpower needs dictate program choices caused much anguish to interest groups dependent on categorical grants for their existence and to some program proponents in Congress and the bureaucracy. It furthermore generated debate over what kind of safeguards for program operators should exist and what programs would be exempted from decategorization.

Special revenue sharing for manpower entailed consolidating numerous categorical grants into a single block grant allocated directly to the state and local governments. Those governments would have the flexibility to decide how to spend the funds for

TABLE 1-2: *Legislative chronology of manpower program reform, 1969–1973*

YEAR	ACTION
1969	Comprehensive manpower legislation is considered for the first time by Congress; two House bills and one Administration bill serve as the basis for the 1970 deliberations.
1970	The Senate bill is introduced. Intensive attention to multiple approaches for reform compromises is acceptable to the House, the Senate, and the Administration. Ongoing work is done in committee, on the floor, and in private sessions. Senator Nelson's bill is the main contender, and very serious efforts are made, with strong bipartisan support, to reach a workable compromise. The House and the Senate pass the bill in December, but Nixon vetoes it because it does not decategorize programs and because it includes Public Service Employment (PSE). It does decentralize administration. The veto is not overridden.
1971	Congressional attention shifts; interest in comprehensive reform flags. Nixon's new proposal on manpower revenue sharing is ignored by Congress, partially because of post-veto bitterness. Congress passes the Emergency Employment Act (EEA), a purely PSE bill, which the President signs because of rising unemployment.
1972	Congress does not act on the manpower revenue sharing proposal. MDTA is extended for one year to allow committees time to work on other manpower reform bills.
1973	Nixon begins to move to implement manpower revenue sharing administratively, without legislation, and plans to let EEA expire. The House acts to block him. The Senate and the House begin serious efforts to shape an acceptable manpower reform bill. The Administration, interest groups, and congressional Republicans and Democrats are all willing to compromise. CETA legislation is signed into law in late December.

Sources: Davidson, 1972:17–95; *Congressional Quarterly Almanac*, 1973: 346–354.

manpower programs with few or no strings attached. The federal role would be passive. This philosophy ("put the money on the stump and run") would, in its ideologically purest form, result in an abdication of federal responsibility, and was anathema to congressional liberals and federal administrators.

Publicly subsidized jobs, also known as federally funded

public service employment (PSE), involved an attempt by the government to counteract troughs in the business cycle and increases in unemployment by creating work and hiring unemployed citizens. Harking back to the WPA, it was of course opposed by congressional conservatives and President Nixon, but as unemployment steadily rose and elections neared, the pressure for adding PSE grew almost irresistible.

THE ACTORS

Major actors (participants) and the positions they supported in the debate that led to the creation of CETA are summarized in Table 1-3. Missing from the table is an entry for governors and state agencies. The states simply were not important forces in manpower reform. Agencies like the Employment Service and Vocational Education were more interested in protecting their turf than in consolidating with the manpower programs. Governors knew very little about manpower (see Levitan and Zickler, 1974:121) and cared less.

GIVE AND TAKE: THE COMPROMISES

Presidential opposition to PSE proved to be the downfall of the 1970 manpower reform bill. Whether the impression was fair or not, PSE evoked the image of dead-end, make-work jobs for many, and was an intensely divisive ideological issue (Davidson, 1972:70–71). In drafting the 1973 CETA compromise, the inclusion of PSE again met with great resistance from the President and conservative Republicans. But compromises were obtained, on both major and minor issues, and CETA became law.

PSE was included as part of the comprehensive manpower reform bill. Growing unemployment made PSE politically essential for Democrats and attractive to many Republicans. The PSE program was tailored to appease critics: jobs were temporary, locally controlled, and to be a transition to regular employment; measures to safeguard against "dead-endism" were included (Davidson, 1972:39). In exchange, congressional extension of the much larger categorical Emergency Employment Act (EEA) public jobs program was dropped.

TABLE 1-3: *Shaping CETA: principal participants and positions*

PARTICIPANTS	POSITIONS TAKEN	PROGRAM OBJECTIVES
President Nixon and conservative congressional Republicans	Favored	Manpower reform Decategorization Decentralization Manpower revenue sharing
	Opposed	Public service employment Strong federal role in administration of programs
Liberal congressional Democrats	Favored	Public service employment Strong federal role in administration of programs
	Questioned	Decategorization Decentralization
	Opposed	Radical manpower revenue sharing
Service deliverers	Favored	Guarantees for programs and service deliverers
	Questioned or opposed	Decategorization Decentralization
Cities and counties	Favored	Decentralization (but argued over how much and to whom) Public service employment
	Opposed	Large role for states in administration
Federal bureaucracy	Favored	Consolidation of programs (but argued over how much and which ones) Strong federal presence in administration
	Questioned	Decentralization
	Opposed	Radical manpower revenue sharing

Sources: Franklin, 1977:268–269; Van Horn, 1979:61–65; Davidson, 1972:17–95.

Manpower programs operating under MDTA and EOA were consolidated and decategorized. No funds were earmarked for individual programs except for the PSE title and the Job Corps program run by DOL. In exchange, clear federal guidelines on eligibility and allowable program activities were included in the law, and a strong federal presence in approving plans and monitoring performance was retained.

Control over manpower planning, administration, and decision-making was decentralized and delegated to local and state governments in the form of a modified special manpower revenue sharing program. Funds were allocated to Prime Sponsors by formula from DOL. In exchange, President Nixon desisted from nonlegislative avenues of implementing manpower revenue sharing.

Other compromises were also reached in CETA: the size of governmental units qualifying as Prime Sponsors was set at 100,000; community action agencies were not added to the jurisdiction of DOL, though the Senate had proposed doing so because the Office of Economic Opportunity was being phased out by Nixon; the funding level earmarked for PSE was kept low enough to avoid a presidential veto, but there was an earmarked PSE amount; the assurance of funding for pre-CETA service deliverers was limited to a recommendation in the law that programs of "demonstrated effectiveness" operated by community-based organizations (CBOs) should be considered for funding (and specific CBOs were named); and the law did not attempt to encompass all manpower programs. Only MDTA and EOA programs were consolidated in CETA. Programs operating under authority of HEW, the Veterans Administration, and Housing and Urban Development were not included. Table 1-4 summarizes the major provisions of CETA as enacted in 1973.

Compromise in 1973 was possible partly because the issues were not new ones. The development of the CETA legislation clearly illustrates that the movement of items on the government's agenda is very slow, and that there are seldom clearcut agreements on new directions. It took Congress, the President, and the interest groups over four years to reach the agreements that allowed CETA to be passed. Nine years later, in 1982, the debate over CETA's replacement involved different facets of the same issues that were debated as CETA was shaped. The basic issues persisted.

TABLE 1-4: *Major CETA provisions, 1973*

CETA TITLE	PROVISIONS
I	Establishes a program of financial assistance to state and local governments (prime sponsors) for comprehensive manpower services. Prime sponsors are cities and counties of 100,000 or more, and consortia, defined as any combination of government units in which one member has a population of 100,000 or more. A state may be a prime sponsor for areas not covered by local governments.
	The prime sponsor must submit a manpower plan to DOL for approval before receiving funds. The plan must set forth the kinds of programs and services to be offered to unemployed, underemployed, and disadvantaged persons.
	The sponsor must also set up a planning council representing local interests to serve in an advisory capacity.
	The mix and design of services is to be determined by the sponsor, who may continue to fund programs of demonstrated effectiveness or set up new ones.
	Eighty percent of the funds authorized under this Title are apportioned in accordance with a formula based on previous levels of funding, unemployment, and low income. The 20 percent not under the formula are to be distributed as follows: 5 percent for special grants for vocational education, 4 percent for state manpower services, and 5 percent to encourage consortia. The remaining amount is available at the Secretary's discretion.
	State governments must establish a state manpower services council to review the plans of prime sponsors and make recommendations for coordination and for the cooperation of state agencies.
II	Provides funds to hire unemployed and underemployed persons in public service jobs in areas of substantial unemployment.
III	Provides for direct federal supervision of manpower programs for Indians, migrant and seasonal farm workers, and special groups, such as youth, offenders, older workers, persons of limited English-speaking ability, and other disadvantaged. This title also gives the Secretary the responsibility for research, evaluation, experimental and demonstration projects, labor market information, and job-bank programs.
IV	Continues the Job Corps (not really part of CETA administratively or budgetarily).
V	Establishes a National Manpower Commission.
VI	Contains provisions applicable to all programs, such as prohibitions against discrimination and political activity.

Source: Adapted from Mirengoff and Rindler, 1976:3.

The Evolution of CETA, 1974–1982

CETA began changing almost as soon as it was signed into law. Part of this change was a simple reflection of over 400 Prime Sponsors' applying their individual interpretations to the legislation as they began to implement it. But the real reasons for alterations to CETA lay in changing conditions. The environment in which CETA had been formed did not remain stable, and national policy-makers modified CETA to try to respond.

The passage of CETA at the end of 1973 coincided with the onset of a serious national recession. As implementation of CETA began in 1974, the state of the economy worsened, and manpower experts in Congress and DOL altered CETA to try to combat rising unemployment. The result was a greatly increased PSE program.

Economic conditions were not the only impetus for changes to CETA, however. Concern with providing manpower services to special client groups accounted for some of the additions. Concern with the need for greater variety in programmatic approaches led to tinkering. And some of the changes reflected DOL's and Congress's own constantly shifting goals.

Whatever the reasons for making changes in CETA, the effects were similar: comprehensive manpower services (the programs authorized under Title I) were displaced by PSE as the primary focus of CETA in terms of both funding and publicity; and CETA was gradually recategorized and recentralized as specific programs and target groups were added to Prime Sponsors' responsibilities by DOL and Congress. Rather than managing a single block grant, within four years Prime Sponsors were administering a series of categorical manpower grants. Recognition of this trend did nothing to eliminate it, however. By 1982 CETA was a series of categorical programs, although the pendulum had swung away from PSE and back toward greater reliance on comprehensive manpower services.

The attraction of creating special-purpose programs with earmarked funds serving targeted groups of clients proved irresistible to members of Congress, interest groups, and DOL. Recategorization greatly restricted the latitude of Prime Sponsors to form a set of consolidated, comprehensive local programs that focused on the needs of long-term, out-of-work individuals (the "structurally unemployed"). Consolidation, coordination, and assistance to the structurally unemployed were major goals of manpower reformers as the legislative debate began in 1969. As CETA evolved, however, these goals were buried, lost beneath a spate of categorical programs nearly as diverse as the MDTA and EOA programs that CETA had replaced (see Table 1-5).

The reauthorization of CETA in 1978 introduced many significant changes. For the first time since the introduction of manpower legislation in the 1960s, a clear and, in principle, measurable objective was stated: to increase the earned income of persons who participated. The programs and activities authorized by the revised act were also clearly designed for the economically disadvantaged, eliminating inconsistencies about eligibility for different titles. The total number of positions for PSE was reduced, and numerous amendments were added to address shortcomings in administration and operation of Title II and VI PSE programs. The 1978 act also changed planning and grant application procedures for all titles, required tighter verification of participants' eligibility, and mandated independent monitoring units in each Prime Sponsorship.

As a result of the reauthorization, the names and content of the various titles were changed. The comprehensive manpower programs of old Title I became Title IIBC; PSE under the former Title II became Title IID; the youth programs of Title III were reauthorized under Title IV. A new program for the private sector was added under Title VII. And a youth conservation corps was included as a new Title VIII.

One thing remained constant in the face of these alterations to the fabric of CETA: the basic decentralized administrative structure. Officials of local governments retained responsibility for planning and operating all the various programs authorized under CETA.

The principal organizational participants and their relationships in providing CETA programs and services to clients are sketched in Figure 1-1. Together, these organizations and groups comprised the CETA delivery system as it had evolved by Fiscal 1982. The solid lines in the figure indicate primary channels of communication, and the dashed lines indicate optional channels of communication exercised in some locali-

TABLE 1-5: *Additions to CETA, 1974–1982*

Program Name, Date, CETA Title	Description of Change
Emergency Jobs and Unemployment Assistance Act, 1974 (added as Title VI of CETA)	Countercyclical PSE program for recently unemployed workers. $2.5 billion authorized for the first 18 months. Grew in size in later years. Implemented at the local level by Prime Sponsors.
Youth Employment and Demonstration Projects Act, 1977 (added to Title III)	Established three separate programs to experiment with youth employment and training: Youth Employment and Training Programs, Youth Community Conservation and Improvement Projects, and Youth Incentives Entitlement Pilot Projects. All Prime Sponsors operated the first two; Prime Sponsors competed for YIEPP grants.
Economic Stimulus Act of 1977 (supplemental funds for Titles II and VI)	Appropriated $6.6 billion to increase PSE enrollments from 310,000 to 725,000 by March 1978 (less than 10 months after funds were allocated). Implemented by Prime Sponsors.
Skills Training Improvement Program (added as part of the 1977 Economic Stimulus Act to Title III of CETA)	Authorized long-term vocational training for experienced workers who were unemployed. Emphasized increased private sector involvement in training. Prime Sponsors competed for STIP grants.
Help through Industry Retraining and Employment, Phase I, 1977 and Phase II, 1978 (created by DOL and funded from Title III)	Established an on-the-job training program for veterans. HIRE I was run by the National Alliance for Business. Poor enrollments resulted in HIRE II being given to Prime Sponsors to operate. Allocations were given on request, but Prime Sponsors did not have to participate.
Young Adult Conservation Corps, 1978 (added as Title VIII in CETA reauthorization)	Work projects for youth in conservation areas modelled after the Civilian Conservation Corps of the 1930s. Implementation at the national level.
Private Sector Initiative Program, 1978 (added as Title VII in CETA reauthorization)	Demonstration program run by Prime Sponsors and newly created Private Industry Councils to increase private sector participation in employment and training programs.
Targeted Jobs Tax Credit Program (added as part of Revenue Act of 1978; not a CETA title)	Established tax credits for employers who hired certain targeted employees. Administered by Prime Sponsors and Employment Service at local level.

ties. The relationships portrayed in Figure 1-1 remained essentially the same throughout the period from 1974 through 1982. Although Private Industry Councils and Youth Advisory Councils were created after 1974, these additions did not alter the general relationships.

The Magnitude of CETA

CETA expenditures between FY 1975 and 1983 totalled over $55 billion. Figure 1-2 shows how annual expenditures grew from just over $3 billion to $9.5 billion within three years. By FY 1983, outlays were back in the $3 to $4 billion range.

The principal cause of CETA's expenditure bulge in the late 1970s was the growth of PSE and then its subsequent phasing out. Growth in other categorical programs accounted for the balance of increases in total CETA expenditures. As the figure clearly shows, outlays for comprehensive manpower programs in absolute dollars changed relatively little between FY 1975 and 1983.

That comprehensive manpower programs took a budgetary back seat in CETA almost from its inception is demonstrated in the bar graphs in Figure 1-3. Title I (IIBC after 1978) accounted for less than half of total expenditures even at its highest point. During the ascendency of PSE, comprehensive manpower programs were dwarfed, making up less than one-fifth of the total spent.

The expenditures described above do not represent the total federal effort in employment and training. Expenditures for programs other than CETA were $4.6 billion in FY 1981 and accounted for 37 percent of the $12.5 billion spent that year on civilian employment and training programs (U.S. Budget for FY 83:108, 109, 123). The federal commitment is undeniably large, but it pales beside the $30 to $40 billion spent annually by private corporations for training their employees (Ripley and Franklin, 1981:3).

Framework for a Political Analysis of CETA

As the foregoing sections have made amply clear, CETA was a multifaceted, changing, complicated set of programs. The data

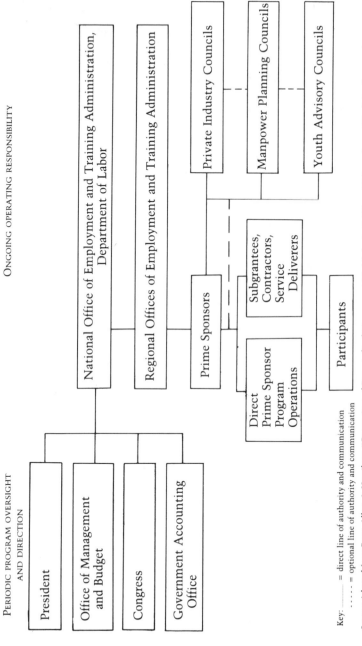

FIGURE 1-1: *Model of the CETA delivery system, Fiscal Year 1982*

PERIODIC PROGRAM OVERSIGHT AND DIRECTION

ONGOING OPERATING RESPONSIBILITY

President

Office of Management and Budget

Congress

Government Accounting Office

National Office of Employment and Training Administration, Department of Labor

Regional Offices of Employment and Training Administration

Prime Sponsors

Direct Prime Sponsor Program Operations

Subgrantees, Contractors, Service Deliverers

Participants

Private Industry Councils

Manpower Planning Councils

Youth Advisory Councils

Key: _____ = direct line of authority and communication
······ = optional line of authority and communication

Source: Adapted from Booz, Allen, & Hamilton, "Comparison of Decentralized Management Models in the Public and Private Sector," Draft Final Report for National Commission for Employment Policy, November 1981: Ch. 3.

FIGURE 1-2: *Expenditures for CETA programs, Fiscal Years 1975–1983*[a]

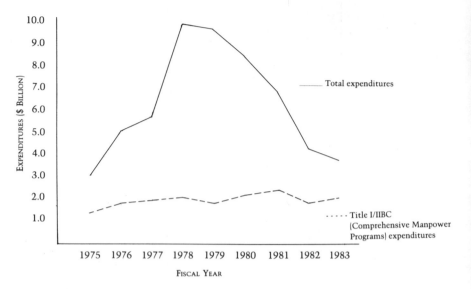

[a]Data for FY 1983 are estimates.
Source: Employment and Training Administration, U.S. Department of Labor.

DATA POINTS FOR FIGURE 1-2: *Expenditures for CETA programs, FY 75–83*

	TOTAL EXPENDITURES	EXPENDITURES FOR COMPREHENSIVE PROGRAMS (TITLES I/IIBC)
FY 75	$3.1 billion	1.3
FY 76	5.1	1.7
FY 77	5.6	1.8
FY 78	9.5	2.0
FY 79	9.4	1.8
FY 80	8.7	2.1
FY 81	6.8	2.2
FY 82	4.1	1.8
FY 83 (est.)	3.7 (estimate)	2.0 (estimate)

FIGURE 1-3: *Major CETA program spending shares, 1975–1983*

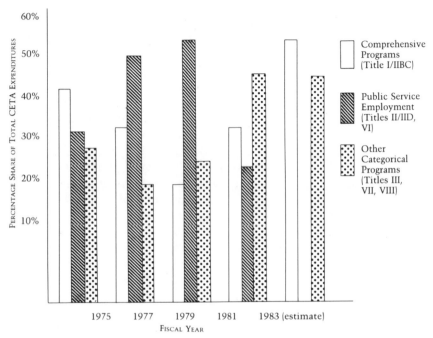

Source: Employment and Training Administration, U.S. Department of Labor

DATA POINTS FOR FIGURE 1-3: *Major CETA program spending shares 1975–1983*

	COMPREHENSIVE MANPOWER PROGRAMS	PUBLIC SERVICE EMPLOYMENT	OTHER CATEGORICAL PROGRAMS
FY 75	41	31	28
FY 77	32	50	19
FY 79	19	54	24
FY 81	32	22	46
FY 83	54	0	46

on CETA activities either existing or required for good analysis can appear to be infinite to any single analyst (or pair of analysts!). Successful analysis depends on selecting some manageable number of the most important factors (variables) with which to work, a manageable number of local sites and programs, and a manageable data base (using some subsets of standardized data specified by the law and considerable original data).

As we begin this task (or, more accurately, as we summarize where we arrived after eight years of working in this substantive field) we think it useful to comment very briefly on our basic interest in CETA—to explain, in effect, why we spent so much professional time conducting these analyses. What drove us to this work was not the employment and training field in and of itself. Rather, we viewed this as an instance of a much larger set of domestic social programs in the United States. These programs all raised the general thematic questions we want to explore as political scientists: the impact of a federal system on implementation, the impact of mandated citizen participation (in this case in the form of councils) on implementation, the causes and results of local decision-making about both allocation of resources and administrative arrangements, and the nature and potential contribution of joint public-private ventures. Other programs could have allowed us to explore many or all of the same questions: the community development block grant program, general revenue sharing, air pollution control, some health programs, and a number of educational programs, for example. However, we felt strongly that political scientists trying to sort out matters in the relatively new and highly complicated area of policy analysis necessarily had to be willing to commit themselves to a long period of research, including a good deal of original research, in the field at a number of the localities in which the programs were implemented. This kind of commitment takes substantial monetary support for the conduct of the research. When CETA was passed we saw an analytic opportunity. We were able to capitalize on the opportunity because of the willingness and desire of the U.S. Department of Labor at that time and for a period of over seven years after the passage of the initial Act to fund research designed to provide some answers to questions that intrigued both us and them. Other scholars during the same period have been able to undertake basic politically-oriented policy analyses in some areas other than employment and training (see, for example, Jones, 1975; Van Horn, 1979; Nathan et al., 1975, 1977; Kettl, 1980; Dommel and associates, 1982), although this type of research still remains relatively rare because of the necessary commitments of time and funding.

Our basic intention, once we have described the phenomena we are studying, is to ask causal or explanatory questions. What causes what in this policy area? What results can be explained in terms of what variations in preexisting or coexisting factors? Our explanations are not always statistical. We do not apologize for that fact; we merely note it. We have made a number of judgments throughout the research about the appropriateness and applicability of different kinds of analysis and have, accordingly, used a variety of kinds of analysis. These range from informed judgments about relationships through bivariate cross-tabulations to multiple regression. Quality of data and number of observations have necessarily governed us as we made the various analytical choices reported here.

Naturally, some of the material in the book will involve individual analyses or specific programs and/or eras in CETA we want to examine. However, the book concentrates on analyzing variations at the local levels ("Prime Sponsors") responsible for implementation. Thus our typical unit of analysis is the Prime Sponsorship and our basic method is to compare experiences systematically, using a wide variety of data over periods of at least several years where possible. *Explanation through systematic comparison over time and between localities* is what we have set out to do. It is through such systematic explanation that we think solid empirically grounded knowledge about American policy will be built.

What phenomena are included in our analyses? At the most general level we explore the links between the non-local (national and regional) context for the program, the context for local decisions, the content of local program decisions, and the results of short-run local program. Figure 1-4 portrays the simplest and most general model of the very broad relationships between major phenomena we examine in this volume.

This model may at first seem static and amenable only to analysis that occurs at one point in time. We are well aware that reality is dynamic and continuously moving. We have used this model as a way to organize our research and our observations, and whenever possible, we used it to take multiple "readings" or observations of the same phenomena over time. Adapted in this way, the model is suitable for longitudinal (across time) analysis. Furthermore, we do not attempt to swallow the vast complexity that was CETA whole with our model. Rather, this model informs the way we approached the general research effort. Specific findings stemmed from more elaborated and often partial use of pieces of the broadest model. Details on those specific uses will be included at the relevant places in subsequent chapters.

Our general model, as diagrammed in simple form in Figure 1-4, both serves a general descriptive purpose and specifies the relationships we want to explore empirically.

Although we intend to present systematic analysis, we hope to do so in a way that allows the reader to understand and become interested in the politics of CETA. We are political scientists and, as such, are convinced that politics are interesting in and of themselves and, moreover, that programmatic results in the United States (and, no doubt, elsewhere as well) stem in part from politics. We have not presented a number of the analyses we conducted over the years but have tried to reassess all of them and present only the most central. At the same time, we strive to inject some of the sense of politics into the book. Much of the analysis cannot be presented as "easy" narrative. We make no apologies for that. But we have made a number of substantive arguments throughout the book and we intend that the analyses support the arguments, not obscure them.

Before turning to specific analyses in Chapters 2 through 5 we need to provide more detail about the kinds of variable clusters we explored as potentially important in explaining variations we observed. Table 1-6 lists those variable clusters. After the

FIGURE 1-4: *General model for examining local employment and training programs*

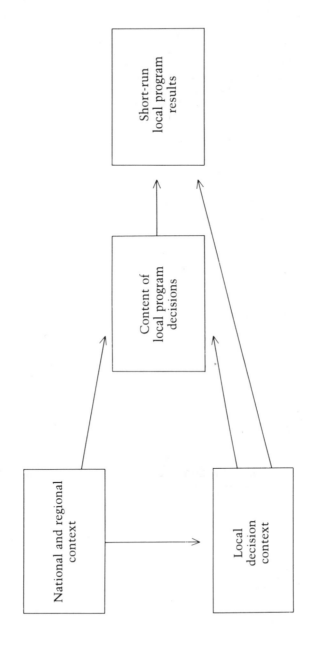

TABLE 1-6: *Variable clusters in the general model for examining local employment and training programs*

National and regional context
  Content of statutes, regulations
  National DOL interpretations and actions
  Regional DOL interpretations and actions
Local decision context
  General local environment
    Socioeconomic characteristics of the population
    Economic conditions/perceptions of those conditions
    Social conditions
    Structure of CETA-related governmental and advisory units
  Local program decisions
    Previous employment and training decisions
    Related social program decisions
  Local influence patterns
Content of local program decisions
  Administrative arrangements
  Local goal specification   .
  Allocational choices
    Program components
    Service delivery agents
    Target groups (recipients)
Short-run local program results
  Client service patterns (enrollment and placement)
  Local goal achievement
  Job placements
  Costs
  Wage gain for participants

following brief introduction, they will be elaborated as appropriate in subsequent chapters.

NATIONAL AND REGIONAL CONTEXT

The content of the statutes passed by Congress and signed by the President are the first layer of the context faced by localities in implementing CETA. Both the national office of the U.S. Department of Labor and the ten regional offices of DOL interpreted these statutes. Regulations written by DOL to elaborate and interpret the statutes formed a significant part of the context. Likewise, specific actions by individuals and offices of both the regional and national levels of DOL were part of the extra-local context in which Prime Sponsors operated their programs. But even within DOL, interpretations and actions varied from region to region at a given time, as well as varying throughout the extra-local system over time.

In principle, the CETA structure provided for some state role beyond the one it played in administering programs for counties that belonged to no other Prime Sponsorship. In practice, this additional state role amounted to very little and thus did not become a factor in our analysis.

LOCAL DECISION CONTEXT

GENERAL LOCAL ENVIRONMENT. A number of aspects of the general local environment are important, or at least potentially so, in investigating local employment and training programs. First, the socioeconomic characteristics of the local population are relevant because they help determine not only the size and nature of the eligible population but also other aspects of community politics. For example, a racially homogeneous community will be missing one element of typical conflict at the local level. A community with a sizeable black population as the only minority may well allocate its employment and training programs primarily to groups and service deliverers committed to serving some of the needs of the black community. And a community with two or more sizeable racial or ethnic minorities may well witness a struggle between those groups for dominance over the employment and training program.

Second, local economic conditions of many sorts are potentially important in explaining what happens with local CETA programs. The basic economic structure of the area in terms of who the employers are and what they do helps explain the nature of the training programs that make sense locally. The health of those local enterprises may help explain the willingness of the employers to get involved in such programs. The perceptions of local economic health—often based partially on perceptions of national economic health—may help shape program choices and expectations about what can and cannot be achieved locally.

Third, local social conditions in a broad sense may help shape the content and nature of local CETA programs. For example, if a community has a history of rocky labor relations, it is likely to be very difficult to get unions and employers to cooperate on programs. If unions simply hold a veto over training programs in some occupational areas, those in control of programming will be forced to select alternative training programs. A community with a history of very tense racial relations can probably expect that tension to spill over and affect decisions about employment and training program choices.

Fourth, the identity, nature, and prescribed relationships of CETA-related governmental and advisory units can help explain what happens in the programs. If, for example, a city purchasing agency or civil service agency has complicated and time-consuming procedures and requirements, the CETA agency may find its flexibility inhibited or may even be driven to seek some sort of independent status. Whether a city manager or an elected mayor really controls a city is important in terms of the questions asked of the professional staff running the program. The city manager may be most concerned with the time-honored virtues of economy and efficiency; the mayor, on the other hand, may be more interested in appearing to favor certain blocs of constituents when selecting programs.

LOCAL PROGRAM DECISIONS. Two sets of decisions already made can have substantial impacts on local CETA programs. The previous decisions made in the employment and training area itself are important. They help set a pattern for choices of programs, service deliverers, and clients to serve that usually form an established model from which subsequent deviations tend to be only incremental. Choices in the pre-CETA days helped determine, in some areas, that certain training institutions were almost automatically funded under CETA. These choices, however, varied considerably between localities.

Local decisions about related social programs can also have an effect on CETA programs. Local politics, for example, may dictate that all major disadvantaged minorities have "their" program. If one minority has been underserved with previous program decisions, then CETA programs may naturally gravitate to them. Use of economic development aid or general revenue sharing might have some marginal impact on use of CETA money. Local decisions about vocational education certainly might either create or deprive a community of certain kinds of public training facilities that have applicability to CETA programs. State and, to some extent, local decisions about the level and ease of welfare benefits may have some impact on the relative willingness of some eligible people to seek CETA training.

PATTERNS OF LOCAL INFLUENCE. At any local level a given program involves both individuals and institutions that have differing resources and capacities and whose preferences are taken with differing levels of seriousness. The differences in levels of influence are related to the general standing of some institutions and individuals in an area and are also specifically related to how their interests in employment and training are perceived and to how well they articulate and work for those interests. In short, all of the politics of local decision-making and the politics of influence-building and use are involved in CETA, as they would be in any other sizeable local program. An analyst of local CETA programs always needs to ask this question: what organizations and individuals, with what capacities and resources, participate in what aspects of employment and training decisions, with what respective weights attached to their views?

Those influencing employment and training programs can generally be classified in seven major categories: (1) the elected political officials with formal responsibility for CETA; (2) the professional staff responsible for day-to-day administration of CETA programs; (3) members of mandated councils responsible for either advice or concurrence on a variety of local decisions; (4) those who work for local interest groups and organizations concerned with these programs (often these individuals are professional staff for service delivery groups); (5) employers in the private sector or subsets of them; (6) political appointees and professional staff who work for other governmental agencies related to CETA; and (7) personnel—the only non-locals—from the regional office of DOL charged with overseeing the program.

CONTENT OF LOCAL PROGRAM DECISIONS

ADMINISTRATIVE ARRANGEMENTS. Local decisions must establish and, from time to time, reaffirm local administrative arrangements for running the program. These include the questions of which city or county or state agencies have responsibility for the program and what form that responsibility takes. Or a new body can be created either outside of existing government or related to it in unusual ways. The question of consortium formation, for example, is both administrative and political. The distinction must be made between administrative units responsible for oversight and those responsible for operations, as the possible division of operating responsibility into a number of different facets is at stake.

SPECIFICATION OF LOCAL GOALS. CETA was structured to establish some national goals that were expected to be adopted at the local level while, at the same time, leaving room for some additional local goals. Individual localities often had the liberty to interpret national goals in ways most pleasing to them. They also took the opportunity to ignore some presumably national goals. And they certainly did add unique goals of their own. Decisions—often implicit and vague—were made at all local levels about this mixture of goals.

ALLOCATIONAL CHOICES. CETA is another instance of the classic situation in which those eligible for service could easily use five to ten times the resources allocated nationally for the program. Thus, virtually every locality faced the situation of having to allocate scarce resources to many more claimants than could possibly be satisfied. The politics of allocational programmatic decision-making were therefore much in evidence in the study of CETA. Three sets of allocational choices were particularly visible and often controversial at the local level.

First, program managers had to decide what kinds of programs to fund. These might include, for example, vocational training in various occupations, on-the-job training with private employers, or exposure to different kinds of jobs through work experience. They also had to decide the relative priority of these program components.

Second, local decision-makers had to pick agencies to provide the vocational training, on-the-job contracts, or work-experience programs that had been decided on. Selection was limited by the range of potential service delivery agencies in a locality, and there was a strong tendency to refund those that had been funded before.

The third choice confronting planners was the need to specify in some detail the clients or "target groups" to be served. This selection process involved analysis of the pool of eligible applicants to decide both how many people the programs could help and what kinds of people to try to reach. These choices included, for example, the relative percentages of different age groups, of males and females, and of whites, blacks, and other minorities.

These three sets of allocational choices were interdependent. Selection of a program strategy would dictate or at least limit choices about service deliverers and client groups. Local political pressures would often cause the first decision to be selection of service providers, which in turn defined what programs were possible and which clients could be reached. In most localities, for example, a decision to fund the local Urban League affiliate was simultaneously a decision to operate an on-the-job training program and to serve disadvantaged blacks.

SHORT-RUN LOCAL PROGRAM RESULTS

PATTERNS OF SERVICE TO CLIENTS. One short-run local outcome that has been of constant interest to us is the question of who uses or is "served" by the programs. We have been intent on describing the characteristics of the participant populations because such characteristics as educational status, sex, race, and age give some clues to the relative level of disadvantage of those served.

LOCAL GOAL ACHIEVEMENT. Another short-run local result that can be observed, although often it is difficult to do so in quantitative terms, is the degree to which local goals—especially those different from presumed national goals—are achieved.

JOB PLACEMENTS. A standard program result specified by DOL and accepted by almost everyone, although often in somewhat different forms, is the placement in jobs of participants who emerge from various programs. These placements may be restricted to private employers who seek profits or they may apply to all employers, including those in the public sector.

Costs. Another standard measure that is widely used, but also widely interpreted in various ways, is costs. The costs are usually specified in "unit" terms, either "per enrollee" or "per placement". The meaning of cost data is not readily apparent. In some ways it may be better to treat such data as indicators of other facets of a program rather than an outcome in itself. But it is a standard measure and thus, politically, it is important to note its use in evaluations by different levels of decision-makers themselves.

At this point, we need simply to note that lower costs are not necessarily better than higher costs. Lower costs may imply efficiency. They may also indicate short-term programs aimed at occupations for which not much training or many skills are needed. Higher costs may represent waste. But, alternatively, they may also represent a serious commitment to training in the more demanding occupations that have a brighter future than the occupations requiring less training. In short, cost data require interpretation; they do not speak for themselves. The same necessity for interpretation applies to all indicators; but the plea for interpretation is particularly strong in the area of costs.

Wage Gain for Patricipants. A final short-run standard measure of results for participants is wage gain, which includes both pre-training and post-training wage, with the difference representing the gain (or, occasionally, loss). But for the data to be useful at all, the gains of participants have to be compared with the gains of non-participants with similar characteristics. Otherwise the supposed gain may represent nothing more than inflation in general or at least inflation in a specific occupational area.

Summary

CETA was the first special revenue-sharing program enacted under President Nixon's New Federalism. The legislative compromises necessary to obtain passage of CETA meant that it was essentially a hybrid block grant that neither fully embraced all federal manpower programs nor fully decategorized all those that it was replacing. Its hybrid nature, the vagueness of its statutory goals, and the uncertain division of power between DOL and the local Prime Sponsors left important questions unanswered that would affect its subsequent implementation.

Major shifts in policy emphasis and funding levels marked CETA's evolution. PSE emerged as a dominant program activity that displaced the original intention to consolidate and integrate programs at the local level. Even after the decline and elimination of PSE, other categorical programs under the CETA umbrella forestalled the ability of Prime Sponsors to develop comprehensive local manpower programs.

With all of its limits, however, CETA still represented a major response—at least by U.S. standards—to a broad set of problems in the labor market. The devolution of decision power to the local level was a landmark decision. "Comprehensive" was at least in the title of the statute, although the claim was overblown from the first. CETA had some promise for producing major forward movement in the way the United States developed employment and training programs.

But CETA wound up as a widely discredited effort. It was less comprehensive when it ended than when it began. In practice, the local administrators were much less autonomous than they were in the theory of the original Act. The replacement fashioned for CETA that came into existence in the autumn of 1983 relied principally on two largely untried levels of administration in employment and training: state governments and the private business sector at the local level. Those levels with the most experience under CETA—the local governmental level and the federal level—were both severely downgraded in the new version of employment and training programs enacted in 1982.

This harsh judgment of CETA was neither fair nor accurate in many ways. Yet, for a variety of reasons, it was the judgment reached by those involved in the national political process. Some local programs provided pockets of excellence in the CETA years. But the cosmic political judgment ignored those pockets.

The following chapters will explore what really happened at the local level and, in particular, will offer explanations for the variations in the quality of local performance. The last two chapters will return to broader themes relating the CETA experience to the nature of American federalism and American politics in general.

CHAPTER TWO

★

Transition to the New System

 CETA WAS SIGNED DECEMBER 28, 1973. A tight dead-line was set for the new system to replace the existing categorical programs outlined in the previous chapter. The new Prime Sponsorships were supposed to be in place and ready to function both administratively and programmatically by July 1, 1974, the beginning of FY 1975.

Much was new about CETA. Some geographical areas that elected to become Prime Sponsorships had never before had employment and training programs. Accordingly, they had neither experience, nor facilities, nor prior interest. Even for the "old hands"—which included the larger cities—there was considerable chaos because of changed roles of old players in the employment and training game and a number of new players suddenly coming into the game. By July 1, 1974, the major responsibility for staffing, enrolling participants, offering training and other services, placing people who completed the programs, and being accountable for funds was in the hands of 403 Prime Sponsorships—states, cities, counties, consortia of cities and counties, and four special rural Concentrated Employment Programs. This number rose to 431 for FY 1976 after some of the initial consortia broke apart and additional mayors and county commissioners saw the advantages of having programs fully under their own control.

As if the chaos of moving to a broader set of players, with new roles and responsibilities for everyone, old and new alike, was not enough, the economy began to sicken almost immediately. In December 1974, the system that had been put into place primarily to rationalize training programs was transformed into a structure in which training took a back seat to public service employment (PSE). PSE had different purposes than training programs—both economic and political—and it served a substantially changed clientele (roughly put, not those people with seemingly permanent barriers to employment but those who happened to be out of work at the time, regardless of other characteristics).

Enrollments and activity in Title I had been building up relatively rapidly after July 1974. This buildup had been paralleled at a much lower level by the original Title II, a small PSE program aimed squarely at the disadvantaged. After Congress passed Title VI to create a large new PSE program intended to counteract the increased unemployment of the recession, Prime Sponsors were deluged with money, new regulations, and instructions to spend and enroll rapidly.

In addressing these first two change-filled years in CETA our major objective was both to map and to explain the major patterns of adjustment and readjustment at the local level. People involved at that level were given new responsibilities and powers. What use did they make of them? And how can the choices made be explained in terms of both political and economic factors?

We wanted to describe the substance of the results at the local level in terms of the nature of the service-delivery systems constructed, the types of specific programs developed to serve clients, and the nature of the clients served. Above all, we wanted to explain why the decisions made were made. This analysis involved, in part, trying to determine who (both individuals and clusters of institutional actors) had what kind of influence over what decisions.

In trying to answer these broad questions we followed two strategies. The primary one was to conduct original research at the time of transition (FY 1975 and 1976) in all of the Prime Sponsorships in Ohio (a total of 14 in the first year and 17 in the second year). Ohio was chosen for the very practical reason that our location there made attracting support for research feasible. However, intellectually it also provided a very satisfactory diversity of types of Prime Sponsorships since Ohio is a large and diverse state and the Prime Sponsorships represented all of the major types that existed nationwide. Our second strategy was to undertake secondary analysis of other studies of other Prime Sponsorships scattered throughout the country. In that analysis we sought answers to the same kinds of questions we had asked systematically in Ohio.

We summarize the major results of our Ohio inquiry in the first major section that follows. Then we turn to a brief summary of some other studies—brief partly because our findings and those of other studies were in agreement. Ohio Prime Sponsorships were, in fact, representative of what happened at state and especially at local levels throughout the nation. Finally, we summarize briefly the major findings about transition to the new system that emerge from our study and the studies by others considered together. We also draw some broader conclusions about the political generalizations that can be offered on the basis of these findings.

The Transition to CETA:
A Systematic Analysis of Ohio Prime Sponsorships

THE NATURE OF THE STUDY

RELATIONSHIPS INVESTIGATED. When CETA began to be implemented and the MDTA categorical programs were changed to the so-called "special revenue sharing" model on which CETA was based, we designed and conducted a systematic study of almost two years in duration of the basic patterns of implementation in all of the Prime Sponsorships in Ohio (14 in FY 1975 and 17 in 1976). We wanted to know how localities reacted to the new world in which they found themselves: what continuities there were, what discontinuities, what inventions, and, above all, how political relationships helped shape program choices and results.

We looked at a variety of both extra-local and local environmental influences, one of which was constant across Prime Sponsorships and the rest of which varied from one Prime Sponsorship to the next. The one constant was the content of the statutes and the federal regulations. Related to this were the interventions by the national government—both Congress when it amended the statutes and DOL when it changed the regulations—that affected all Prime Sponsorships, at least in principle. Other external interventions, principally interpretations and actions by the regional office in Chicago (the region responsible for Ohio Prime Sponsorships as well as those in five other states), were, in theory, constant across Prime Sponsorships. But, in fact, they varied because each Prime Sponsorship directly interacted with a different "federal representative," who had differing competences and interpretations of his or her own power and of the meaning of the federal regulations. Thus directly contradictory answers on substantive questions could be given, at least for a short time and sometimes for a long time, to different Prime Sponsorships, even though they might adjoin each other geographically in a single state. This variation was even more dramatic when boundaries between the ten federal regions were crossed.

The state of Ohio played a very limited role in Prime Sponsorships other than the so-called Balance of State for which it was directly responsible (58 of the 88 Ohio counties in FY 1975), which represented the small-town and rural residue of the state after the heavily populated areas were organized in their own Prime Sponsorships. And the few interventions it attempted varied in content between Prime Sponsorships, although they were generally so weak and ineffectual as to be invisible both to the local administrators and to analysts like us.

Within Prime Sponsorships we assessed the socioeconomic characteristics of the population, local economic and social conditions, various features of governmental and advisory structures that influenced CETA, previous employment and training programs, attitudes of individuals towards CETA, and the patterns of relative influence over CETA decisions by four major categories of local actors (elected officials, professional staff, the advisory council mandated by the statute, and local service deliverers) and other local interest groups.

The decisions in which we were interested for these two years included those about program components, identity and importance of service deliverers, and target groups in the eligible population. We also followed closely the decisions by local jurisdictions about whether to join with others in a consortium and about distribution of funding within geographic areas of a Prime Sponsorship.

The major "result" we thought we could fairly assess at this early stage of CETA's evolution was the pattern of clients receiving services: what kinds of individuals used the programs that were operated by the Prime Sponsorships?

Sites. Although the Ohio Prime Sponsorships were not a statistically representative sample of the more than 400 Prime Sponsorships that existed in the country during FY 1975 and 1976, they did exhibit a broad range of labor market and demographic conditions, program sizes, and types of Prime Sponsorship organization. (These variations are detailed in Appendix Tables A 2-1 and A 2-2.)

Data Base. A large, varied data base was used in analyzing the implementation of CETA in Ohio. It consisted of interviews (both closed- and open-ended) with many of those involved with the manpower system in Ohio; observations of meetings of manpower planning councils and other related groups; a vast quantity of pre-CETA and CETA documents (including Cooperative Area Manpower Planning System [CAMPS] materials, instructions from the Chicago regional office, field assessment letters and backup materials from the regional office, field memoranda, minutes of council meetings, CETA plans, project planning summaries, budget information summaries, project status summaries, financial status reports, and quarterly summaries of participant characteristics); newspaper clippings; and relevant census and employment service data.

A summary of interview data and observational data collected is contained in Appendix Table A 2-3. These data were supplemented by information that came from a large number of telephone calls and informal conversations interspersed with the more formal data-gathering visits.

AN OVERVIEW OF THE GENERAL FINDINGS

The following pages briefly summarize our major findings

about the transition to CETA in Ohio. Subsequent sections offer a more detailed analysis of local patterns of influence, local decisions about program components, and client patterns.

INFLUENCE PATTERNS IN LOCAL DECISION-MAKING. On Title I decisions professional staff members wielded dominant influence. Elected political officials became involved when dollar allocations were at stake—either to delivery agents or to geographical areas within a Prime Sponsorship. The mandated advisory councils varied greatly in their importance. In some localities they were purely rubber stamps; in others, particularly where the political officials were not involved, they developed more influence. Service deliverers retained some importance in choosing their own clients, but, compared to the pre-CETA days, their influence on the overall shape of the system declined. Federal representatives were found to have little influence at the local level as individuals.

Political officials, virtually all of whom cared very little about the basic shape of the Title I programs in their areas, became much more personally involved in decisions about public service employment (PSE). But professional staff members continued to share influence in this area. No other actors had any particular influence in dealing with PSE.

TITLE I PROGRAM COMPONENTS. In general, the use of training programs (classroom training and on-the-job training) declined in these first few years in favor of employment programs (both work experience and PSE).

TITLE I SERVICE DELIVERERS. In making choices about service deliverers, those with the decision power no longer simply protected the status and funding of existing deliverers. They were willing to make some changes, sometimes on the basis of evaluations of past performance and sometimes on the basis of the political preferences of political officials and/or advisory councils. The state Employment Service, a major presumptive deliverer in the pre-CETA days, had particular problems in retaining a significant role in the new locally-run systems. The role of a public agency was easier to reduce than those of community-based groups. The former had no clout at the polls; the latter did.

Professional staff were explicitly constrained in their decision-making about service deliverers. They most often said the reasons for choosing specific agencies to provide services were prior program decisions and/or prior decisions about clients. The content of these decisions led to choices of service providers. The third most often cited reason for choice of service deliverers was the absence of alternatives.

PSE PROGRAMS. Although theoretically forbidden to do so by federal regulations, the localities with the most serious budgetary problems tended to use PSE money to rehire laid-off local employees or to substitute federally-funded workers for regular municipal employees. This possibility helps explain the interest of elected officials and city managers (in localities in which they were more powerful than elected officials) in PSE.

PARTICIPANTS. Who received services? In general, Title I participants looked quite different from the PSE participants. The former were likely to have less formal education and were much more likely to be black, economically disadvantaged, female, and young. Because Title II PSE participants, who initially were quite disadvantaged, quickly began to resemble Title VI participants, all PSE participants tended to be relatively less disadvantaged than Title I participants. In short, jobs went to the less disadvantaged, who also tend to vote. Training went to the more disadvantaged, who vote less frequently.

In these first few years, however, the proportion of participants in Title I programs as well as in PSE who were economically disadvantaged also declined at a steady rate, and the relatively most disadvantaged part of the general eligible target population got less and less service. Other characteristics of those served pointed the same way: an increase in average formal education for participants in all three titles and a decrease in the proportion of blacks served.

It should be noted, however, that these were only general patterns; some localities made decisions about participants that ran directly counter to the general state and national patterns. A few localities emphasized service to the most disadvantaged.

AN EXPLANATION OF LOCAL PATTERNS OF INFLUENCE ON TITLE I DECISIONS

Depending on what was at stake, the general pattern of influence varied among Prime Sponsorships. Local factors, especially local politics, produced local variations, although there were also some commonalities. Table 2-1 summarizes the broad patterns of political influence on CETA Title I decisions in the 16 local Ohio Prime Sponsorships (Balance of State is omitted) in 1976. On three major types of decisions—program mixture, selection of service deliverers under Title I, and clients to be served—staff was the most consistently important. In general, political officials were next most important, although since they intervened selectively, they were not consistently important. The other groups listed—especially advisory councils ("manpower planning councils," as they were generally called in 1975 and 1976) and service deliverers were more consistently present. In only a few individual cases was staff of secondary importance and in only the rarest of cases was staff missing altogether as an important decision-maker. In short, CETA programs quickly became institutionalized, with the professional staff as the most important decision-makers. However, like bureaucrats in the United States at all levels of government, these bureaucrats held office through a mixture of civil service and political appointments and, most importantly, they were expected to be skilled at building political coalitions and making political decisions. They lived up to these expectations. Professional and political considerations together influenced CETA decisions from the outset of the program.

Three sets of factors helped explain the variations in influence among the different groups involved in making CETA decisions: the orientation of the participants (their attitudes, experience, interest and commitment to CETA); staff structure and other features of local government; and economic conditions. We will discuss each briefly.

ORIENTATION OF ACTORS. Professional staffs throughout the Prime Sponsorships studied were the most important group in

TABLE 2-1: *Patterns of influence on CETA Title I decisions, Ohio Prime Sponsorships, 1976 (participants in manpower decisions are listed in descending order of importance)*

TYPE OF DECISION	STATEWIDE PATTERN	VARIATION AMONG PRIME SPONSORSHIPS (NUMBER OF CASES)
Program mix in Title I	Staff/political officials	Staff/political officials (5) Staff/manpower planning council (4) Staff/service deliverers (3) Political officials/staff (2) Political officials/manpower planning councils (1) Manpower planning council/service deliverers (1)
Selection of Title I service deliverers	Staff/political officials	Staff/political officials (6) Staff/manpower planning council (3) Staff/service deliverers (3) Political officials/staff (1) Manpower planning council/staff (2) Manpower planning council/political officials (1)
Title I client decisions	Staff/political officials	Staff/political officials (4) Staff/manpower planning council (5) Staff/service deliverers (6) Political officials/staff (1)

CETA decision-making, although their influence varied from place to place.

The degree of staff autonomy was determined by the experience of the staff, especially the director, and the level of interest in CETA on the part of the political officials. Where staff experience was high and the interest of the political officials was low, the staff was autonomous. Even an inexperienced staff could gain autonomy from officials who lacked interest, simply because the staff's own direct interest and involvement soon provided experience. Where political officials' interest was high and staff experience was low, the staff had low autonomy. In cases where an experienced staff and interested political officials coexisted, the usual result was low staff autonomy, though to a lesser degree than in Prime Sponsorships with interested political officials and an inexperienced staff.

Those political officials most active in CETA decision-making wanted either to change the existing manpower system in their locality or to prevent change in a system they found satisfactory. Their attitude toward their own involvement usually determined the influence of other actors. Most active political officials did not appoint forceful, aggressive staff members.

The influence of manpower planning councils depended on two principal factors: the attitude of the staff and the political officials toward council participation as well as the attitude of the council members themselves. If staff and officials supported an active council, then the necessary groundwork for an influential council was present, although the council did not automatically achieve that status. Absence of such support, however, meant that there was virtually no chance that a council would have influence. If the council members believed that their recommendations were being taken seriously and that the time they devoted to CETA benefitted the programs, they participated vigorously. In those cases, if staff and official support were present, the council could achieve some influence.

The influence of service deliverers in CETA decision-making declined dramatically in 1975 and 1976 compared to their pre-CETA standing. Decline was greatest in Prime Sponsorships in which the service deliverers were kept off the advisory councils.

In such cases they had no official forum in which to present their views. They remained influential in Prime Sponsorships in which they were firmly entrenched through the years of previous manpower experience. The continued high influence of service deliverers occurred where the political officials were not motivated to change the existing programmatic emphasis.

STAFF STRUCTURE AND LOCAL GOVERNMENTAL FEATURES. Certain features associated with the organizational structure and the location of the Prime Sponsor staff in local government affected the relative influence of local actors. In some Prime Sponsorships, the CETA staff operated as part of a regular city or county department. The staff in these cases became much more responsive to the demands of political officials than was the case when the CETA staff operated in other administrative organizations. This responsiveness was particularly noticeable during mayoral races or in partisan turnover in city or county government. Those Prime Sponsor staffs not closely affiliated with the regular machinery of local government had greater autonomy and greater insulation from political considerations.

Among consortia, there were two possible locations for the Prime Sponsor staff. They either became part of the city or county government of one of the consortium partners or they served as the administrative staff of an independent legal entity that embodied the consortium. Overall, the political officials in a multijurisdictional consortium were more active in CETA decision-making than those in single-jurisdiction Prime Sponsorships, often to insure that their individual jurisdictions received a "fair" (that is, maximum possible) allocation of CETA funds.

The form of local government also affected the influence of the different actors in a Prime Sponsorship. In most municipalities that gave the mayor considerable authority, the mayor was active in CETA decisions. City managers, on the other hand, did not take such an active role. Furthermore, those city managers who participated did not try to restrict the activity of other interested groups such as the planning council or the service deliverers. The Prime Sponsorships in which the political officials appointed relatively weak staffs and tried to restrict the participation of other actors in CETA decisions were all large cities with strong mayors.

ECONOMIC CONDITIONS. Unemployment rates in Ohio Prime Sponsorships in FY 1975 and 1976 ranged from 7.5 to 15 percent. In most Prime Sponsorships rising unemployment heightened the interest of political officials in CETA and especially in PSE. One mayor expressed it this way: "When unemployment is low, the manpower division is just another agency; now it is important. The benefits are spread around and the programs are a political asset, not a liability."

Fiscal crises in some local governments also roused the interest of political officials in CETA. Attempts were made to use CETA funds to support local government personnel who were laid off. During such crises the political officials usually had one of their cabinet-level deputies assume direct control of the local PSE programs. In Prime Sponsorships where local governments had fiscal crises there was also greater use of PSE under Title I. Naturally enough, any mayor trying to keep a city afloat fiscally looked for pots of money wherever they existed.

AN EXPLANATION OF LOCAL DECISIONS ON PROGRAM COMPONENTS

We wanted to determine systematically what factors were associated with local decisions to allocate resources among different program components. To measure programmatic emphases, data on planned expenditures from original FY 1976 Title I plans were collected for the major types of program activities defined by DOL: classroom training, on-the-job training, work experience, and public service employment (which was permitted under Title I during FY 1975 and 1976).

Three groups of variables reflected differing programmatic emphases most accurately: previous program choices; environmental constraints; and, to a more limited extent, the priorities of employment and training decisionmakers.

PREVIOUS PROGRAM CHOICES. One plausible explanation for any given set of program choices is previous program choices (see, for example, Lindblom, 1959; and Davis, Dempster, and Wildavsky, 1966; for critiques of those views see Gist, 1974; Natchez and Bupp, 1973; and Ripley and Franklin, 1975). Some argue that, typically, decision B is only a slight variant of the previous decision A.

There is substantial evidence that Prime Sponsorships as a rule did not make large or non-incremental changes in their plans over time. Correlations for relative emphasis on different programmatic components at each local level at different times in FY 1975 and 1976 revealed relatively little change over the two-year period. What was in place tended to stay in place. A qualitative analysis of the specific changes in individual Prime Sponsorships also indicates that change was relatively gradual. In most cases, substantial planned changes were rescinded in practice because the constraints on change proved too great.

ENVIRONMENTAL CONSTRAINTS. Another possible explanation for change and variation in local program priorities is what we called local environmental constraints. For example, widely dispersed population would seem likely to make institutional training more difficult, regardless of preferences. Similarly, an absence of established training facilities, at least in the first years of CETA, would also make training difficult to undertake. On-the-job training (OJT) would seem unlikely in areas in which manufacturing employment was relatively low, because almost all such opportunities are in manufacturing establishments.

Tests of the relationships between these environmental factors and the planned program expenditure shares offered a good deal of confirming evidence. Low population density correlated positively with a relatively strong emphasis on work experience, whereas high population density correlated positively with a relatively high emphasis on OJT and classroom training. High population density correlated both positively and significantly with an emphasis on PSE, a relationship that makes sense, as it was the large cities that had the fiscal crises, real or imagined, that led them to use Title I for PSE.

The presence of established vocational education programs and facilities showed high negative correlation with work experience and positive correlation with classroom training. This pattern suggests that Prime Sponsors will utilize classroom training when facilities are available, work experience when they are not. Two significant relationships also emerged when type of program was correlated with the ratio of manufacturing jobs to population. The strong negative correlation between the ratio and work experience suggests that in the relative absence of manufacturing jobs a CETA system can be expected to emphasize work experience. There was a strong positive correlation between the manufacturing employment ratio and emphasis on OJT.

PRIORITIES OF LOCAL DECISIONMAKERS. Changes and variations in program choices may also be partially explained by the priorities of relevant contributors to the manpower system. In systematic interviews virtually all local personnel in Ohio in the spring of 1976 were asked to rank order their program preferences, using the four major program components analyzed here. Ideal preferences differed considerably from planned expenditures. This finding lends weight to the interpretation that the shift to Title I PSE and work experience at the expense of classroom training and OJT was largely a response to events over which individual planners had no direct control—primarily fluctuating economic conditions—rather than an expression of their preferences for employment programs over training programs. The best correlation between preferences and planned expenditures for FY 1976 came in the case of work experience. The only other relatively high correlation was between the preference of all actors and planned OJT spending. The rest of the correlations were very low and, for PSE, negative. The findings again suggest that the decrease in classroom training and the increase in Title I PSE were not really in accord with "ideal" preferences.

AN EXPLANATION OF CLIENT SERVICE PATTERNS:
WHO RECEIVED SERVICES?

Why did patterns of service to different classes of participants emerge as they did? The focus in our analysis was on levels of service and changes in those levels for the economically disadvantaged and blacks. These characteristics were chosen because it was argued, before the passage of CETA, that these two groups would suffer most in loss of services if manpower programs were decentralized and decategorized (see, for example, Mangum and Snedeker, 1974:309). The first few years of CETA witnessed a large decrease in service to these groups in Title I and stabilization at relatively low levels of service in Titles II and VI.

We found that variations in patterns of service to participants were accounted for by the attitudes and preferences of manpower actors, the characteristics of the eligible population, DOL policy, and decisions about programs and vendors.

ATTITUDES OF ACTORS. The attitudes of manpower actors about the kinds of participants that they preferred to serve under Title I were important in explaining actual patterns of service to participants. Elected officials were the least concerned with high levels of service to the economically disadvantaged and to blacks, as Table 2-2 shows. Staff were most concerned about the disadvantaged, and advisory council members were most concerned about services to blacks.

Our expectation was that how successfully attitudes were translated into action depended on influence patterns. Attitudes held by more influential actors would be reflected in patterns of service to participants, while attitudes of less influential actors would not have a systematic effect. An analysis (which took into account the proportion of blacks and the economically disadvantaged in the eligible population) did indeed show that combinations of preferences with influence patterns explain a good deal of why varying mixtures of participants were served as they were in different Prime Sponsorships.

UNIVERSE OF NEED. The characteristics of the population eligible for CETA services (known in employment and training jargon as the "universe of need") were measured using Employment Service data on active job applicants. The analysis showed that this factor affected patterns of service to participants, but it was not controlling or direct. Intervening were the perceptions of staff members and service deliverers about changes in the eligible population and general economic conditions (perceptions that were based more on impressions than data). Thus, for example, the relative need to serve blacks declined, but the actual service

TABLE 2-2: *Local preferences about patterns of service to clients,*
Ohio, 1976

		PREFERENCE PATTERNS (FIGURES ARE PERCENTS)	
GROUP SURVEYED	NUMBER SURVEYED	ECONOMICALLY DISADVANTAGED SHOULD BE 50 PERCENT OR MORE OF ALL TITLE I PARTICIPANTS	BLACKS SHOULD BE 50 PERCENT OR MORE OF ALL TITLE I PARTICIPANTS
Staff	109	86	57
Service deliverers	78	81	55
Political officials	37	70	24
Council members	174	75	65

patterns decreased much more rapidly because of perceptions that distorted the need for service. Similarly, although data for Ohio showed the need to serve the economically disadvantaged to be stable, the actual level of service decreased substantially.

DOL ACTIVITIES. The 1973 statute set eligibility requirements for Title I that broadened the potential pool of individuals who might seek manpower services. The categorical programs were more closely tied to the most disadvantaged in the population. The CETA Title I allocation formula also created a flow of manpower dollars to more suburban areas, usually predominantly white, away from central cities, with much larger black populations (see Mirengoff and Rindler, 1976). Title II also had reasonably broad eligibility requirements, and with the coming of Title VI (and the close linking of Titles II and VI in most minds) PSE focused on the recently unemployed person who tended to be less disadvantaged in other ways.

Thus the trend away from service to the disadvantaged and, to some extent, the trend away from service to blacks was dictated by Congress in the basic statute and in the addition of Title VI. (Proponents of these changes of course argued that there was nothing unfair about them but that, in fact, CETA represented a fair distribution of resources among that part of the population genuinely in need of manpower services.)

In a number of ways it seemed that the policy of the regional office in the case of Ohio also reinforced the trend toward relatively less service for the most disadvantaged (see Van Horn, 1978). In 1975 and 1976 the regional office took only minimal steps to monitor the eligibility of enrollees in Prime Sponsorships. There was no attempt to determine whether patterns of service to clients corresponded to the actual nature and incidence of need.

Emphasis from the regional office on spending at the planned rate, especially for PSE and especially in 1975, also led to diminished service to the most disadvantaged. It was much easier to locate and enroll the relatively less disadvantaged and especially the recently unemployed who might be quite middle class in all other ways. In effect, the regional office encouraged Prime Sponsors to commit greater funds to programs that could be implemented quickly with high costs per enrollee, thus spending the money rapidly. The result was to reduce services for the participants less ready for jobs, who also tended to be the most economically disadvantaged.

PROGRAMMATIC DECISIONS. Decisions about the type of programs offered and the choice of those who would provide them have direct impact on the type of participants enrolled. For example, Perry and others (1975) report that minorities have traditionally been enrolled in work-experience programs. One might also speculate that the most economically disadvantaged have also tended to cluster in work-experience programs. Thus, those Prime Sponsorships that stressed work experience may also, in effect, have been deciding simultaneously to serve a higher proportion of blacks and economically disadvantaged. On the other hand, those Prime Sponsorships that stressed PSE were probably at the same time building in a relatively lower stress on minorities and the economically disadvantaged.

Because of factors such as the physical location of specific service deliverers, their selection often had a direct impact on which participants were recruited and enrolled. Service deliverers located in a black ghetto are most likely to serve blacks; those located on a suburban beltway miles from the central city and with no public transportation serving them, are much less likely to be able to serve blacks and economically disadvantaged. Furthermore, the history of service to particular groups by specific agencies often was well-developed before CETA began.

The Transition to CETA: *The National Perspective*

Fortunately, on a number of questions we raised about the transition period we were able to check our findings based on Ohio Prime Sponsorships against findings from national studies conducted in different samples of localities and states during the same period. Specifically, two reports from a national study of CETA that was conducted during most of the life of the program covered the early years (Mirengoff and Rindler, 1976, 1978) and an additional study analyzed original research in 45 other Prime Sponsorships and combined that information with analysis of data from the DOL in-house (and short-lived) evaluation effort in 66 sites (Snedeker and Snedeker, 1978). We did additional analysis on raw data collected by DOL on all Prime Sponsorships in the nation. Thus, when all of this analysis is added to our own detailed analysis of the Ohio cases we are confident we have a very accurate picture of the first two years of CETA. And the picture is very consistent no matter which set of data is used.

The most interesting transition issues for us are those dealing with the allocation of resources under the new decentralized, decategorized system and the comparisons of how the CETA system changed relative to the MDTA base. We concentrated on the most important national changes brought about by CETA. In the sections that follow we focus on the changes in FY 1975 and 1976 that occurred in the nature of the service delivery system—the structure, organization and identity of service delivery agencies; changes in the types of manpower programs offered; and changes in the characteristics of persons receiving manpower assistance.

CHANGES IN THE SERVICE DELIVERY SYSTEM: STRUCTURE AND ORGANIZATION

The "service delivery system" includes the interrelationships of agencies, programs, and administrators who are involved in providing manpower services to participants within a given locality. The manpower delivery system encompasses front-end services such as recruitment, admission, and assessment; program activities such as classroom training, on-the-job training, and work experience; and post-program services such as job development, job referral, and placement.

Pre-CETA manpower programs at the local level were manifestly devoid of coordination, organization, and integration. There was no system. Fragmentation of numerous programs operating at the local level with literally no relationship to each other was one of the main problems at which manpower reform was directed (see Davidson, 1972). By consolidating programs and improving coordination among individual manpower programs, CETA was expected to bring order to local service delivery systems, eliminating duplication and filling program gaps.

The most visible and significant structural alteration resulting from the transition to CETA was the immediate creation of new bodies—the Prime Sponsorships—with the responsibility and authority to coordinate CETA programs. No such hierarchical arrangement existed for MDTA and EOA programs. The nearest models were the Concentrated Employment Program and the pilot Comprehensive Manpower Program (CMP). Both operated only in a limited number of jurisdictions and had little success (see Williams, 1980:30–34, on CEP; Levitan and Zickler, 1974:91–95, on CMP).

Although Prime Sponsors had the authority to design a service delivery system from scratch, the extent of change introduced to the pre-CETA arrangements was limited and incremental, especially in FY 1975. As Snedeker and Snedeker (1978:136) note: "Relatively few sponsors attempted a total reorganization or upheaval of established delivery patterns during the first months of CETA. In most cases, initial delivery changes were implemented gradually and on a modest scale. Early delivery decisions were heavily influenced by existing program operations."

That alterations in local service delivery systems were neither rapid nor drastic was a result of the implementation context. Caught up in the normal turmoil of implementing the newly decentralized Title I and II programs, Prime Sponsors were involved with activities like finding offices, hiring and training staff, and submitting plans and grant applications. The normal implementation routines were compounded by the phasing out of MDTA and EOA programs (due to expire in December 1974) and by the unexpected addition of a large new Title VI PSE program in December 1974. Under these conditions it was simply easier to do no more than tinker with the Title I program delivery system. There were other factors that contributed to the difficulty of making early changes: many staff were new and inexperienced; even experienced staff lacked data on which to base decisions about service delivery systems in the first year; technical assistance from DOL in putting new delivery arrangements in place was inadequate; entrenched service deliverers, not without political clout, were often able to resist attempts to change their programmatic turf.

Options available to Prime Sponsors ranged from a totally comprehensive service delivery system on the one hand to a categorical system on the other. The comprehensive service delivery system meant that "all activities and services offered in one geographic area would be unified . . . accountability would be centralized . . . participants would be exposed to a full range of training and service options" (Mirengoff and Rindler, 1978:138). In a categorical system pre-CETA programs and service deliverers continued to operate with little change in their scope of services and with little opportunity for integration of programs or for exchange of participants between programs. The mixed model of service delivery combined aspects of both the comprehensive and the categorical models.

The major operational difference among the various models of service delivery systems was the absence of any centralized or coordinated services in the categorical model. In this disaggregated delivery system, separate programs were indeed separate from beginning (recruitment) to end (placement). In the comprehensive model, the Prime Sponsor centralized at least one of the major functions—for example, admissions, training, or placement—either by operating the service directly or by contracting with a single delivery agent for its provision. In addition to standardizing procedures, the centralized function served as a clearing point for all participants. The range of choices and options available to participants was thereby increased—participants were exposed to the offerings of the entire CETA system, not just those of a separate service deliverer.

Among the 24 local Prime Sponsors studied by Mirengoff and Rindler (the four Balance of State sites were excluded from this analysis), one-third had adopted a service delivery system that was primarily comprehensive in nature by the end of FY 1976. One-fourth of the sites had a mixed system, and the remainder (42 percent) had a categorical delivery model (Mirengoff and Rindler, 1978:138). Prime Sponsors with an array of entrenched MDTA and EOA service deliverers were least able to shift to a comprehensive system. Conversely, Prime Sponsors starting with few previous programs were in better position to design consolidated and coordinated programs.

Snedeker and Snedeker (1978:140–41) classified service delivery models using different labels but with similar operational meanings. The distribution of 66 Prime Sponsorships from the DOL evaluation sample differs from the Mirengoff distribution—one-fourth of the sites were in the functional group (corresponding to the comprehensive system), one-half had a mixed system, and one-fourth were in the program group (corresponding to the categorical system).

The most frequently implemented change in service delivery arrangements was to centralize admissions to the programs within a single agency. Even among Prime Sponsors where admission was centralized, however, there was limited exchange of participants among the various Titles. Since the service system was redesigned, participants were exposed to more manpower services under Title I, but their assignment to Title I instead of Titles II or VI depended on the extensiveness of intake services within the Prime Sponsorship. In most localities, admission for the PSE titles was separate from Title I program admission, and client mobility between PSE and non-PSE programs was limited.

CHANGES IN THE SERVICE DELIVERY SYSTEM:
SERVICE DELIVERERS

Decisions about which agencies would provide programs and services to participants had previously been made by DOL, but under CETA such decision-making was transferred to the new

Prime Sponsor staff. Although the law said that programs of demonstrated effectiveness ought to be given special consideration, no presumptive service deliverers were mandated. All program operators—previously secure in their funding from DOL—now had to compete at the local level for funding from Prime Sponsors. Several striking changes resulted from the decentralized decision-making.

First, the number of agencies providing manpower services increased substantially, jumping from about 1440 in FY 1974 to over 2400 in FY 1975 (U.S. DOL, Oct. 1975:6; the national estimates are projections based on DOL's sample of 66 state and local sites). This increase was a one-time rise, however, reflecting the extension of administrative responsibility to areas that had never had it before.

Second, a new class of program operators emerged: the Prime Sponsors themselves. DOL's estimates showed that in 61 percent of all local Prime Sponsorships, in-house staff were engaged in delivery of programs or services; an even higher proportion (71 percent) of the sample sites used by the National Academy of Sciences study operated programs directly (Mirengoff and Rindler, 1978:143–145).

Third, there was a major shift by CETA Prime Sponsors away from using the Employment Service (ES) as a service deliverer. Though ES had previously enjoyed an assured role in providing MDTA classroom training and on-the-job training as well as being heavily involved in local EOA programs, the level of ES participation under Title I in FY 1975 declined about 30 percent from the 1974 level for comparable programs. Although 80 percent of all Prime Sponsors continued to use ES to provide some services, it lost one quarter of its manpower-related staff positions between FY 1974 and 1976 as the size of its CETA contracts shrank (Mirengoff and Rindler, 1978:150–151). A large proportion of all local Prime Sponsors reduced the level of services provided by ES.

Fourth, vocational education agencies (which under MDTA had shared a monopolistic role with ES in operating classroom training programs) continued to receive about the same level of total funding under CETA as they did under MDTA. However, under CETA there was a significant decrease in the administrative autonomy of state vocational education agencies, and at the local level, the choice of organizations providing vocational education changed as Prime Sponsors became more involved in choosing curricula and making program decisions that had previously been made by the schools.

Finally, community-based organizations (CBOs) did not suffer under the transition to CETA as many observers had feared. In fact, the "big three" CBOs (the National Urban League, the Opportunities Industrialization Centers, and SER) all significantly increased both the number of projects funded and the financial value of those contracts. Community action agencies (CAAs) did not fare so well as the other CBOs, however. Over half of the sites in the DOL survey reduced or eliminated funding for CAAs between FY 1974 and 1975, generally because CAAs were politically controversial or because Prime Sponsors absorbed the roles they had previously played (Snedeker and Snedeker, 1978:170). Although CBOs continued to play a central role in the delivery of manpower programs under CETA, they had to make adjustments in both their programs and the participants they were required by Prime Sponsors to serve. Like ES, their autonomy was challenged, and they were forced to adapt to the Prime Sponsors' new delivery systems. Unlike ES, however, since they served special clienteles, they were able to persuade Prime Sponsors of their unique ability to reach and serve CETA's intended clients—minorities and the poor, groups that ES was perceived not to serve effectively. The skill of CBOs in staying in the new system both reflects their political skill and helps explain why service to blacks, hispanics, and a few other minorities did not diminish more than it did. They provided a countervailing political and bureaucratic force to those elected officials and staff members who had little or minimal interest in service for minorities.

CHANGES IN PROGRAMS

The general types of programs (classroom training, on-the-job training, work experience, public service employment) operated under Title I changed little from pre-CETA programs. The vast majority of Prime Sponsors indicated that they deliberately chose to retain most pre-CETA programs. Changes tended to be modest and incremental (Mirengoff and Rindler, 1978:134).

But the allocation of expenditures and enrollees among basic activity clusters in Title I underwent notable changes in the transition from categorical programs to CETA programs. Data on all U.S. Prime Sponsors collected by DOL showed large drops in the percent of funds allocated to classroom training and on-the-job training activities in FY 1976 compared to 1974. The declines were balanced by large increases in public service employment (PSE) and a moderate growth in supportive services. The share for work experience remained fairly stable. Table 2-3 summarizes the shifts in types of programs operated.

The shifts were due in part to the changeover to new decision-makers and the subsequent alteration of program priorities and vendor selection at the local level. The declining economy played some role in stifling on-the-job training but was not a dominant explanatory factor (Mirengoff and Rindler, 1978:123). The most important factor was rather the pressure on Prime Sponsors from DOL to spend funds quickly and to boost enrollments during the first years of CETA. Work experience, PSE, and supportive services were all activities that could be implemented quickly with both rapid enrollments and spending.

TABLE 2-3: *CETA Title I expenditures by program type, Fiscal Years 1974 and 1976*
(figures in percents)

PROGRAM TYPE	FY 1974	FY 1976[a]
Classroom training[b]	42	33
On-the-job training	18	9
Work experience	37	38
Public service employment	0	11
Services and other	4	9

[a]Excludes transition quarter.
[b]Includes CETA 5 percent vocational education funds for governors.
Source: Adapted from U.S. DOL data reported in Mirengoff and Rindler, 1978:119.

The most dramatic change in employment and training in the 1970s began shortly after implementation of CETA started. The growth of PSE in Titles II and VI of CETA was phenomenal (see Baumer and Van Horn, 1984, for a comprehensive analysis of PSE; Mirengoff and Rindler, 1978: Ch. 7, offer a concise survey of the early implementation of PSE in CETA). The Public Employment Program (PEP), authorized by the Emergency Employment Act of 1971, was the immediate predecessor of PSE in CETA, but its scale was much more modest—$2.25 billion authorized for 2 years, and 175,000 persons enrolled at the peak of hiring. PSE in CETA began modestly enough (the initial authorization was for $400 million), but the addition of the new Title VI midway through FY 1975 added a $2.5 billion authorization. By the end of FY 1976, over $3.4 billion had been spent on Titles II and VI, and 721,000 persons had been enrolled. The types of PSE jobs funded by CETA were very similar to the jobs funded by PEP, although turnover in those jobs was higher in CETA than in PEP (Mirengoff and Rindler, 1978:167).

Perhaps the greatest difference between PEP and PSE in CETA was in the transition of participants to permanent unsubsidized employment. Under PEP, transition was a primary goal: the Republicans had insisted on that in 1972 as the price for having a public jobs program. Over half of all PEP employees moved into regular employment. But the placement rate for PSE employees in CETA was less than 30 percent (Mirengoff and Rindler, 1978:232). The lower rate reflects DOL's priorities: in FY 1975 and 1976, the emphasis was on hiring and on spending funds, and transition received little attention.

The PSE buildup in FY 1975 and 1976 fostered a number of consequences that neither DOL nor Congress had foreseen. The most serious of these was the dependence of municipalities on PSE for fiscal relief from severely strapped local budgets. Despite maintenance of effort provisions in the law, PSE funds were substituted for local funds or were used to supplement local budgets to avoid increased tax rates. Almost from the outset PSE produced problems that were ultimately to prove fatal politically to the overall image of CETA with the public and, even more importantly, with Congress. Though the training part of CETA generally worked and produced better results over time, PSE became fixed in the minds of most observers as the whole of CETA, and it clearly had grave problems.

PATTERNS OF SERVICE TO PARTICIPANTS

Some observers, especially representatives of CBOs, expressed concern that minorities and the poor would lose manpower services as a result of the transition to CETA. The legislation stated that CETA Title I participants must be economically disadvantaged, unemployed, or underemployed, but in the first two years of CETA Prime Sponsors were relatively free to set local service priorities within the broad eligibility parameters. As a result of expanded eligibility (pre-CETA programs focused primarily on the disadvantaged), extension of manpower programs to suburban communities, and the rising unemployment rate, the pool of persons eligible for CETA programs was much broader than the pre-CETA base. Those receiving manpower assistance under CETA included many who were not the most disadvantaged.

Changes in patterns of service to participants are discussed using the following comparisons: (1) persons enrolled in pre-CETA and CETA programs; (2) persons enrolled compared to persons hired; and (3) persons in PSE and non-PSE titles of CETA. We examine demographic characteristics that are associated with a greater competitive disadvantage in the labor market—minority status, welfare dependency, being female, being young, having limited education, and being poor. [Data for the following discussion were collected by DOL and represent national averages of all Prime Sponsors. These data are summarized in Appendix Table A 2-4. See Baumer, Van Horn, and Marvel, 1979, for a separate analysis using a similar approach.]

PRE-CETA AND CETA PARTICIPANTS. The most noticeable participant-related effect of the transition to CETA was the greatly increased number of persons served. Pre-CETA manpower programs served just over half a million people in FY 1974; comparable CETA Title I programs served over 1.7 million in FY 1976.

As the number of persons served was increasing, the type of persons enrolled was changing from the pre-CETA pattern. Several important trends confirmed the fears of some early observers. Between FY 1974 and 1976, fewer economically disadvantaged participants were enrolled in CETA as a fraction of all enrollees (the proportion dropped from 87 percent to 76 percent). Fewer young people were enrolled (the proportion dropped from 63 percent to 57 percent). And the proportion of persons who were better educated increased (from 34 percent to 45 percent). On the other hand, the level of service to minorities remained stable, and the proportion of welfare recipients enrolled in Title I programs increased slightly (from 23 to 26 percent).

A look at PSE enrollees reveals that the PEP program enrolled a much smaller share of economically disadvantaged individuals than did the PSE programs in CETA (34 percent compared to 45 percent). There were, however, more welfare recipients in the CETA PSE programs than in the PEP program (14 percent compared to 10 percent). But these shifts were due less to the effects of PSE than to the narrowness of the PEP program. The latter was a countercyclical program targeted on the unemployed generally and especially on veterans, whereas CETA PSE, at least in Title II, focused nominally on the disadvantaged and persons who were unemployed for a longer time.

PERSONS ENROLLED AND HIRED. What differences existed between participants who entered various CETA programs and those hired into regular unsubsidized employment? Did Prime Sponsors skim off the easiest to place? Was the tendency to enroll a less disadvantaged clientele in Title I evident in the placement function as well? Available evidence indicates that this was indeed the case.

As DOL did not collect data on characteristics of persons hired from the categorical programs, we cannot make a comparison with the pre-CETA programs. But within Title I programs, the data clearly show that the persons most likely to be hired from CETA programs were white and well educated, while the economically disadvantaged and minorities got a smaller share of jobs (see Baumer, Van Horn, and Marvel, 1979). The same tendencies were present among the PSE titles, although the magnitude of differences was greater in Title I.

PSE AND NON-PSE ENROLLEES. The congressional shift in emphasis in the first year of CETA from traditional programs to

PSE programs had a significant impact on the characteristics of persons served in the two types of programs.

A comparison of the characteristics of participants in Title I programs and the two PSE titles shows that there were major differences in the kinds of persons who were enrolled. Title I program participants were much more likely to be economically disadvantaged, nonwhite, less educated, receiving welfare, female, and young. The titles did discriminate, and the benefits to participants were unequal: PSE provided participants with a job and a wage of up to $12,000, while Title I program activities paid either a minimum wage for work experience or a training allowance. In short, the best benefits went to the least disadvantaged clients (Baumer, Van Horn, and Marvel, 1979).

Summary

In this chapter we have examined some of the effects of the transition from categorical manpower programs to CETA, using data from several national studies as well as our own research on implementation in Ohio Prime Sponsors. By the end of the second year of implementation, many changes had occurred in local employment and training system as a result of the transition.

Manpower was clearly institutionalized at the local level and incorporated into the local public administration agenda. New administrative structures were created, and Prime Sponsors assumed responsibility for planning, managing, and evaluating local manpower programs. The professional staff consistently had the most influence in decisions about manpower. Elected officials were less involved in Title I decisions and more involved in PSE decisions. The factors that explained patterns of influence included attitudes, interest, commitment and previous experience; the staff's location within the Prime Sponsorship; and economic conditions.

The nature of the delivery system changed gradually during the first two years. Prime Sponsor staff became active in delivering programs; the role of Employment Service and community action agencies as service deliverers was sharply reduced; most CBOs received more funding than they had before CETA. In most sites complete or partially comprehensive service delivery systems began to be fashioned, consolidating activities and coordinating the movement of participants from intake through programs to placement.

The types of programs funded in Title I shifted away from classroom training and on-the-job training toward PSE and supportive services. This trend was caused more by DOL pressure to spend funds and economic recession than by staff preferences for PSE. Factors found to be important in explaining program choices in the first two years of CETA included previous program decisions, environmental constraints, and attitudes and preferences.

Manpower programs served a clientele better off than that before CETA. A smaller proportion of enrollees in Title I programs were young, poorly educated, and economically disadvantaged; PSE enrollees were more likely to be better educated, white, and male than Title I participants. CETA brought about a reduction in services for the most disadvantaged and an increase in the range and number of persons who received assistance during the first two years of implementation. The factors found to explain patterns of service to participants included attitudes and preferences of influential actors, characteristics of the eligible population, DOL policy, and decisions about specific programs and service deliverers.

The degree of change that occurred in delivery systems, programs, and participants varied among Prime Sponsorships as a result of different local conditions. Factors promoting change included the new set of actors (Prime Sponsor officials) in charge of manpower decision-making; altered relationships among pre-CETA manpower actors; the spread of manpower services to suburbs and rural areas; dissatisfaction with pre-CETA programs and agencies; and the worsening recession, which led to increased unemployment, fiscal strains on municipal budgets, and a nationally imposed PSE priority. Countering these forces were a variety of factors that retarded dramatic change: the lack of time available to develop alternatives to the status quo; retention of pre-CETA programs and service deliverers for reasons of good performance, political considerations, or lack of alternatives; staff commitment toward certain types of programs and participants; and increasing DOL pressure on Prime Sponsorships to focus on PSE at the expense of Title I.

What broader conclusions can be drawn from a careful examination of the first two years of CETA? We offer the following comments both as a way of providing a partial political interpretation of what was happening in these years and as a way of providing general statements against which experience in the succeeding years of CETA can be gauged. Four broad statements seem to be warranted on the basis of the data and an interpretation of the meaning of our analysis.

★ The authority of full-time bureaucrats (the professional staff) was usually unchallenged except when elected officials were attracted by money directly under their control which they thought they could use for political advantage. Challenges by existing service delivery agencies were usually met by allowing them some share in the programs. Aggressive advisory councils could be important, but usually only because local staff wanted them to be important. They hardly ever generated an important role for themselves, beginning life very much the creatures of the staff and, to a much lesser extent, the elected officials.

★ Substantive decisions were based primarily on the realities of relative political influence among the various actors and very rarely, if ever, on more objective analysis of data on needs and evaluation of program effectiveness. Professional staff dominated decision-making both because they were at the center of programs and were paid to manage them full-time but also because they tended to become the most politically skillful on a day-to-day basis.

★ The emphasis on PSE began immediately to distort CETA's original focus on training for the most disadvantaged. Some of the distortions came about simply because of the design Congress included in Title VI (as well as the discarding of the original purpose on the small Title II PSE program). Others came about because of perfectly understandable political and fiscal greed on the part of those who ran Prime Sponsorships. Mayors and county commissioners and governors saw the opportunity to spread some jobs with the presumed favorable results in terms of votes for re-election in time and the opportunity to rescue their jurisdictions from already present or pending fiscal crunches by funding regular local services with PSE money. Efforts to support the basic local services also had the added political advantage of helping local officials avoid tax increases, always politically unpopular.

★ The most disadvantaged part of the eligible CETA clientele faced an uphill fight in preventing deterioration of service. Only some staff and even fewer political officials were much interested in them, the latter partially because they tended to vote less frequently than others still eligible for CETA. In these early years Congress and the Department of Labor (both nationally and regionally) also showed relatively little concern for the most disadvantaged. However, the most disadvantaged—particularly those minorities served by vigorous local community-based organizations, the most important of which were local branches of national organizations— were not without resources. Locally, some of the CBOs had the twin advantages of already being in place (and therefore favored by inertia) and, more importantly, of having politically skilled individuals working for their interests. Nationally, those with similar political skills could keep pressure on both Congress and DOL to counteract any tendencies to forget minorities and the most disadvantaged. Service did deteriorate, but less rapidly than it would have without the presence of these active countervailing pressures. And in some localities it not only did not deteriorate but may even have improved.

In short, CETA quickly became a thoroughly politicized decision-making system and, therefore, many of its substantive results can be meaningfully understood only in political terms.

CHAPTER THREE

★

Local Program Management

 IN CHAPTER 2 WE EXAMINED THE OPENING
YEARS OF CETA by focusing on general transitional
patterns and a few sets of decisions and results that
seemed to be particularly important for the future. The present
chapter focuses on local management: specifically, data drawn
from the local CETA programs a few years after they began and
presumably had been able to achieve some stability. We examine in more detail the dynamics of local program choice in
this analysis. We also begin to analyze more meaningful data on
the results for individuals who had been exposed to CETA
programs and services.

CETA was never stable at the local level primarily because
Congress and the Department of Labor could not refrain from
constantly tinkering with it in increments ranging from fairly
small and peripheral to extremely large and central. Naturally,
local politics and, to a much lesser extent, the fluctuations of
local economies also kept local CETA programs in a constant
state of flux. Under such conditions the concept of "management" must be broad.

We use the concept of management to encompass a range of
activities and decisions by program administrators. Our conception of management goes well beyond the traditional concerns
of agency personnel policy. Staff organization, hiring and pro-

motion policies, and salaries are important and can help to shape agency morale and performance, but they do not account for all aspects of management. We are also interested in the practical details of program implementation because this is an integral part of management. But most important, *local management of CETA programs was political management.* Political management means deciding about who gets what—for example, what programs to fund, what services to offer in-house and what services to subcontract, which agencies to fund, which participant groups to enroll, what role to grant to the local citizen advisory council. Political management also involves weighing competing claims from local interest groups and resolving conflict between contending parties. These kinds of management decisions are important not just because they are intrinsically interesting to political scientists but because they affect the effectiveness of services provided to participants. In short, local management decisions help shape program outcomes. This link between management and outcomes is the focus of this chapter.

One of the premises of CETA was decentralizing program management to the local level. Major responsibility for decision-making and implementation was transferred from the federal government primarily to localities. In this chapter we examine how local actors responded to their new responsibilities several years into the program and the programmatic consequences of their actions. Beginning with a general introduction to the nature of management in CETA, we then analyze the local management efforts and consequences of those efforts in a sample of 15 Prime Sponsorships throughout the United States that we studied in 1976 and 1977. Finally, we briefly summarize our general conclusions about the nature of local management.

The General Nature of Management in CETA

FEDERAL IMPACTS ON LOCAL MANAGEMENT

Local management of CETA programs was a central feature of CETA. Several studies demonstrated that local management and planning decisions made considerable difference in the performance of local CETA systems. In fact, variations in local management were shown to be the single most important category of explanatory factors associated with program perform-ance at the local level (see Ripley and associates, 1978 and 1979d; Mirengoff and Rindler, 1978; and Snedeker and Snedeker, 1978). Aspects of management such as developing high quality staffs, attracting business participation in CETA programs, developing effective techniques for monitoring and evaluating the perform-ance of service deliverers, integrating programs with each other, developing and using good data for planning, and managing (but not avoiding) local conflicts to prevent them from disrupting delivery of services to participants were all found to be impor-tant.

But local management occurred in the context of provisions in the statutes and regulations and management by the national and regional offices of DOL. That context could constrain or encourage what local managers of CETA could achieve. The extra-local constraints grew as CETA evolved. Tension between local managers and DOL was widespread and consistently high because of local resentment of the constraints.

Federal interventions shaped local options and gradually but continuously encroached on local flexbility. Federal manage-ment directives changed frequently. Emphases switched from levels of enrollment to rates of expenditure to eligibility of participants to liability of Prime Sponsors. Attention shifted errati-cally from one title to another. There was no logical progression from one emphasis to another. Furthermore, DOL changed its management priorities before local managers had time to comply with previous directives.

Federal directives tended to concentrate on administrative and procedural aspects of management rather than on broader issues of local political management. But regardless of whether federal directives were focused on broad or narrow management issues, they generated political implications for local managers. DOL and Congress, however, were insensitive to the difficulties that Prime Sponsors faced in adjusting to the frequent changes; they continued to impose additional priorities and restrictions.

Continuous fluctuations and delays in CETA funding were a major problem for local CETA administrators. Congress rarely passed appropriations before the beginning of the fiscal year for which they were intended, and local managers usually had to make program decisions before they knew how much money they would have. Planning estimates provided by DOL for local managers were often incorrect, and reductions or additions necessitated repeated administrative activities to adjust to the changes—revisions of planning documents, adding or subtracting service deliverers or program activities, raising or lowering enrollments. A rational funding cycle was nonexistent; forward funding or stability of funding were tantalizing and unattainable ideals.

National intrusions by both Congress and DOL sometimes helped push Prime Sponsors toward good management and good performance. All too often, however, those intrusions made it more difficult, if not impossible, for local managers to arrive at sensible decisions that were shown by research to produce better program outcomes. It should be emphasized that Prime Sponsors varied greatly in size, resources, and managerial capability. Small Prime Sponsors had a particularly difficult time coping with the effects of changing national efforts at managing CETA. The following examples suggest the general problem:

* The proliferation of categorical programs and mandated target groups coming from the national level prevented local managers from integrating their programs.

* Burgeoning reporting requirements from DOL forced the local staff to scramble simply to fill out the national reports, even though the data had little use locally.

* These reporting requirements supplanted the useful role DOL could have played in working with Prime Sponsors on a cooperative basis to develop essential data for both planning and local monitoring and evaluation. As in many other cases, DOL was torn between its desire to have comparable data on all Prime Sponsors and to know everything about program operation. As a result, it required over-reporting by Prime Sponsors, and many of the data collected were not only irrelevant to local program managers but were not used anywhere.

* Local conflict was often intensified, sometimes beyond reasonably manageable proportions, by national intrusions requiring new services to specified "significant segments." These well-intentioned intrusions sometimes put the Prime Sponsor staff in a position of being unable to meet all demands by competing local groups

and thus helped convert local operations into defensive
holding maneuvers rather than integrated delivery systems related to local needs.
★ Proliferation of local programs through national mandates
complicated local monitoring and evaluation efforts.
Evaluation tended to be a rarely occurring luxury. Even
though monitoring was shown to be critical to the effectiveness of local programs, with many Prime Sponsors
its use was limited to desk reviews and cursory compliance activities. Rarely were monitoring and evaluation used to assess alternative strategies for dealing with
local manpower needs.
★ In terms of vision, talent, and performance in implementing CETA, Prime Sponsors ranged from highly
skilled and successful to submarginal. But the strongest
and the weakest were all treated equally by DOL, to the
detriment of both. There were no particular incentives
to improve performance, the strongest receiving no special rewards and the weakest receiving little constructive attention. Harassment seemed to be DOL's major
tool for encouraging good performance and punishing
what was regarded as poor performance.

THE LOCAL MANAGERS

Management at the local level in its most elementary terms
meant first, that professional staff would have a concept of
program design and second, that they would implement that
concept. Constructing a program design required the CETA
administrators to translate the potential in the CETA legislation into a set of programs appropriate for the specific local
context. They had to understand the outlines, content, and purpose of the local service delivery system. This system included
programs, agencies, the enrollees to be served, and the types of
jobs awaiting participants after leaving CETA. Furthermore, the
program design had to be adjusted constantly as the national
context altered and additional administrative requirements
were imposed. Implementing the program design required,
therefore, a thorough knowledge of what kind of program was
desirable for the Prime Sponsorship, an ability to sell that design

to others in the service delivery system, and finally an ability to adjust it or to resist adjustments as changes in the national CETA context occurred. Implementing the program design required pushing and pulling, selecting and creating, cajoling and sometimes threatening the service deliverers, the elected officials, the CETA staff, and the advisory council members, as well as juggling existing financial and other resources to achieve the design.

Prior to CETA there was great diffusion of administrative responsibility and little management in the sense of coordinating and creating an integrated service delivery system at the local level. CETA introduced the opportunity for local managers to coordinate and integrate existing programs, service deliverers, and goals or to devise new ones. To be successful, managers had to combine a variety of skills: interpersonal (leadership, supervision, delegation, and negotiation), technical manpower (planning, monitoring, evaluation, and contracting), political (managing competing demands from particular groups for services, from agencies for contracts, and from interest groups for a role in the decision-making process), and personal (tenacity, commitment, experience, and dedication). (See Snedeker and Snedeker, 1978:210.)

As Levitan and Mangum (1981:55) observed, managerial effectiveness was marked by the ability of administrators "to conceptualize the CETA system for their locality, derive a set of objectives consistent with the local economic and political mix, design a realistic program consistent with those objectives, and then direct the human and financial resources of the prime sponsorship toward the achievement of those directives."

Perhaps one of the most difficult things for a Prime Sponsorship director to accomplish in the face of the constant federal interventions that redefined the rules of the game was to create a competent staff. Turnover and "burnout" were problems in many areas, although precise data on the extent of the problems are not available. Levitan and Mangum (1981:59) found that strength of leadership on the part of the local CETA director and a well-defined sense of mission in the agency were important to attracting and retaining competent and dedicated staff. Staff competence could be supplemented by in-house training, exposure to a variety of assignments, and personnel leaves to other agencies. CETA staff grew significantly between 1975 and 1980 when CETA itself was growing. It reached a peak of about 30,000, but extensive decreases occurred in 1981 and 1982 when PSE was phased out, and in 1983 when CETA was being replaced by the Job Training Partnership Act.

In many cases, management at the local level was characterized by a big gap between the ideal and the actual. Prime Sponsor directors and staff often recognized what they wanted to do and what CETA was originally intended to allow them to do—build new systems, be creative, and innovate—but continued federal intervention locked them into increasingly narrow options. Merely coping and surviving became agency goals in many Prime Sponsorships. A few Prime Sponsorships were able to resist the federal encroachments and to promote local goals and programs over nationally imposed ones. But most Prime Sponsorships were able to cope only by lowering their expectations for local management. They reacted to federally imposed crises and priorities rather than creating and implementing their own agendas. This is not a condemnation of those Prime Sponsorships, but simply an acknowledgement of the pressures they faced.

Local Management and Program Performance: A Systematic Analysis

We want to go beyond the general contextual description offered earlier of local management and the problems local managers faced to specify the kinds of differences local management decisions and styles could make in program results. Some have argued that program outcomes are foreordained regardless of what local managers do. Since much policy and legislation is predicated, at least implicitly, on the belief that management and administrative actions do make a difference, it seems worthwhile to investigate carefully the extent and nature of the impact of management. That is what we set out to do in a major study conducted in 15 localities in 1976 and 1977. The most important results of that study are reported and analyzed in the rest of this chapter.

THE NATURE OF THE STUDY

RELATIONSHIPS INVESTIGATED. CETA embodied the belief that local Prime Sponsors knew best how and when to respond to specific local conditions in order to achieve the general goals of the program. Nationally, there was great variation among Prime Sponsorships in terms of types of conditions faced, the types of programmatic responses generated, and the results of the responses.

Our central research question can be stated simply: under what conditions did different management choices seem most likely to enhance program performance?

We began with the belief, supported by our 1974–1976 work in Ohio, that Prime Sponsor performance was influenced both by a variety of conditions that are external and antecedent to management decisions and by those decisions themselves.

We systematically investigated a number of aspects of seven different external local conditions in Prime Sponsorships:

* Economic conditions.
* Demographic characteristics.
* The history of employment and training programs.
* Local government structure.
* The attitudes of various actors with some actual or potential influence over decisions toward employment and training programs.
* The formal administrative location of the CETA unit.
* The resources allocated to the staff of the CETA unit in terms of both budget and personnel (number, qualifications, pay, nature of personnel system).

The first six of these conditions are relatively hard, if not impossible, to change through specific actions by local staff members. We also systematically investigated eight different areas of local management decisions in which the potential for short-run change in response to local staff choices is considerably greater:

* Administrative and programmatic integration or separation of public service employment (PSE) programs with other CETA programs.
* Service delivery operating responsibilities (the balance between in-house programs and those subcontracted).

★ Service deliverer selection processes.

★ Monitoring of programs, (that is the nature and extent of data collection on individual programs).

★ Evaluation of programs (that is, the analysis of program data and comparison of alternative program strategies).

★ Staff relations with other key actors: political officials, Manpower Advisory Councils, business, and unions.

★ Management of actual or potential conflict in the manpower system.

★ Other aspects of program design (most were specific to individual localities, but we looked at the place of the Employment Service in all cases).

We looked at the performance of Prime Sponsors in a number of different ways that will be specified in the body of the analysis that follows. In general, we investigated performance in relation both to presumed national goals for CETA and to explicit and implicit local goals.

SITES. We studied 15 Prime Sponsorships throughout the nation in 1976 and 1977. They were selected as a purposive sample of all Prime Sponsorships in those years (431 in FY 1976 and 445 in FY 1977). Although our sample was not so large that we can generalize about all Prime Sponsorships in a strict statistical sense, we selected Prime Sponsorships in which we expected broad variations in the elements of their programs and management. We were not disappointed in this expectation. (Appendix A, Tables A 3-1 and A 3-2, and Appendix B contain details of the selection of sites and the characteristics of the study sample.)

DATA BASE. A very large part of the data base used for this analysis was created from interviews and documentary materials at the 15 sites. In addition, we used the data for the study of all Ohio Prime Sponsorships in 1974–1976 and some data for all Prime Sponsorships collected by DOL. Data for the study of management in the 15 sites were primarily of two kinds. First, a great range of data on all of the external conditions and the management decisions noted above were collected. These data came mostly from the sites themselves and many were based on detailed interviews (see Appendix A, Table A 3-3). They also came from the national and regional DOL offices and state offices of the Employment Service. Second, aggregate data on performance were collected for all Prime Sponsorships in the country.

GENERAL FINDINGS

Our broadest finding was that CETA at the local level was not a highly constrained system. Local decision-makers, particularly very competent and committed local professional staff members, had a great deal of latitude in determining who received service and how well the programs performed. Factors over which they had considerable control were the most important in explaining quality of performance. The difficulties with DOL summarized earlier in this chapter were real. But skillful local management could still make a positive contribution.

WEAK CONSTRAINTS. We found some factors to be either nonexistent or quite weak as constraints on the patterns of service to participants and various other aspects of program performance. These findings are particularly important because they refute the notion that certain factors, often claimed to be strong constraints beyond the control of local personnel, are dominant. Specifically:

★ The history of pre-CETA manpower programs in localities was of diminishing importance by 1976 even in those areas in which there was a sizeable pre-CETA manpower establishment.

★ The demographic composition of a community did not, except in very broad terms, determine the nature of those individuals whom the Prime Sponsorship served.

★ The level of unemployment at the local level was only a mild constraint on the options open to the CETA staff and on the level of program performance.

★ The aggregate nature of persons served was only a mild constraint on performance. The relatively most disadvantaged (often alleged to be "hard to serve") could be given the highest priority and the programs could still perform very well.

★ The activities of the regional DOL offices had no consistent, major impact on local decisions and program performance. They were an annoyance though not necessarily one with lasting deleterious program effects.

In their study of 12 Prime Sponsorships, Levitan and Mangum (1981:128) confirmed these results: "the placement success of a prime sponsor is not foreordained by participant characteristics, economic conditions, or service patterns." Their regression analysis showed that 60 percent of the variance in placement rate was dependent on local management and emphasis on placement as a goal.

EXPLANATORY FACTORS. The analysis in our study was detailed and complex and we will report only the most important phenomena affecting program performance. When all of the necessary caveats and details have been adduced and the central tendencies have been determined, a relatively simple set of consistently important relationships emerged from this study. Local management decisions about the manpower system (for example, the use of data in decision-making, the openness of the decision-making process, the use of monitoring and evaluation) were clearly related to program performance.

We defined program performance in three different ways: characteristics of persons served, achievement of locally determined goals, and performance on standard indicators of placement and cost efficiency. In addition to local management decisions, two other sets of factors were related to program performance: the preferences, priorities, and commitments of the most influential actors and the mix of programs.

In the sections that follow, we examine the explanatory features associated with each dimension of program performance, paying special attention to the role of local management decisions.

PATTERNS OF SERVICE TO PARTICIPANTS

In assessing patterns of service to participants, we focused on the level of service to females, economically disadvantaged persons, and minorities. We investigated many possible explanations in seeking to explain variations in characteristics of persons served in CETA programs. Three sets of factors had systematic influence: decisions about the balance of local programs, attitudes of influential actors, and—less directly—management practices at the local level.

DECISIONS ABOUT PROGRAM MIX. We explored the possibility that the selection of programs and service deliverers helped determine the type of participants that received service. Typically, work experience programs are widely thought to be associated with higher service to the economically disadvantaged and nonwhites, while an emphasis on PSE has been associated with a relatively lower stress on minorities and the economically disadvantaged (see Perry et al., 1975). The available data did not permit us to conclude that a causal relationship existed between program choice and client patterns. But the strength of the relationship between program expenditures and patterns of service to participants can be examined.

Table 3-1 shows the relationships between spending choices and enrollment patterns. The data on percent of total expenditures for each of the four major program types in Title I were correlated with the percent enrollments for three demographic groups at the end of FY 1975 and 1976.

Only the correlations involving PSE and the disadvantaged and women were statistically significant at the .05 level, but other relationships were of interest, including spending on OJT and classroom training with the enrollment of economically

TABLE 3-1: *Correlation between program spending shares and selected demographic characteristics of enrollees, 15 study sites, Fiscal Years 1975 and 1976*

PERCENT EXPENDITURES ON PROGRAMS	DEMOGRAPHIC GROUP					
	ECONOMICALLY DISADVANTAGED		WHITE		FEMALE	
	1975	1976	1975	1976	1975	1976
Classroom training	0.38	0.21	−0.43	0.21	−0.05	0.01
On-the-job-training	−0.21	−0.08	0.01	0.42	−0.03	−0.28
Work experience	0.06	0.02	0.31	−0.25	0.42	0.32
Public service employment	−0.59[a]	−0.53[a]	−0.03	−0.21	−0.63[a]	−0.46[a]

[a] = significant at the .05 level.

disadvantaged clients, where a negative relationship was present. On the other hand, positive relationships were found between expenditures on classroom training and enrollments of economically disadvantaged clients.

A similar analysis was undertaken for the 17 Ohio Prime Sponsors. The same inverse relationship was found between Title I PSE and the percent of economically disadvantaged clients. However, positive relationships were found between Title I PSE and the proportion of participants who were white or female. The relationships between work experience and the level of economically disadvantaged clients and the proportion of white clients were positive, the same as in the 15 national sites. The relationship between work experience and females was negative, implying that increases in expenditures for work experience are associated with decreases in service to females in Ohio, which contrasts with the national sites.

These relationships suggest that the types of programs funded can have a noticeable effect on the resulting levels of service to certain client groups. However, the choice of service deliverers is also very important in this regard. Community based organizations in a central city often serve a very different combination of participants than a suburban service deliverer operating the same type of program. Thus, in attempting to establish a system that emphasized service to clients, Prime Sponsors had to take into account the history of a deliverers's service to particular groups. The conclusion supported by these data, however, is that program choice alone does have an important and defineable effect on patterns of service to participants.

ATTITUDES OF INFLUENTIAL ACTORS. Local demographic and economic conditions were not directly translated into patterns of service to participants. Rather, demographic and economic conditions were filtered through the perceptions and preferences of manpower actors: political officials, Prime Sponsor staff, members of manpower planning councils and service deliverers. The preferences of human actors were more important than factors over which they had no control.

We sought data on the attitudes about preferred patterns of service to clients from all manpower actors in sites studied. Our survey permitted us to rank the sites according to their desire to serve economically disadvantaged, nonwhite, and female clients. This ranking was then compared with the ranking of actual service patterns (measured in absolute percentages). In general, we found a high degree of congruence between the attitudes of manpower actors and the relative degrees of service. For example, congruence between preferences for service to females in both Title I and PSE and actual service patterns was strong in 11 of the 14 Prime Sponsors for which data were available. And the fit between preferences and service to non-whites in all Titles was also quite good. In the economically disadvantaged category, however, only 9 of the 14 Prime Sponsorships achieved high degrees of congruence. These data lend support to the general argument that Prime Sponsor manpower actors exercised a substantial measure of control over the nature of participant service patterns and that the resulting patterns accorded closely with their general preferences.

We also attempted to weight the preferences of the actors in terms of their relative influence on decisions. For Title I decisions we found that the Prime Sponsor staff was influential in all but two Prime Sponsorships. In the 13 Prime Sponsorships with high staff influence there were clear relationships between the preferences of the staff and service to the economically disadvantaged. Prime Sponsorships that served relatively fewer of the economically disadvantaged also tended to be managed by staffs with a weaker commitment to serving this group.

In PSE decisions, political officials played a more central role in the selection of clients, and they were generally not committed to serving the disadvantaged. The attitudes of the professional staff were also important. Here again the commitment to serving the disadvantaged under PSE tended to be weak or non-existent (often corresponding to the attitudes of political officials) and much lower than the levels for Title I. Eight of the Prime Sponsor staffs had little or no commitment to serving the disadvantaged in PSE, while only three staffs expressed such an attitude for Title I programs. However, it is important to note that committed staff members and elected officials could, indeed, serve disadvantaged individuals with PSE if they chose to do so. Six of our national sites exceeded the national average for service to the disadvantaged with PSE jobs in September 1976. Four of these had staffs and/or elected officials with very strong commitments to serving the poor.

MANAGEMENT PRACTICES. Observations in individual sites suggest that certain management procedures were critical to a well run program and therefore to a conscious choice of participants. For example, the extent to which a staff had relevant data on the universe of need and control over admission procedures, even if decentralized, influenced the direction exerted over who were served. An accurate assessment of what groups were in most need of service and the demographic composition of applicants, as well as a current accounting of enrollees' characteristics were prerequisites for effective targeting of participants.

EXPLAINING LOCAL GOAL ACHIEVEMENT

One of the justifications offered for the establishment of CETA was that it would permit local jurisdictions to pursue employment and training goals that were responsive to unique local needs. Although national goals and standards would still be promulgated, sufficient programmatic latitude would be given to Prime Sponsors for them to avoid the lock-step approach to manpower training presumably found under the categorical programs.

During detailed field work at our 15 sites, we made two basic discoveries. First, presumed national goals for CETA tended not to be very explicit or important at the Prime Sponsor level. Second, there was considerable diversity in the local goals that had been set. We specified both the explicit and implicit local goals that had been adopted at each of the 15 sites and also reached judgments on their level of success in achieving the goals. The goals varied greatly in scope, content, and level of ambitiousness. However, when the goals from the 15 sites were considered together most of them fell into four areas of concern: placement and retention (13 Prime Sponsorships), nature of participants (12 Prime Sponsorships), managing the manpower system (12 Prime Sponsorships), and substantive program activities (6 Prime Sponsorships).

The Prime Sponsors had, in general, set attainable goals for themselves. Of the more than 60 separate goals we identified at the 15 sites, we judged that about 80 percent of them were being achieved with at least moderate success. The goal category with the lowest degree of success was placement/retention.

Relatively low levels of success tended to appear in relation to goals that had only recently been adopted. In these instances the Prime Sponsor had little time to effect desired movement toward the goal. Success was also less likely in cases of goals that were overly ambitious and/or ambiguous.

There was a positive correlation between the priority given to each goal by the professional staff and the degree to which it was attained. Goals of higher priority were more likely to be achieved than those of lower priority. More than simple pronouncements of goal intentions were required for a high degree of goal achievement. Commitment of resources and clear, deliberate means-to-ends actions were also required. And these necessary ingredients were more likely to be found where the staff consciously thought of a goal as high priority.

Two local management factors were associated with a high degree of local goal achievement: quality of staff and organizational arrangements for operating programs. Those Prime Sponsorships with staff that we judged to be of higher quality than others also were achieving their goals better, perhaps in part because the staff was perceptive enough to set reachable goals. Second, those Prime Sponsorships that subcontracted all service delivery tended to do better in goal achievement than those that attempted to manage all or part of the programs directly. As will be discussed below, both of these factors had favorable effects on program performance measured using standard indicators.

EXPLAINING PLACEMENT RATES AND COSTS

EXPLANATORY FACTORS AND PERFORMANCE MEASURES. There are many factors that can affect Prime Sponsor program performance and goal achievement, some of which can be readily identified and measured, though others are more qualitative in nature. The general factors we examined included staff characteristics and management decisions, involvement of actors other than the staff in manpower decisions, characteristics of participants served, expenditures for program activities, enrollments by program activities, economic conditions, and size of the Title I budget allocation.

A major focus of the explanatory approach used here was to identify what the Prime Sponsor staff could do to change program performance, with emphasis on factors over which the staff had some control. While it may be interesting to know about differences in program performance between rural consortia and urban Prime Sponsorships, there is little a staff could do to change the nature and composition of a Prime Sponsorship, even if such a change might improve performance. It is more useful for a staff to know whether factors that are at least partially under their control, such as spending for different program activities, are related to changes in program performance.

Table 3-2 summarizes the explanatory factors we used and indicates the relative degree of staff control over each feature analyzed. Within the three basic categories of degree of staff control, no rank ordering is implied.

The indicators of program performance were derived from standard measures used by DOL to assess Prime Sponsor performance. They included favorable termination results (placement into unsubsidized employment), negative results (nonpositive terminations or "dropouts") and three measures of cost efficiency. (Appendix C contains details on the measurements used.)

In discussing the results of our analysis we focus on factors that had systematic influence and on factors widely believed to be influential for which we discovered no influence on performance. Thus we looked for important links both present and absent. Our focus was limited to explaining performance of programs operated under Title I, the basic training title of CETA. The following sections discuss the impact of individual factors on performance.

UNEMPLOYMENT RATE. The conventional wisdom among manpower practitioners suggested that Prime Sponsor performance suffered as unemployment rates increased. Prime Sponsorships with high unemployment were expected to have lower placement rates and higher costs for placements and enrollments.

TABLE 3-2: *Explanatory factors used in analyzing performance and degree of staff control over them*

Factors over which staff has little control
Unemployment rate
Funding allocation trend
Pre-CETA manpower experience of staff
Administrative integration of Titles I, II, and VI

Factors over which staff has some control
Quality of top staff
Quality of all staff
Nature of operating responsibility
Involvement of business
Involvement of advisory council
System-wide commitment to placement
Level of conflict
Quality of program evaluation

Factors over which staff has relatively high control
Staff commitment to placement
Quality of program monitoring
Use of requests-for-proposals
Involvement of Employment Service
Programmatic integration of Title I
Characteristics of persons enrolled
Characteristics of persons placed
Expenditures for program activities
Enrollments in program activities

Numerous different crosstabulations and correlations for different groupings of Prime Sponsors showed that the association between unemployment rate and placement rates was very weak even when time lags were introduced into the analysis. All of the results of this part of the analysis indicated that while unemployment certainly provided some constraints on placement, the constraints were very weak.

CETA staff did not live in a universe tightly determined by the unemployment rate. Neither they nor the Department of Labor could accurately explain poor program performance simply by referring to a high unemployment rate. Other factors helped explain poor performance. And, even in the face of high unemployment, there was much that could be done by a staff that could result in good performance.

QUALITY OF STAFF. The analysis indicated that there was a clear association between quality of the staff and performance. Specifically, Prime Sponsors with staff judged to be only fair were much more likely to have higher costs per placement than Prime Sponsors with good or very good staffs, and they were somewhat more likely to have lower placement rates.

Although staff quality is difficult to change, it is a partially manipulable factor and can be improved gradually through a variety of management moves.

NATURE OF OPERATING RESPONSIBILITY. One of the features of CETA most attractive to some Prime Sponsors was the opportunity it provided to centralize program operations and make all or most manpower services an in-house responsibility. A commonly cited rationale for this model of program operation was that it allowed the staff to maximize control over program operations and thus perform better. We examined the link between the nature of operating responsibility and program performance measures to see whether Prime Sponsorships with totally in-house operations did better than Prime Sponsorships that subcontracted all services.

In Prime Sponsorships where operations were handled completely in-house or as a mixed operation (combining in-house and subcontracted delivery), placement was likely to be lower and costs higher than in Prime Sponsorships where services were all subcontracted. Our analysis suggests that, assuming there were competent potential subcontractors, subcontracting for service delivery was likely to be more productive than the retention of all or a substantial part of the system for in-house delivery by the Prime Sponsor.

STAFF COMMITMENT TO PLACEMENT. We hypothesized that staff attitudes would be an important factor affecting program performance. To test the hypothesis, we examined the link between the staff's articulated commitment to placement as a goal for Title I and the Prime Sponsor's performance on the placement measures. There was a direct correlation between these two factors. The commitment to placement also carried over to affect cost per placement: Prime Sponsors with a high commitment to placement had lower costs per placement.

Commitment to placement alone was not a guarantee of better placement rates, but it was an important first step for a staff to take because it led to other actions that helped implement the commitment.

NATURE OF PROGRAM MONITORING. We expected Prime Sponsors with high quality monitoring of programs to have better placement rates and lower costs. The expected relationships received moderate support from our analysis.

Of the Prime Sponsors with limited program monitoring, a majority had lower placement rates, as we expected. But of the Prime Sponsors where monitoring was good or very good, only half had higher placement rates, and the other half had lower placements. There was no relationship between quality of monitoring and nonpositive termination rate. A moderately strong inverse relationship was present between the quality of monitoring and the costs per placement.

Program monitoring is an important key to good performance, although the strength of the relationships reported here suggests that it is far from sufficient by itself. But in addition to its effect on program performance as measured here, it should be noted that good quality program monitoring served other important purposes at the local level. No Prime Sponsorship staff was likely to exercise much effective control of a manpower system without good monitoring.

USE OF RFPs. The use of requests-for-proposals (RFPs) to generate competition among potential service deliverers was directly linked to program performance. Such use was related to lower cost per placement and higher placement rates.

Although there are some local political costs involved in implementing an RFP system for program choices, these results indicate the costs are more than offset by improvement in placement rates and to a lesser extent by more cost-efficient operations.

CHARACTERISTICS OF PERSONS SERVED. Some participants have greater disadvantages in the labor market and are more difficult to serve and place than others. This condition accounts for Prime Sponsors' "creaming" (that is, helping the individuals easiest to place) in admissions, referral, and placement. Many practitioners have suggested that serving the hard-core disadvantaged client is incompatible with an emphasis on placement and cost efficiency.

Our analysis examined the association between levels of service to several client groups and program performance to test the assumption that characteristics of clients restrict program performance. Six characteristics can be identified for enrollees who were difficult to place: economically disadvantaged, welfare recipient, limited education (less than high school), unemployed, female, and nonwhite. The percentages of each group served and placed were correlated with the program performance measures.

The general conclusion emerging from our analysis was that characteristics of participants were only weakly related, at most, to performance measures. Such characteristics did not accurately predict placement rates, nonpositive termination rates, or cost for placements and enrollments. In many cases the association between participant characteristics and performance measures was in a direction opposite from what was expected, and in many other cases no association at all emerged.

To test for the possibility that the unemployment rate could be masking relationships between participant characteristics and the performance measures, we used the technique of partial correlation to control statistically for the level of unemployment while examining the associations between characteristics of persons served and the performance measures. The results of the partial correlations did not reveal any systematic relationships. Again we conclude that unemployment rate basically does not affect the nature of the participants served. No systematic relationships emerged, even with controls for the indirect effect of unemployment.

It is clear that characteristics of clients do not dictate levels of performance on placement rates and cost indicators. The absence of relationships between clients generally regarded as difficult to serve and the performance measures indicates that a number of Prime Sponsors were able to serve high levels of clients who would be called "difficult" according to the six above-mentioned characteristics and still obtain relatively high levels of placement rates and low costs, while other Prime Sponsors with lower levels of "difficult" clients were unable to obtain higher placement rates and lower costs.

PROGRAM MIX. The apportionment of expenditures and enrollments among different program activities (classroom training, OJT, work experience, PSE) affected program outcomes. The comparative utility and effects of training programs versus work experience programs have been long discussed by those interested in employment and training programs. Work experience programs are not generally regarded as placement intensive, while classroom training and OJT impart specific skills that presumably enhance the placement potential of participants. Work experience, especially in-school programs for youth, is a relatively "cheap" program: more people can be served in work experience for a given amount of money than can be served in classroom training or OJT. Thus Prime Sponsors with a large proportion of their Title I expenditures going to work experience could be expected to have lower placement rates, higher nonpositive termination rates, and higher costs for placements, although the cost of serving each enrollee would be lower.

The results from our analysis confirmed most expectations. OJT is clearly the most efficient and work experience the least efficient means of obtaining placements. Classroom training investments, though more likely to lower cost for placements, were not associated with increasing placement rates.

A SUMMARY OF IMPORTANT EXPLANATORY FACTORS. Table 3-3 summarizes those management factors that we found to be related to good performance (defined as high placement and low cost). Very weak and nonexistent relationships were excluded from the table. Management factors that pushed in different directions for the two different performance indicators are omitted. The information in Table 3-3 clearly shows that for most of the management factors good performance in placement was linked to good performance on costs.

Some of the factors that were found not to have any rela-

TABLE 3-3: *Association between operational factors and good program performance*

FACTOR	NATURE OF ASSOCIATION	
	HIGH PLACEMENT	LOW COST
High quality staff	Positive	Positive
High degree of subcontracting for service delivery	Positive	Positive
High staff commitment to placement as a goal	Positive	Positive
High quality ·of program monitoring	Positive (weak)	Positive
Use of requests-for-proposals	Positive	Positive (weak)
Relatively high level of expenditures for on-the-job training (OJT)	Positive	Positive (weak)
Relatively low level of expenditures for work experience	Positive (weak)	Absent
Relatively high enrollments in OJT	Positive	Absent
Relatively low enrollments in work experience	Positive	Positive

tionship to performance are also important. Critically, none of those factors over which the staff has the least influence was found to be consistently highly related to performance. Even unemployment had only a modest impact. Thus local CETA staffs were not facing a situation over which they could fairly claim to have little or no control. Equally important, the nature of the participants served in terms of aggregate demographic and economic categories did not have much impact on performance. This means that the hard-core, most disadvantaged part of the population eligible for CETA could be served without sacrificing good placement and cost performance.

Conclusions

Three broad conclusions emerge from this review of local management. First, despite the complexities of CETA administration and the constant changes introduced by Congress and

DOL, local Prime Sponsor staff still had significant latitude to choose different options as they made decisions about service delivery, programs, and patterns of service to participants. This latitude decreased over CETA's lifetime, and administration was difficult even when latitude was greater. But ultimately it was local program managers who made their own choices. DOL and Congress could have facilitated local performance even more by providing a stable environment. The destabilizing effects of national actions no doubt reduced the overall quality of local performance and probably made good performance on the part of marginal Prime Sponsorships very unlikely. But strong Prime Sponsorships could perform well despite nationally induced destabilization.

Second, local management decisions did affect program performance. Choices about the balance among types of programs affected patterns of service to participants (e.g., an emphasis on Title I PSE was linked to lower levels of economically disadvantaged participants, while emphasis on classroom training was linked to higher levels). Client patterns were also affected by the type of service deliverer, and by the attitudes and preferences of influential decision makers.

Achievement of local manpower goals was facilitated by the presence of high quality staff and reliance on subcontracting. Placement rates and cost efficiency were enhanced by a number of local practices, including subcontracting, use of RFPs, and the commitment of the staff to placement as a goal.

Third, non-manipulable factors over which local decision-makers had little direct control (such as the unemployment rate and pre-CETA program history) had little direct effect on program performance. When compared to previous administrative situations, CETA at the local level was not a highly constrained system. What the local managers did made a real difference in terms of how well people were served. And, most important, what they did in terms of "management" necessarily involved grappling with and "managing," as far as possible, a variety of political factors.

CHAPTER FOUR

★

Local Planning and Program Performance

 IN ANY ORGANIZATION, planning activities are central to orderly program implementation. Planning allows program managers to set goals and objectives, to choose strategies for reaching them, and to review progress in achieving them. Though sometimes regarded as a set of technical and apolitical activities monopolized by staff, in CETA planning was conducted in public and immersed in local politics.

Both the Department of Labor's planning requirements and the limited funds available to Prime Sponsors for the basic training title (funds that shrank with time) forced local actors to choose among different target groups, programs, and service deliverers. The decisions made by localities could be distributive or redistributive in nature, controversial or free of conflict, but because they were choices and because they affected the allocation of benefits (programs, services, contracts, dollars) to various groups, they were political decisions.

Considered in this light, manpower planning activities and decisions can be viewed as a special subset of local program management activities and decisions. We analyzed planning in this way. Our conception of planning is very broad. We believe that any planning system is set in a broad local context that directly affects both the nature of that system and program results. We also assume that, within broad limits related to the context, the nature of the planning system has the potential for affecting program results.

In a generic sense planning is one potentially important structured intervention between the contextual factors in a Prime Sponsorship and the results of programs. Theoretically, "good" planning should result in improved program performance because it will help develop the most productive programmatic responses to contextual factors and/or it may help alter those portions of the context that are susceptible to deliberate, short-term manipulation.

In this chapter, we first discuss the nature of manpower planning and examine its context, the actors involved, and temporal changes in planning. The second section summarizes our systematic analysis of manpower planning in a national sample of twelve Prime Sponsorships in 1977 and 1978. The chief purpose of that section is to investigate the relationship of planning to program results. The final section presents conclusions about planning, management, and performance results.

The Nature of Manpower Planning

OVERVIEW OF PLANNING

Manpower planning at its simplest and broadest relates supply—human resources—to demand—available or potential employment opportunities. But in the context of CETA and pre-CETA employment and training programs, which were aimed at the unemployed and economically disadvantaged, manpower planning takes on a more specialized meaning. As Levitan, Mangum, and Marshall (1976:279) describe it, manpower planning consists of efforts to improve the employability, employment opportunities, and incomes of persons experiencing difficulties in successfully competing for jobs in the labor market. During the pre-CETA period and nearly all of CETA, manpower planning was focused almost exclusively on supply: manpower planners were concerned with the needs and abilities of the clientele served by manpower programs. Even after the Private Sector Initiative Program was passed in 1978, attention to demand—that is, the needs and interests of employers who provided jobs—was limited. It will presumably receive greater attention, however, during the implementation of the Job

Training Partnership Act, which succeeded CETA in the fall of 1983.

The essential technical elements of manpower planning for the disadvantaged segment of the labor market have been well defined by Mangum and Snedeker (1974) and by Levitan, Mangum, and Marshall (1976:ch. 13). They identify seven component activities: 1) establishing broad policy goals (for example, decreasing unemployment or reducing welfare dependency); 2) identifying barriers to achieving the broad goals (barriers can be societal, political, personal, or resource-based); 3) examining alternative approaches to goal achievement and assessing them as to feasibility, resources required, and likely consequences; 4) setting measurable objectives to gauge progress toward goal achievement; 5) designing specific programs and implementing them; 6) monitoring program implementation and evaluating results (monitoring focuses on operational questions, while evaluation focuses on impacts, but both ask how well and at what cost a program is operating); and 7) information feedback and continuous program adjustment.

Specialized manpower planning tasks derived from these generic planning activities include: 1) analysis of the characteristics of the eligible population and selection of priority groups to receive service; 2) analysis of labor market conditions to identify current and future job openings accessible to CETA participants; 3) analysis of the barriers to employment facing CETA clients (for example, no job skills, no work history, racial discrimination, lack of education); 4) designing a combination of programs and services to remove or overcome the barriers to employment (such as income maintenance, job creation, remedial education, training, supportive services); 5) selection of vendors to provide the programs and services; and 6) monitoring, evaluation, and feedback of results (these tasks require a working data information system).

Manpower planning is inherently political because it involves making choices about who gets what. Nonetheless, planning can be a dry and pointless exercise if planners lack the political support and resources to get their recommendations implemented. The pre-CETA planning situation for example, was little more than an information exchange because planners from various agencies were making recommendations about how funds should be spent without having the power to implement their recommendations. With CETA, however, local Prime Sponsors were given authority to control the allocation of resources as well as to plan for them, so planning was plunged into local politics. Manpower planners, CETA agencies, and to some extent advisory councils became the arbiters of competing claims from groups and agencies wanting a slice of the CETA pie.

CONTEXT FOR PLANNING

Prime Sponsor staff had to learn to balance the needs of the labor market, the needs of the CETA-eligible population, the expressed or implicit political needs of the elected officials, pressures from service deliverers, and cooperation and interest from private employers. They also had to set feasible priorities, and they had to operate in an environment of changing federal regulations and funding uncertainty.

THE NATIONAL CONTEXT. Each locality responsible for CETA planning and management was subjected to interventions from the federal level that circumscribed local flexibility. The most obvious constraints on local planning were, first, the DOL's requirements that Prime Sponsors submit a formal plan in order to receive grant funds for each title. Analysts and most Prime Sponsor staff made a distinction between the plan as a formal document submitted to comply with grant requirements and planning as a continuous interactive process between managers and programs, a process designed to elicit management information. The plans mandated by DOL were collections of standardized statistical and narrative information that often failed to describe what Prime Sponsors were really doing. Prime Sponsors exerted much effort in producing planning documents for DOL that were of limited local utility (Mirengoff and associates, 1982:42–45).

DOL emphasized compliance with prescribed plan formats and also projected "participation" from various demographic groups instead of program substance and quality. DOL's focus was on the form of the plan, not its content. DOL paid little or no attention to long-term program goals and results.

The addition of categorical programs during the life of CETA meant that planning had to occur for each program separately, rather than for integrated programs and resources. Almost immediately after 1974 Prime Sponsors lost the opportunity to plan comprehensively because of actions taken by Congress and DOL.

Because planning as defined by DOL was tied to annual funding cycles, Prime Sponsors were at the mercy of the vagaries of congressional appropriations. Uncertainty over timing and amount of funds meant that contingency plans had to be patched together and later modified and resubmitted when actual funding levels became known. The jerky funding cycle plagued staff efforts to plan rationally, and was clearly the most serious nationally-induced problem facing Prime Sponsor staff as they tried to manage their programs (Levitan and Mangum, 1981:65–68).

Not content to leave the prescribed outlines and contents of plans alone, DOL constantly tinkered and revised. Especially after the 1978 CETA amendments, these changes caused great administrative hassles for staff, complicated the planning process, and increased the amount of time necessary for preparing plan documents for DOL. The changes, however, did not increase the relevance of the documents to local managers.

The definition of Prime Sponsorships as political jurisdictions meant that manpower planning was focused on portions of labor markets. DOL's consortium incentives were insufficient to encourage jurisdictions to combine to serve full labor market areas. Many consortia that did form operated on a pass-through rather than an areawide basis (each consortium partner simply got a fixed percentage of the funds). Cities and counties were the operational units in CETA, even though very few of them coincided with labor market boundaries. Finally, the pressures of the federally defined planning cycle and its requirements forced Prime Sponsor staff to take a short-range, immediate view of planning. Very few Prime Sponsors were able to think strategically about what they wanted to happen more than a few months from the present, let alone a year or more in the future. The annual appropriations cycle, the press of implementing numerous programs and adjusting to frequently changing federal regulations and directives forced all but the most able staffs into a short run, planning-for-the-present stance.

THE LOCAL CONTEXT. The exact configuration of the key elements in the local planning context—the actors involved, the planning recommendations, and the previous program history—varied in each locality, but certain patterns existed in all sites.

Professional staff were consistently the most influential actors in planning. The role and influence of the advisory councils, service deliverers, and elected officials varied depending on local tradition and precedent, attitudes of the staff, and political clout. In the next section we examine the influence of different actors in more detail.

The principal challenge facing manpower staffs was to determine which programs to continue, drop, or add, which service deliverers to fund, and what target groups to serve. What staff needed most to do was to identify the criteria to use for making recommendations and decisions. Data could be quantitative or qualitative, political or objective, or some mix. But the key to using the data was to apply criteria systematically when making planning recommendations.

The ability of the planning staff to get their plans adopted depended largely on their political sense, that is, their ability to interpret the local situation and anticipate what was feasible and what was not. If they wanted to proceed with proposals that would generate conflict, their success depended on their ability to forge a coalition in support of the change and to document the need for the change, preferably with hard data. The advisory council and an open public planning process could be used constructively by staff to promote and legitimate recommendations. But if service deliverers had a dominant role on the council, they could obstruct change.

Some planning staffs tackled poorly performing and entrenched service deliverers and won (for example, because they had data to document the poor performance, they had support of the elected officials and the council, and had alternative programs and deliverers to put in place). Some staff tackled the status quo and lost. Others declined to try to make changes except incrementally.

Sawyer (1974) identified key local factors associated with successful pre-CETA planning: the support of chief elected officials, the support of the top administrators in the manpower agency, a public planning process, and staff competence. These factors continued to be key elements for good local planning in the CETA era.

THE PLANNERS

To the extent that planning refers to the technical aspects of collecting and analyzing data on the labor market, demography, and program performance and preparing narrative documents for DOL, then planning is clearly a staff function. Throughout the period of CETA's existence, professional staff had the training, experience, and bureaucratic responsibility for preparing statistical analyses, mastering the regulations, and submitting acceptable planning documents to DOL. Planning in CETA, however, was not just a paper exercise but a real allocation of resources, and numerous actors beyond staff were involved. Staff members were unquestionably the most important participants because they had the data and prepared the first drafts of proposals. But they were not the only participants. In most Prime Sponsorships, generating a first draft of a plan was only the beginning of a public process of review and comment, consulting, reviewing data, and adjusting recommendations. This public process involved the local elected officials, the advisory council, and service deliverers.

ELECTED OFFICIALS. Most of the time elected officials were not personally involved in manpower planning. The actual analysis and plan writing were, of course, staff responsibilities. The role of the elected official was either to support or to overturn staff recommendations if controversy generated by those recommendations required intervention. Much of the time planning decisions in CETA were routine and handled by staff. But elected officials were final arbiters. They were the ones who signed the plan that went to DOL and they were the natural focal point for complaints and appeals by those at the local level who felt their interests had been given short shrift.

Some elected officials consistently became involved in decision-making about service deliverers, programs, or target groups because they had strong preferences about what the outcomes should be. More often, however, elected officials intervened only on an intermittent basis to protect a favored deliverer or program. In some Prime Sponsorships, elected officials refused to reverse decisions that had been ratified by staff and the advisory council in a public planning process. They consciously used the public process as a buffer for upholding decisions and resisted the temptation to make decisions for political reasons. Oftentimes, elected officials did not have to become personally involved in defending or overturning planning recommendations because the staff were sensitive to what their preferences were and avoided making recommendations that would not have their support.

ADVISORY COUNCILS. Manpower advisory councils (MACs) were statutory creations dating from the original CETA law in 1973 (later amendments added youth councils and Private Industry Councils). Advisory councils included a variety of mandated members—representatives of community based organizations, the Employment Service, education, labor, and business. MACs were advisory: they were to submit recommendations on programs, goals, procedures, and plans, but final decisions were reserved for the Prime Sponsor.

MACs were intended to provide a forum for broad participation in manpower planning. In practice, however, participation from the general public was nonexistent. Attendance at council meetings was limited to those with a direct interest in outcomes. The assumption that decentralization would lead to broad public accountability was not realized through the MACs (or any other mechanism). Manpower issues were not noticeable to the general public.

The MACs had variable roles in influencing plans and decisions. Mirengoff and Rindler (1978:56–57) found that MACs made a substantial contribution in only a few sites during the first year of CETA planning. By the end of the second year, MACs were important in a third of the study sites. A separate study in FY 1980 showed that in about half of the sites, MAC recommendations on most issues were adhered to by staff (Levitan and Mangum, 1981:60).

Three types of council roles emerged (see Mirengoff and Rindler, 1978:53). *Informational* MACs were "kept" bodies, convened only to receive information from staff and to rubberstamp recommendations; they had no independent initiative. *Consultative* MACs were not totally passive bodies, as they were asked for their views and input. *Participatory* MACs, active in planning and reviewing operations, used a committee structure to get work done; issues most commonly addressed were the ranking of target client groups and program proposals.

The key determinant of the role a council would have and whether it would be effective was the attitudes and policy of CETA staff and elected officials. If staff and political officials regarded councils as an asset and gave them real assignments, they could be very constructive aids to planning. If, however, staff and political officials regarded councils as a federally imposed nuisance and limited them to a minimal, reactive role, the MACs were unlikely to achieve anything. A productive MAC needed a productive partnership with the staff. Without such a relationship, MACs could not function independently.

SERVICE DELIVERERS. Service deliverers were among the most knowledgeable participants in the planning process, but they obviously had a vested interest in having their funding continued. Although service deliverers were permitted by the regulations to sit on councils, they were not allowed to vote on issues affecting their funding. They met the letter of the law, if not the spirit, by engaging in logrolling agreements with other service deliverers (vote for me and I'll vote for you) and by actively lobbying other members. Usually they were successful in getting refunded as long as their program performed reasonably well. In a few cases clearly marginal performers were retained on the CETA dole to avoid a local political battle, but by the end of FY 1980 most staffs and MACs had dumped the least effective deliverers (see Levitan and Mangum, 1981:60).

CHANGES IN THE PLANNING PROCESS

For a discussion of changes in CETA planning, two periods are particularly notable. The first was the transition from the pre-CETA planning system known as CAMPS—the Cooperative Area Manpower Planning System (see Mirengoff and Rindler, 1976:48). In 1968 CAMPS began to try to increase coordination among the fragmented categorical programs. Participants were representatives of local public agencies involved in MDTA and EOA programs. There was no citizen participation and no involvement from non-MDTA or EOA manpower programs. The major flaw in the CAMPS planning process was that local recommendations, which were submitted to regional DOL offices, had no influence on the actual allocation of resources. DOL made the decisions about how funds would be spent, and locally developed plans were often ignored. The CAMPS process helped to develop a core of manpower planners at the local level and it stimulated some communication, even if not coordination, among manpower agencies. But as it was little more than a paper exercise, CAMPS had no impact on outcomes.

But planning in CETA was plagued with its own problems. Categorical programs, for example, impeded comprehensive planning; uncertainties and cuts in funding forced Prime Sponsors to take cautious approaches to planning and operations. The administrative burden of preparing separate plans for each CETA program was recognized during the 1978 CETA reauthorization. The variety of changes introduced constituted the second milestone (and, as it turned out, millstone) for manpower planning (For a discussion of the effects of the 1978 amendments, see Mirengoff and associates, 1980:ch. 2.)

The 1978 amendments were intended to simplify the planning process, to reduce Prime Sponsor paperwork, and to increase the involvement of advisory councils. But these desired effects were not achieved. Separate annual plans were replaced by a single and supposedly one-time-only Master Plan and by a single annual plan covering all programs operated by the Prime Sponsor. However, the Master Plan had to be changed and revised. The annual plan required great detail and time to prepare (it represented, in effect, only a stapling together of various separate program plans, not an integrated plan for all programs.) Parts of the annual plan had to be modified frequently to take into account the erratic funding levels set by Congress. The new requirements for additional data actually increased the planning workload for Prime Sponsor staff, while the changes in the composition of the advisory councils had no effect on councils' roles or influence.

Throughout CETA's lifetime the major planning difficulty encountered by Prime Sponsors continued to be the uncertainty resulting from late notification of funding levels. One year forward funding was actually authorized in CETA legislation, but it was never put into practice. Appropriations were rarely enacted before the beginning of the fiscal year, although planning was supposed to begin up to nine months in advance.

Other major problems that plagued CETA staff were the inadequacies of local demographic and labor-market data, the frequency with which Master Plans had to be revised, and the redundancy and unnecessary detail required by DOL in the annual plans (see Mirengoff and associates, 1982:42).

The many pressures that forced Prime Sponsors to plan rapidly also limited their use of evaluation. In all but a few sites, staff did not assess the impacts of programs and weigh alternative approaches to programs (Snedeker and Snedeker, 1978:208–10). Although they did short-term program monitoring, they were under such pressure from DOL that their monitoring of their own subcontractors emphasized immediate concerns like expenditures and enrollment levels and placement rate, not quality of programs.

PSE PLANNING

The sudden addition of Title VI in late 1974 and the subsequent buildup of PSE forced Prime Sponsors to squeeze in time for PSE planning, which was quite different from planning for the basic training title (Title I before 1978 and Title IIBC after the 1978 amendments). Because PSE planning began so abruptly, Prime Sponsors had only six weeks to submit their first Title VI plan to DOL. Subsequent PSE expansion occurred under great pressure for speed at the local level. Since PSE planning was separate physically and functionally from Title I planning, the respective programs were categorically separate and the local staffs responsible for PSE planning and operations were usually different. PSE staff were often located in a different administrative unit and reported to a different individual than did the Title I planners.

Elected officials were much more closely involved in PSE planning than in Title I. The involvement of elected officials was much greater in jurisdictions experiencing serious fiscal problems. Usually no one else beside the staff and elected officials was involved in PSE planning. Substantive participation of the advisory council was virtually nonexistent.

The main PSE planning decision, the allocation of jobs among various government and nonprofit agencies, was made by the chief elected official and staff. The extensive information required by DOL on wage rates, occupational summaries, and demographic characteristics was totally irrelevant to the basic local planning decision of how PSE jobs would be distributed within the Prime Sponsorship. The PSE planning information requirements constituted an even greater burden for staff than did the Title I requirements. (See Baumer and Van Horn, 1984, for a thorough study of PSE planning and implementation.)

Prime Sponsor Planning and Program Performance: A Systematic Analysis

AN OVERVIEW OF THE STUDY

During FY 1978 we undertook a detailed study of manpower planning in a dozen Prime Sponsorships throughout the nation (for the full final report see Ripley and associates, 1979d). Our interest was not simply to describe the nature of planning activities and systems but to examine the effects of planning on program performance. The empirical literature in the early years of CETA stressed the difficulties and diversity of local manpower planning efforts but did not look beyond planning to programmatic consequences. In the study summarized briefly here, our intent was to link planning systems and decisions with program outcomes. Three key sets of relationships served as the focus for the research: general context and planning systems, general context and performance, and planning systems and performance.

We collected data on local planning (such as history of CETA programs, local economic conditions, demographics, and previous planning history), the nature of current planning activities (including local goals, target groups, labor market information, selection of program vendors, monitoring, evaluation, and the character of the public planning process) and program results (measured using local goal achievement, quality of job place-

ments, and standard indicators of placement rates and costs).
We used quantitative data from Prime Sponsor files, standard
reports, and national DOL data as well as information from over
400 interviews conducted and 50 meetings attended during field
work.

The twelve sites selected for the study were chosen to maximize variation of type, general economic condition, size, and
geographic location of Prime Sponsors. In addition, sites were
chosen because they were known to take planning seriously and
to do it relatively well. (Appendix Table A 4-1 profiles the study
sites at the time of the research.)

MODELS OF PLANNING

DERIVATION OF THE MODELS. We view *planning activities* as a
specific subset of *general management activities.* Both management and planning activities, decisions, and decision-making
processes are set within a *general local context.*

Planning decisions cover five major areas: identification and
choice of local goals; identification and choice of participant
target groups to be served; identification of target occupations
for training and placement; identification and choice of program
mix; and identification and selection of service deliverers who
are to deliver the training and employment services.

Management decisions include all planning decisions, as well
as other decisions necessary to organize, implement, and operate an employment and training program. Examples include
arrangements to manage actual or potential conflict; choice of
the nature of and use of monitoring and evaluation of programs;
and the nature of staff relations with such key figures as political
officials, advisory council members, and service deliverers.
These management factors are important in considering planning because they form part of the context of planning decisions
and thus may influence them.

General context consists of conditions external to the CETA
program that are generally not open to short-term change
through the actions of the local program staff. Included are such
factors as economic conditions, the history of employment and
training programs in the locality, and the structure of local
government. The general context is important insofar as it influences the nature of planning.

Our purpose, at the most general level, was to explain how and why Prime Sponsors plan. We began with the belief that the nature of Prime Sponsor planning is influenced by two broad factors: the general context and general management decisions. Testing this assumption led us to pose three central questions, which are discussed in sections that follow:

1. What major variations exist in the nature of planning decisions?

2. Which factors in the general context and in the set of management decisions are important influences on the nature of planning and which are not?

3. How do the important factors influence the nature of planning?

We analyzed the nature of planning in the twelve study sites on five dimensions of variation and applied each of these to the five planning decision areas. Determination of the five dimensions was based on preliminary analysis of planning system characteristics; these five were the ones that occurred most frequently and with greatest significance.

Stability of relations among actors, the first dimension, was analyzed according to which actors participated in each decision; the extent and consistency of their influence; and the reasons for their influence. Overall stability of each decision area was also examined.

Conflict over planning decisions was similarly analyzed, considering not only the level of conflict but also how well conflict was managed and channeled to productive ends. A comparison of FY 1978 with FY 1974 and 1975, when local decision-making patterns were being established, indicates that most sites had declined in overall level of conflict. But there was also some variation in 1978.

Degree of routine planning is a summary measure that takes into account the presence of decision-making routines and their success. Such routines included regular use of RFPs, substantial reliance on the advisory council, and the development and use of standard data analysis formats.

Feedback mechanisms were assessed along two lines: whether they were present and whether they worked. They were interpreted to include both "hard" (for example, Management Information Systems (MIS) formal evaluation) and "soft" (for example, informal reports from job developers) information.

Deliberate attention to long-range decisions, the final dimension, was defined as decision-making that looked beyond a one-year time span. Prime Sponsors assessed positively on this measure consciously allocated time and resources to the long-range planning function.

On the basis of the major variations we observed, we constructed three general models of planning systems and labeled them *Crisis Management* planning, *Operations Management* planning, and *Future Oriented* planning. Table 4-1 summarizes the broad characteristics of the three models.

It should be noted that these models are derived from twelve Prime Sponsorships that were reputed to take planning seriously. In other studies we came across a number of sites in which planning was quite rudimentary and, in many important senses, nonexistent. Thus, a fourth model is implicit: *No Consistent Planning.* However, since we are presently reporting on sites in which at least some consistent planning was observed to take place, we limit ourselves to discussing the contexts for and results of these three models. But we are not asserting that all Prime Sponsorships in the country necessarily fell into one of the three categories. A number would belong in the No Consistent Planning category, and there would also be a greater number in the Crisis Management category than is indicated by our identification of only one of our twelve sites. And there would probably be a smaller proportion of Future Oriented sites than is indicated by our identification of 25 percent of the study sites fitting that model. In short, we do not claim that the breakdown of our twelve sites reflects the breakdown among all Prime Sponsorships. But we are confident that the four models would adequately describe all cases nationally.

In the *Crisis Management* model (only one of our twelve sites) the influence structure is highly unstable. Influence of actors changes from moment to moment and from decision to decision. Little trust or stability in communication is present. In addition, when conflict arises, which is often, it is unmanaged (that is, there are no routines established and accepted for conflict resolution). A critical characteristic of the Crisis Management system is the malfunctioning of the information feedback system. Although good qualitative and quantitative informa-

TABLE 4-1: *Characteristics of planning models*

Dimension of variation	Crisis Management model	Operations Management model	Future Oriented model
Stability of relations among key figures	Unstable	Stable	Stable
Conflict over planning decisions	Unmanaged	Well-managed	Well-managed
Degree of routine in planning	Lack of successful routines	Many routines	Many routines
Feedback mechanisms	Absent or malfunctioning	In place and utilized	In place and utilized
Deliberate attention to long-range decisions	None	None	Important

tion may in principle be available, without a feedback pipeline the information will not be utilized in making important decisions. In sum, the Crisis Management planning system is characterized by a reactive decision-making process that focuses, of necessity, on unpredictable problems, often organizational in character, that continually emerge from an unstable environment. No patterns of influence are established among actors, and a generally chaotic system seems to prevail. But, even in the midst of turmoil, planning is not abandoned. This fact creates a model of planning instead of a model of non-planning.

In contrast, the *Operations Management* system (eight of our twelve sites) is characterized by a stable and smoothly working structure of influence in which actors recognize their own and other actors' positions. In addition, conflict is well managed (that is, routines for resolving conflict are established, accepted, and practiced). Planning activities, whether qualitative or quantitative, generate important information, organize it, and communicate it to the important decision-makers. A feedback operation is in place and is utilized. Finally, the decision-making process focuses mainly on short-term performance with a time frame usually a year or less in length.

The *Future Oriented* planning model (three of our twelve

sites) differs from the Operations Management model only in its deliberate attention to long-range decisions. Future Oriented planning systems will not necessarily have any different or better monitoring systems. Both qualitative and quantitative information is gathered and relayed to important actors so as to improve ongoing programs incrementally. Yet the Future Oriented system commits significant organizational time, energy, and capital, both human and financial, to the mapping of strategies for long-range goals.

Our research did not lead us to concude that there is an inherent ranking among the models of planning. Clearly there are high programmatic costs for a Prime Sponsorship that has no consistent planning and there are also high costs for the Crisis Management model—a system in chaos can have little hope of fulfilling its goals. Neither the Operations Management nor the Future Oriented model seems intrinsically superior to the other. Depending on the conditions and evolutionary state of the Prime Sponsorship, either style may be appropriate and productive.

PATTERNS OF INFLUENCE. In general, only Prime Sponsor staff, service deliverers, advisory councils, and political officials were actively engaged in the planning process at the local level. The influence of each group, moreover, varied according to the type of decision. It is also worth noting that in only one case was the Employment Service important in making any planning decisions and in no cases were representatives of DOL important.

We found, as we expected, that staff members generally had the most influence on decisions, usually because of their control over information. In the Crisis Management site, however, staff members were significantly less dominant than in other sites, while service deliverers were very important. At the other extreme, in the three Future Oriented sites, staff members were active in all five areas of decision and very seldom shared their influence with others. The influence of service deliverers, in addition to that of staff, was common in Operations Management sites, where it was most significant in decisions about selection of service deliverers and program mix. The influence of advisory councils was found most frequently in selection of target occupations and service deliverers, although the type and level of influence did not strongly correlate with other factors. Influence of political officials appeared in some decisions but was not frequent, though it should be noted that the infrequent *participation* of political officials in decision-making may mask the greater indirect *influence* these officials may actually have because of anticipatory decision-making by the staff.

PLANNING DECISION AREAS. In analyzing local goals, we found a closed process in which staff chose goals based on value judgments with little use of data. Although there were variations in this pattern, they were not so numerous as variations in other areas. Future Oriented sites tended to have more specific long-term goals, although not usually stated formally.

The selection of target groups was most commonly the focus of attention by staff, service deliverers, and advisory council members, who made high use of socioeconomic, monitoring and evaluation data. The pattern we observed suggests that the selection of target groups, because it directly affects allocation of resources, is next most controversial after the selection of service deliverers and therefore receives serious consideration. At most sites the decision about target occupations was treated as a technical one. Little nonstaff participation was noted, and staff made extensive use of data.

The choice of program types split into two fairly clear patterns: one in which it was derived from other decisions and made with input from service delivery agencies, and the other in which staff decided the issue and applied it to the selection of service deliverers. The first pattern was more common; the second appeared only in the three Future Oriented sites.

The selection of service deliverers likewise displayed two patterns: the three Future Oriented sites used a closed decision-making process that was not greatly influenced by the political clout of individual groups; most of the others, however, employed more open systems that were susceptible to pressure from service deliverers and advisory council members.

All planning systems that we observed focused almost exclusively on CETA matters. Even in the Future-Oriented sites we did not see any systematic integration of CETA planning with community development planning. In short, CETA planning focused only on planning activities with relation to the supply side of the labor market. Planning linked to non-CETA programs with concrete actions on the demand side of the labor market remained largely virgin territory.

THE RELATIONSHIP OF PLANNING AND CONTEXT

GENERAL CONTEXT. Four groups of factors were used to describe the general context: the nature of the local economy (unemployment rate, economic growth, and percent of jobs in the service sector); the nature of the local population (percent of people unemployed, percent economically disadvantaged); size of the basic (Title I) CETA program; and organizational characteristics (consortium partner, hierarchical location of agency). When these factors were related to the types of planning models, the effects were found to be minimal. The distribution of contextual factors among the three models was practically random.

MANAGEMENT DECISIONS AS CONTEXT. Four groups of indicators were selected to represent management activities. The first offered an estimate of the importance of staff in shaping the nature of planning in terms of two variables, the quality of key staff and the presence of discontinuities in key staff tenure. The second dealt with the nature of relations between the staff and other important groups such as political officials, service delivery contractors, advisory councils, and business representatives. The third examined some measures of the nature of data obtained for use in decisions, centering on the quality and extent of monitoring and evaluation information. Finally assessed was the extent to which optional program activity influenced the nature of planning. Optional program activity was defined as successful competition by a Prime Sponsor for one of the grants awarded by DOL on a competitive rather than a formula basis. [The program possibilities at the time of the study were the Skills Training Improvement Program and the Youth Incentive Entitlement Pilot Projects (YIEPP), Tier I and Tier II.]

Analysis of the associations between the management variables and the three planning models showed that strong relationships did exist between the kinds of management choices made by the Prime Sponsor and the nature of the planning systems (see Appendix Table A 4-2). Specifically, the Future Oriented sites were distinguished by a set of particular variations on the management indicators. They invariably had excellent key staff and experienced no discontinuities in key staff or administration. Staff were uniformly the most influential figures with only minor participation by service deliverers. The Future Oriented sites had a high degree of business involvement, above-average political support, success in obtaining supplemental funding, and uniformly high-quality monitoring.

In Operations and Crisis Management sites, in contrast, service deliverers had significant influence (in seven of nine cases). Three were handicapped by discontinuities in key staff, in two cases severely. Few sought or had the involvement of business. Political support above average levels was present in only four of nine cases. A majority did, however, win optional grant competitions, for the large Tier I YIEPP program in two cases. Only three of the nine possessed monitoring systems that were judged high in both extent and quality.

Thus, although no contextual factor emanating from management decisions was unique to the Future Oriented sites, their characteristic pattern included high-quality staff who dominated decision-making, stronger than average political support, thorough monitoring, and active involvement of business.

SUMMARY: CONTEXT AND PLANNING. Though the general context was not related to the type of planning models, the context of management decisions showed a clear association. This observation is significant because most of the management decisions examined were manipulable by staff. Once again, as we found in the previous two chapters, local implementers by and large controlled their own destinies.

EXPLAINING PERFORMANCE:
CONTEXT AND PLANNING SYSTEMS

In the present section we examine the link between planning and program performance. We look also at the effects of context and management decisions on performance, to test both previous findings (reported in Ch. 2 and 3) and conventional wisdom prevalent among manpower practitioners. Performance was measured using the same variety of quantitative indicators of terminations and costs we used in Chapter 3 (these are summarized in Appendix C).

GENERAL CONTEXT AND PERFORMANCE. Seven indicators measuring economic conditions, demographic conditions, and program decisions were used to represent general context. Multivariate regression analysis was employed to determine the effect of these factors on program performance. We were interested in two issues: the combined effect of the explanatory factors on a given performance measure and the influence of a single factor relative to other factors. The following conclusions emerged from the analyses:

1. The proportion of variance in the dependent performance measures explained by the combined effect of unemployment rate, distribution of funds among programs, and demographic characteristics of participants was low—less than one-third. Thus there was a great deal of latitude for staff to affect program performance even after these factors have been taken into account. This result was true for other comparison groups of Prime Sponsors as well as for the study sites.

2. The unemployment rate was the single least important explanatory factor affecting change in the performance measures among the planning sites. The implication is that the unemployment rate may have had more effect in the hearts and minds and perceptions of staff than it actually had on the program performance of Prime Sponsors. Attitudes about the impact of unemployment may be a much greater constraint on performance than the actual unemployment rate. And, of course, attitudes can be very real in their impact.

3. The demographic characteristics of participants did not control performance. For only two measures of performance was a demographic characteristic (the percent of enrollees without a high school education) found to be the most important explanatory factor. For the other measures of performance, demographic characteristics were not important explanatory variables.

4. The proportion of expenditures for training activities (combining classroom work and OJT) was not important in accounting for variance in the placement measures in the twelve sites. These results were surprisingly different from common expectations about the association between higher commitments

to training and better placement rates. Regression analysis using comparison groups of Prime Sponsors upheld the expected relationships, however. So it would be premature to dismiss the impact of the proportion of spending on training activities.

MANAGEMENT AND PERFORMANCE. Management characteristics were chosen to reflect qualities of and processes within the CETA staff organization itself. We focused attention on three broad categories of management indicators: staff characteristics, administrative characteristics, and relations with other actors. We correlated these with the performance indicators. Management features were not related to performance on the two cost-efficiency measures. Placement rates had a strong positive correlation with quality of staff, quality of monitoring, and business involvement. Nonpositive termination rates varied inversely with quality of staff and quality of monitoring. In short, quality of staff and quality of program monitoring were consistently important.

PLANNING SYSTEMS AND PERFORMANCE. In general, we expected that Prime Sponsorships with a Crisis Management planning system would demonstrate worse performance figures than sites with either an Operations Management or a Future Oriented planning mode. We did not predict much difference in the performance measures between the Operations Management and Future Oriented planning sites, as the decision-making processess for planning are basically the same and are sound in both models. Evidence generally confirmed these expectations.

Regardless of how performance was measured or analyzed, the Crisis Management site showed poorer performance than the other sites. There was little difference between the performance of Operations Management and Future Oriented planning sites, although Future Oriented sites showed slight but sometimes significant superiority in the selected measures of performance. Both types of sites were able to meet planned levels of performance.

EXPLAINING PERFORMANCE: A SUMMARY. As in the previous section, where we saw that the staff was able to control the nature of their planning systems by conscious manipulation of selected elements of their management environment, the most striking theme emerging from the analysis of program performance is the degree of control that Prime Sponsor staff can exert over program performance. If the indicators of context and management characteristics are classified in terms of the extent to which the staff can directly control or shape them, a very interesting pattern emerges. *The explanatory factors readily manipulable by staff are those that tended to have a high positive correlation with performance variations; the explanatory factors over which the staff can exert less direct control were not strongly associated with performance variations.* Cynicism about the potential for achievement at the local level would be inappropriate on the basis of our analysis of data. Improvements in program performance are little constrained by the less manipulable elements of context such as economic conditions and demographic characteristics, despite the contrary assertions of conventional wisdom.

The factors that we found to be most strongly associated with better performance were the quality of the staff, the nature and extent of business involvement, and the quality of monitoring, all of which are highly manipulable by staff.

Conclusions

CETA planning was set in a local context of previous manpower programs, existing service deliverers, established patterns of influence, and demographic and economic conditions. The local context was significantly shaped by federal intervention, including imposition of administrative complexity, delays in appropriations, recategorization of programs, and the overloading, then phasing out of PSE. Emerging as a product of the combined local and federal context, CETA planning emphasized contingency and short-range issues. Strategic and long-range planning were virtually impossible due to the unpredictability of funds and policies, as well as day-to-day administrative pressures.

The formal planning document required by DOL often bore little relation to the operational intentions and needs of Prime

Sponsors. The DOL plan was part of a routine to get funds. Real planning occurred in a Prime Sponsor's negotiation with subcontractors and the advisory council over key local choices— whom to serve, what programs to operate, which vendors to fund.

CETA staff were the most influential group in manpower planning. Though elected officials, the ultimate authority, were always indirectly important, they were usually not directly involved. Advisory councils were influential only if the staff and elected officials wanted their participation. Probably no more than one-third to one-half of all MACs achieved real significance in local planning decisions. Service deliverers derived their importance through representation on the MACs, lobbying of MAC members and elected officials, and political pressure. Broad citizen participation in CETA planning was nonexistent.

Three types of planning systems were identified in the systematic analysis of planning and program performance: Future Oriented, Operations Management, and Crisis Management. A fourth model, No Consistent Planning, was implicit.

General contextual factors such as economic and demographic conditions did not determine what kind of planning systems emerged in individual Prime Sponsorships. Each Prime Sponsorship could design the kind of planning system desired for programmatic reasons and was not forced into a specific planning mode by external factors. The general management context in a Prime Sponsorship was, however, related to the kind of planning system that emerged.

Future Oriented planning systems were characterized by a pattern of staff-dominated decision-making, a stable and high-quality staff, stronger than average support for staff from political officials, thorough monitoring, and the active involvement of the private business sector.

In Prime Sponsorships with operations management planning systems there was more likely to be less staff domination of decision-making (usually involving significant sharing of influence with service deliverers), more turnover in key staff, low involvement of business, and less well-developed monitoring systems.

Management characteristics and planning both had stronger influence on program performance than any contextual variables. This is a very encouraging finding, for it means that Prime Sponsorships—particularly the staff—have the latitude to focus on management decisions and planning, over which they have considerable control, in order to improve performance. Conventional wisdom suggesting that economic conditions and demographic characteristics of participants determine or at least highly constrain performance received no empirical support. The factors we found to be most strongly associated with better performance were the quality of staff, the nature and extent of business involvement, and the quality of monitoring.

Five major conditions promote effective planning if present and impede it if absent:

1. Goals are essential. These need to be consciously addressed and articulated. And this process needs to be repeated; it cannot be assumed that goals will be adopted if announced only once. Lack of clearly articulated goals or the presence of goals that are almost all implicit can create problems in both planning and, ultimately, performance.

2. Some form of public planning process or provision for major input from actors outside the staff is very useful in promoting planning decisions that are responsive to conditions in the "real world" and also in promoting decisions that are widely accepted as legitimate by the major participants in the system. The advisory council is usually the centerpiece in a public planning process.

3. Both good monitoring and well-developed Management Information Systems (MIS) are essential for linking planning to operations and using both to improve performance. Evaluation is more rare, but where it exists it is a useful addition to the basic monitoring and MIS activities.

4. Perhaps most important as a foundation for many of the other conditions, Prime Sponsorships need to be very careful to develop a solid staff—ample in number, well-trained, willing to stay with the job at hand for a period of years, and committed both to the overall success of the program and to some concrete programmatic goals.

5. The CETA staff needs to have a productive relationship

with its subcontractors. Where those subcontractors are strong performers with a strong independent political base, this relationship may well have to be based on negotiation and compromise aimed at creating a "family feeling" about the whole system.

In short, a careful analysis of the relations among general context, management context, planning, and program results shows planning—theoretically a dry and abstract activity and usually treated that way by social scientists—to be thoroughly political. Decisions made during planning cycles represented the outcomes of contention among competing sets of values and interests at the local level. Planning was thoroughly immersed in the political arena. It was not an arena widely visible beyond those individuals and groups with immediate interests to pursue. But to those with such interests the planning decisions about various kinds of allocations determined how well their interests would be served and their turf preserved. Despite the relative invisibility of this kind of local planning and decision-making, we think it can be understood only as intimately involved in a larger set of political processes. And local program results can be understood only if these relatively invisible processes are observed and analyzed carefully in systematic fashion.

CHAPTER FIVE

★

Stalking the Private Sector

 SINCE THE 1960's employment and training policy has included some role for the private as well as the public sector in planning, implementing, and evaluating federally funded programs. In recent years, the nature and magnitude of the invitation to the private sector has broadened significantly, reflecting a twofold concern: first, that programs operated by the government had not lived up to public expectations and that the private sector could do a better job; and, second, that the private sector should be heavily involved in training programs since most jobs are in the private sector (five out of six jobs is the most commonly cited figure). In 1978 a major addition to CETA—Title VII, known as the Private Sector Initiative Program—was made to increase the role of the private sector. And the program replacing CETA expanded that role even more.

This chapter will examine past experiences in involving the private sector in employment and training program—specifically in Title VII of CETA, which aimed expressly at fostering business participation. The first section of this chapter briefly describes efforts made prior to PSIP to involve the private sector and sketches the evolution of the latter program. The chapter focuses on an analysis of the performance of PSIP from 1979 through 1981 based principally on research conducted and directed by the authors and supplemented by two other implementation studies. In the concluding section, the link between private sector participation and PSIP program performance is discussed as well as conditions that contribute to positive program performance.

In 1982 Congress passed the Job Training Partnership Act, a new program replacing CETA and modeled heavily on PSIP. An understanding of PSIP, particularly the limits of business participation and the conditions that promote and impede it, leads to a better understanding of current and future jobs and training programs that seek the involvement of the private sector.

The Evolution of PSIP

PROGRAMMATIC PREDECESSORS

PSIP represented an extensive effort to make the private sector a full partner in operating a segment of the nation's employment and training programs. Before turning to the analysis of PSIP, however, it is useful to examine its programmatic predecessors and the factors that affected its formation.

The origins of PSIP were influenced in part by changing attitudes toward the relationship of the public and private sectors. PSIP resulted from perceptions of the performance of the programs that had preceded it, especially those operated under Title I of CETA. The performance of these programs in terms of traditional measures like placement rates and costs was viewed, perhaps unfairly, as disappointing. To a large extent this dissatisfaction was fed by a backlash toward the heavy reliance on public service employment (PSE) in the mid to late 1970s that had dominated CETA spending (National Commission for Manpower Policy, 1978:5; Sawhill, 1978:68). Accompanying the disenchantment with the results and direction of public sector employment and training programs was a growing "pro-private sector" sentiment and sensitivity. This relatively simplistic and uncritical appreciation of the presumably untapped potential in the private sector was stimulated in part by a developing literature on privatization (for examples, see Spann, 1977; Savas, 1978; Davies, 1971) as well as an ideological conviction that the private sector was inherently more efficient than the public sector. In fact, there were a number of reasons besides ideological conviction supporting the argument that the private sector could be more efficient in running a program than a public agency:

> 1) the fact that private profit-maximizing firms have an incentive to minimize costs . . .; 2) the size of private firms is not restricted by political boundaries . . .; 3) the monopolistic nature of government bureaucracies; 4) the lack of innovation in governmental bureaucracies due to reasons of cost, institutional constraint, size, and urban government complexity; 5) the lack of a motivational incentive on the part of the public sector to reduce costs and increase efficiency; and 6) the type of "market place" the public sector deals in.   (Goodman, 1982:20–21)

Added to these factors was the failure of previous employment and training programs to do as much as possible to obtain participation of the private sector. In fact, as Table 5-1 indicates, until 1977 private sector involvement in a variety of employment and training programs was minimal (Ripley and Franklin, 1983). These PSIP predecessors included: (1) MDTA vocational training and OJT; (2) the National Alliance of Business's Job Opportunities in the Business Sector (JOBS) program, an OJT program run by a business intermediary group; (3) CETA vocational training and OJT; (4) Help through Industry Retraining and Employment (HIRE) I and II, an OJT program for veterans, run initially at the national level but later transferred to Prime Sponsors; (5) the New Job Tax Credit (NJTC), a tax credit for employers hiring additional employees; and (6) the Skills Training Improvement Program (STIP), a vocational training program specifically oriented to the private sector.

An extensive and comprehensive review of literature on the participation of the private sector in the above-mentioned programs (see Ripley and Franklin, 1981) indicates that these programs varied widely in both the extent to which they were oriented to employers and the degree to which employers were responsive. Until the STIP and NJTC programs in 1977, employment and training program efforts to stimulate involvement of the private sector were sporadic and limited at both the national and local levels. Although STIP and NJTC sparked a significant new business participation, each had important limits. NJTC operated only for one year, and it was not directed toward disadvantaged persons. The STIP program operated in fewer than half of all Prime Sponsorships.

Reasons for the responsiveness of employers or the lack of it prior to PSIP were, of course, complicated. The degree of responsiveness was related in part to specific elements of program design and marketing, but it also was limited by an array of attitudes within the private sector, ranging from cautious skepticism to overt hostility toward government programs (see Ripley and Franklin, 1981: 49–51).

DEVELOPMENT AND OVERVIEW OF PSIP[1]

The reauthorization of CETA in 1978 was the occasion for a major examination and redirection of the overall CETA program. This examination focused on the heavy emphasis given to PSE since the inception of CETA as well as on the performance of CETA training programs. A PSE backlash in Congress was growing as a result of widely publicized abuses in local program administration and the realization that dependence on public sector employment did nothing to encourage participation of employers in the private sector who had most of the nation's jobs. The data on CETA program performance between FY 1975 and 1978 reinforced attitudes that changes were needed. Placement of enrollees into unsubsidized employment was low, and placement into jobs in the private sector was even lower. On-the-job training accounted for less than 10 percent of the total CETA expenditures. For four years CETA Prime Sponsors had been told by Congress to emphasize PSE. Now, during the reauthorization debate, they were criticized for not emphasizing ties with and placements in the private sector. Policymakers were changing their attitudes.

Within the Administration and Congress the desire to increase the role of the private sector in employment and training was growing. The Committee for Economic Development (CED), a group composed primarily of businessmen, was vital in providing both inspiration and concrete suggestions that led to the demonstration PSIP program. The CED study, *Jobs for the Hard-To-Employ: New Directions for a Public-Private Part-*

1. The discussion in this section is based in part on Goodman (1982:93–114) and Seessel (1980:37–47).

TABLE 5-1: *Private sector involvement in public employment and training programs prior to the Private Sector Initiative Program*

Program and years of operation	Implementation responsibility and relationships	Specific efforts to generate employer responsiveness	Amount of local employer responsiveness	Impacts in terms of private sector jobs for eligible clients
Manpower Development and Training Act (Vocational Training and On-the-Job Training), 1962–1974	National DOL contracts to local deliverers. Relations with local businesses were at discretion of deliverer.	Minimal and scattered. No national emphasis on private sector involvement.	Minimal.	Minimal.
National Alliance of Business–Job Opportunities in the Business Sector, 1968–1974	National business group oversaw pledges from national corporations. Local business group branches got both pledges and contracts from local businesses.	Relatively high, at least rhetorically. Focus on large national corporations.	Relatively high at rhetorical level from national office. Minimal for contractual positions for specific slots.	Minimal.
CETA (Vocational Training and On-the-Job Training), 1974–1982	Local political jurisdictions had implementation responsibility. They could write contracts with any deliverer, including business.	Generally minimal; some local exceptions. No special emphasis at national level on employers until 1978.	Generally minimal. A few exemplary demonstration programs.	Minimal overall, but great variation in individual sites.

Help Through Industry Retraining and Employment, Phase I, 1977–1978	National business group (NAB) oversaw effort, both voluntary and contractual. Local political units administer with help from business intermediary groups.	Some, aimed primarily at large national corporations. Minimal effort with small corporations.	Relatively high at the rhetorical level from the national office. Minimal in localities, and with small corporations.	Minimal.
Help Through Industry Retraining and Employment, Phase II, 1978–80	Local political units responsible for administration and oversight of contracts with local deliverers. Veterans' groups and others may assist.	Varied by locality; some direct approaches to local businesses.	Moderate interest from small and moderate sized corporations. Almost no interest from large corporations.	Minimal.
New Jobs Tax Credit, 1977–78	Self administered by employers (reporting on tax returns)	Moderate national publicity. Main factor was absence of restrictions on hiring—no target groups or eligibility requirements.	Fairly heavy, much more than previous, targeted, tax credits.	Generally good, but no data kept on employment of disadvantaged workers.
Skills Training Improvement Program, 1977–80	Local political units responsible for administration & oversight. Grants awarded on competitive basis.	Considerable, through involvement in program design, creation of employer oversight committees, and use of some private sector deliverers.	Generally high; participation present in about two-thirds of the sites with the program.	Generally good. Most of the placements occurred in the private sector.

Source: Adapted from Ripley and Franklin, 1981

nership (1978) documented a variety of cases of successful involvement of the private sector in employment and training programs in local communities. It pointed up the importance of a "business intermediary" group that worked with public agencies and relieved employers of much day-to-day administrative detail. The National Alliance of Business (NAB) was a particularly enthusiastic supporter and lobbyist for this notion, since the major cases cited by CED involved local NAB offices. Even before its publication, the CED report was circulating within DOL, influencing thinking both there and in the White House. Receptive to the idea of a business intermediary organization, the Administration wanted to create a program within the CETA framework that would be *of* business and *for* business. Although existing CETA legislation contained in principle the flexibility to allow increased participation by the private sector, the Administration wanted a separate title with a new organizational structure in order to emphasize the new commitment to the private sector.

The PSIP program was first announced publicly in President Carter's January 1978 State of the Union address. The program was only in outline form, but the President asked for $400 million for FY 1979. As the basic structure of the program evolved, conflict arose over several issues.

The existence and role of Private Industry Councils (PICs), the proposed intermediary organizations, caused great concern. Business groups favored a new organization with broad powers to implement Title VII. CETA Prime Sponsors and existing service deliverers (especially CBO's) questioned duplication and anticipated threats to their own authority. A central concern was that Prime Sponsors would be held accountable for actions of independent PICs.

Another concern was the role that NAB would play in PSIP. Many groups and individuals in and out of the business sector, resenting NAB's inside track in the development of PSIP, resisted implicit assumptions that NAB should provide PSIP services.

Compromises within the legislation addressed these and other issues, but they did not eliminate inner tensions from the new program. On the one hand, the law creating PICs required that at least half of the members be representatives of the private sector, and granted them tangible resources: the choice of a variety of roles, ranging from advisory to operations; a broad mandate to innovate and experiment with ways to involve the private sector and to expand employment opportunities in the private sector for economically disadvantaged citizens; the right to incorporate; an invitation to look at employment and training programs beyond Title VII; a PSIP budget separate from the other CETA titles, and concurrent signoff authority with the Prime Sponsor on the Title VII plan.

But on the other hand, the law bound PICs to the existing CETA system. Prime Sponsors had the power to curb PIC activities. PIC funds were channeled through the Prime Sponsorships, and Prime Sponsors were financially liable for Title VII expenditures. Prime Sponsors were responsible for appointing members of PICs. Prime Sponsors made decisions about staffing for PICs, although PICs were supposed to be consulted. The Prime Sponsor had the ultimate authority to heed or ignore PIC recommendations. Thus for a PIC to be effective, a cooperative working relationship between the PIC and the Prime Sponsor was essential.

PSIP was intended to stimulate innovative approaches to manpower programs and problems, but it was also a system of checks and balances between the newly created PICs and the Prime Sponsors. The degree of latitude granted to each—or left undefined—in the law and the regulations required a balancing act. In each of the more than 470 Prime Sponsorships, that balancing act took different forms—unique treaties among local actors were reached depending on local conditions and those arrangements changed over time. The uncertainty in PSIP, while complicating life for administrators and PICs, was an inevitable result of an attempt by the federal government to address a national problem by using a decentralized administrative structure without surrendering centralized control over the process and the results.

Implementation and Impact:
A Systematic Analysis

NATURE OF THE STUDY

During the first three years of the implementation of PSIP we directed an on-going evaluation of the program in 25 sites in the

United States. Between the spring of 1979 and the late summer of 1981, our research staff visited each site seven times, interviewing people, attending meetings, observing programs, and collecting data. During the study over 1,600 interviews were conducted with a wide variety of local actors, including CETA Administrators and staff, PSIP Directors and staff, PIC Chairpersons and members, service deliverers, and employers, among others. Additional data were drawn from local plans, quarterly program reports, and other documents, as well as from interviews with individuals in public and private organizations in Washington.

The sites in the study were chosen to provide a diversity of geographical location, size, urban/non-urban character, and program experience. Balance of State sites were excluded. The sample was not scientifically drawn, and it did not purport to be representative of all PICs and PSIP programs in the country. Nonetheless, the congruence of findings from our study and two other major implementation studies discussed below suggest that the sites provided a typical range of experience. The study sites are profiled in Appendix Table A5-1.

The focus of our implementation study was on describing and explaining implementation patterns and short-run performance. We devoted special attention to PIC development, multiple indicators of program outcomes and success, change in CETA programs, business participation, and program innovation (see Ripley and associates, 1979a, 1979b, 1980a, 1980b, 1981a, 1981b, 1981c).

THE IMPLEMENTATION CONTEXT FOR PSIP

The extent of PSIP achievement in three years was more limited than some of the program's most ardent boosters will admit. Before discussing the nature and extent of PSIP accomplishments, however, we want to sketch the environment in which PSIP had to operate. That PSIP had not created a brave new world of every Prime Sponsorship in two or three years is not surprising, considering the harsh national and local context in which it was thrust. But in view of the obstacles, its accomplishments are at least moderately encouraging.

During the implementation of PSIP, the CETA system of

which it was a part was in almost continuous turmoil. Due to President Reagan's government-wide budget cutbacks, CETA funding in Prime Sponsorships declined drastically in FY 1981: the PSE titles were virtually eliminated and other titles were cut, though less severely. These cuts resulted in shrinking administrative cost pools and massive staff layoffs. Also contributing to the fiscal woes was uncertainty about the future of CETA when its authorization expired at the end of FY 1982. Constant speculation about the direction the impending reauthorization would take heightened problems of local staff morale and motivation.

PSIP had limited resources with which to carry out its mandate. In relation to total CETA funds PSIP's share was quite small—5 percent in FY 1980, and 12 percent in FY 1981. Although PSIP's share rose as other titles were cut and it was not, its allocations were always far less than the authorized amounts, and even these small amounts were not efficiently transmitted to individual localities. DOL delays in making allocations coupled with fluctuations in planning estimates made administration difficult for staff and irritated employers involved in PSIP. In addition, as CETA Administrators saw their budget evaporate, some could not resist raiding PSIP budgets, which typically were underspent. Such encroachments varied in magnitude but often contributed to tensions between PICs and Prime Sponsors.

The national recession made life difficult for all manpower programs, including PSIP. As unemployment increased and layoffs rose, PICs saw even well-planned programs founder. Customized training for employers became very difficult to arrange, and placements suffered. Even training programs that had been designed to meet employer specifications fell through when employers were unable to hire trainees because of unforeseen worsening economic conditions.

The final factor in the harsh environment confronting PSIP was a set of negative attitudes. Program history prior to PSIP had suggested that with few exceptions in individual localities, involvement of the private sector was likely to be modest. Both public and private sectors viewed each other with mixed emotions, including caution, skepticism, distrust, and hostility.

Employers who had been involved in public employment and training programs were usually less than delighted with their experiences. Negative business attitudes on the eve of PSIP were summarized by two studies (see de Lone, 1978:218–219; Robison, 1978:151–152). Complaints included criticisms of the erratic flow of funding and planning, bureaucratic red tape, insensitivity to the concerns of the private sector, an overemphasis on income subsidy programs and an underemphasis on motivating participants to work.

Like most new programs, PSIP was introduced with much fanfare and many glowing statements of what it would accomplish. Unfortunately, such hyperbole created expectations that could not possibly be achieved, even under favorable conditions. Claims that PSIP would turn CETA around in two years simply ignored the length of time necessary to create solid local infrastructures, orient new PIC members to regulations and opportunities, and set up operational programs.

PSIP RESULTS: KEY DECISIONS ABOUT LOCAL IMPLEMENTATION

Implementers of any new program must address basic issues of organization, planning, and expenditures. In PSIP, the central decisions to be resolved involved the relationship of PICs to the Prime Sponsor structure, recruitment and organization of the PICs, their role, and the purposes for which PSIP funds would be spent.

These decisions were not made in a set order, not were they fixed and immutable. At the beginning of PSIP, these basic decisions were made by CETA directors, local elected officials, the interim PIC chairpersons, and local business organizations like NAB or the Chamber of Commerce. PIC members became involved in the decisions after PICs were formed.

Whether PICs were separate from or integrated with Prime Sponsors was probably the most consistently sensitive issue throughout PSIP's implementation. The degree to which PICs were independent—possessing programmatic autonomy, separately hired staff housed in a separate physical location, and existing as an incorporated body represented a cluster of important symbolic issues. Independence and incorporation, however, did not preclude a PIC from pursuing a close, cooperative working relationship with the Prime Sponsor. The alternative, a PIC that was integrated into the Prime Sponsor's administrative structure, did not have to produce a rubberstamp council. But those for and against "autonomy" in any specific locality usually painted the choices in these stark terms.

Building PICs from scratch occupied much attention in the early days of PSIP. Business members and others had to be recruited, selected, and trained; bylaws had to be written and a committee structure put into place. In many localities the initial PIC member recruitment was virtually random, while in others a strategy helped to guide selection of members. PICs differed greatly in the pace at which members were presented with and were able to absorb information on local CETA programs and PSIP options.

The role of PICs emerged less as a conscious initial decision (though this occurred in some sites) than as a response to members' interests, suggestions of Prime Sponsors, and local precedent. A variety of roles were possible: designing and operating programs directly, advising on or evaluating programs; focusing only on PSIP or on all local CETA programs; becoming involved in a network of agencies and issues broader than just employment and training. PICs could be aggressive in setting their own agendas or timid and passive.

Decisions about program operations were usually made after basic initial decisions about size, structure, and status of PICs. How to spend PSIP dollars was a regularly recurring item on the agendas of PICs as new funds were allocated or underspending forced reprogramming. The two main types of programs chosen by PICs were similar to ones operated under CETA Title IIBC: vocational skills training and on-the-job training. PICs also often increased the amount of customized training with employers, job search and self-directed placement programs for participants, and coupled vocational training and on the job training.

Employment generating services (EGS) were a special category of expenditures unique to PSIP. Up to 30 percent of PSIP outlays could be spent for activities that did not relate to direct services to participants or administrative costs. Only a few of PICs ignored the EGS option and spent all their money on programs serving clients directly, and many PICs spent well under the 30 percent allowed, but three distinct EGS activities were common: marketing, labor market information, and economic development networking. The most popular use of EGS was for marketing, which included publicity designed to increase awareness in the local business community about PICs and PSIP programs. Marketing strategies varied from low key, small-scale campaigns targeted narrowly on specific sectors to full-blown public relations campaigns replete with glossy ads and large media budgets. Labor market information was collected and analyzed to help make decisions about programs and placement activities. Networking with local economic development agencies was aimed at promoting information-sharing about potential opportunities for creating jobs and improving consultation and inter-agency coordination so that employment and training resources could be integrated with local development activities.

Several patterns of implementation at the local level can be traced in the PSIP experience. Implementation takes place as a series of activities. More than one may occur simultaneously, and different weights will be given to them at different times. The first step is a period of *institution-building*, which seems to be a necessary condition to allow later stages to be reached. Institution-building involves assembling the new elements required by the program and integrating them into the local context of agencies and actors. It includes, for example, selection and training of PIC members, setting goals, hiring staff, and working with established agencies to define mutual responsibilities and activities. Second, *planning* is necessary to make decisions about programs, activities, service delivery agencies, and clients to be served. In the third stage, *operational programs* emerge, clients are enrolled and trained, and graduates are placed in jobs. The final stage, *impact*, is reached after the preceding activities have operated long enough to achieve a record of achievements that affect participants, the employer community, and the local employment and training system.

Of the study sites, most were engaged almost exclusively in institution-building in 1979 and continued it at a moderately intensive level during 1980 and into 1981. Planning began in most localities by early 1980. By the first half of FY 1981, the center of gravity had shifted to planning and the early stages of program operation. By the end of that fiscal year, many programs reached the impact stage, but the pace varied from site to site. Program operation was the dominant activity.

PSIP RESULTS: PIC DEVELOPMENT

The centerpiece of the PSIP legislation was the PIC, which was mandated for every Prime Sponsorship. These new employer councils, intermediaries between the employment and training needs of employers and the resources of the public sector, were to match needs and resources and to plan and oversee PSIP implementation.

The emergence of PICs as mature institutions in their local settings occurred gradually and at variable paces. Our study identified features that, when present, facilitated the ability of PICs to play their mediating role. Empirically derived from observation of the 25 PICs, these indicators of strong institutional health of PICs included PIC goals, activity of members, the role of the Chairperson, impact on programs, visibility, and relations with CETA staff.

PIC GOALS. The direction a PIC chose for itself was determined by its goals. PICs without goals floundered or made random choices about programs and expenditures. To be achieveable, goals had to be addressed in a deliberate manner by PIC members and staff. Although goals had to be clear, fairly specific, and widely understood and shared by members, they could change as achievements and conditions required. By the end of FY 1981, eleven of the 25 study sites had goals meeting these criteria.

ACTIVITY OF PIC MEMBERS. Typically, in any group of volunteers, continuous participation and leadership rest with a core of activists. This central group should be large enough to sustain decision-making that takes into account different points of view and interests, and it should consist of at least a majority of the full membership.

The interest, activity, participation, and leadership of members from business was very important in determining how much orientation towards the private sector the PIC possessed. We found that within the core of activists, the private sector accounted for between 30 and 90 percent of the members, with 60 percent the average. Nine of the study sites exhibited both membership criteria: at least half of their total PIC membership was in the activist core, and half or more of that group was composed of employer representatives.

THE ROLE OF THE CHAIRPERSON. Potentially the most important member of the PIC, the Chairperson had responsibility for molding the PIC into an effective group. If the PIC were to have a positive impact, the Chairperson had to be an effective leader within the PIC—interested, informed, and active. He or she had to promote timely decisions, oriented toward goals, in a process that was efficient but permitted all points of view to be heard. The Chairperson had to nurture a spirit of cooperative problem-solving among members.

Outside the PIC the Chairperson also had significant responsibilities for obtaining access to employers in the local business community. To do this successfully, the Chairperson had to make active use of contacts with important parts of the local business community to promote programs sponsored by the PIC. By the end of FY 1981 two-fifths of the study sites had Chairpersons that were effective both inside the PICs and with the local business communities outside the PICs.

IMPACT ON PROGRAM DECISIONS. The stance a PIC took, as a body, toward initiating ideas for PSIP goals, strategies, programs and activities, was a critical measure of its institutional development. PICs that were new or still immature were naturally more dependent on initiatives of non-PIC members, but mature PICs took major initiatives and/or made major amendments to initiatives of others.

A second aspect of the roles of PICs in shaping PSIP is the extent to which the programs and activities that had been implemented bore a "PIC imprint." Strong PICs had a substantial amount of direct impact on the shape and content of PSIP programs; they were not simply providing window dressing for superficial compliance with legal requirements. This aspect of PIC impact is related to the first one. It requires first that PICs do more than passively ratify non-PIC initiatives, and second that PIC initiatives be implemented. Of the 25 study sites, 14 met the joint criteria that PICs were active in initiating their own ideas or amending the ideas of others and that PICs had a high or moderate direct impact on the shape of PSIP programs implemented through the end of FY 1981.

PIC IMAGE. After several years of PIC programs coupled with marketing and "missionary work" of individual PIC members, some PICs were beginning to develop a positive image in their local business communities. Specifically, strong PICs were achieving both visibility and credibility in the eyes of employers who did not sit on the PIC. But among the 25 sites, only seven had achieved both positive visibility and credibility in the local business community.

RELATIONS WITH CETA STAFF. Hostility in the critical interaction between a PIC—as well as its independent staff if it had one—and the CETA Prime Sponsor staff impeded the timely and efficient development of programs by distracting attention, consuming time, and draining energy and morale. Conversely, cooperation between the PIC and the Prime Sponsor allowed PSIP to proceed with reasonable efficiency and harmony. In eleven of the 25 study sites this relationship was unequivocally cooperative and productive by the end of FY 1981.

A COMPOSITE RANKING. To summarize the overall development of PICs as institutions from FY 1979 through 1981, we assigned a simple unweighted score of one point to each site for each positive situation for the six clusters of indicators just discussed. The judgments were added to produce an aggregate score. A six was the highest possible total, a zero the lowest. Table 5-2 shows the distribution of PICs at the end of FY 1981.

That only one-fourth of the sample demonstrated the characteristics of a mature and healthy local institution emphasizes the difficulties that faced these organizations. Institution-building requires time and major commitments. Progress was assisted by members' and staff attitudes and by the willingness

TABLE 5-2: *Development of PICs, Fiscal Year 1981*

Category	Number of PICs[a]	Evaluation score	Percent of sample[a]
Strong	6	5-6	24
Intermediate	10	2-4	40
Weak	9	0-1	36

[a] Number of sites studied was 25.

of the PICs to cooperate with the Prime Sponsor. In a later section we discuss the relationship between the level of PIC health or strength and PSIP program performance. We assume a strong PIC can facilitate better programs and will test that assumption in the present analysis.

PSIP RESULTS: BUSINESS PARTICIPATION

Stimulating the involvement of employers in employment and training programs was PSIP's general purpose, and by the end of FY 1981, business participation in PSIP was widespread. While sitting as members of PIC constituted one important way for employers to contribute to PSIP, other concrete forms of involvement from employers both on and off the PIC were equally important. Our study was particularly interested in participation involving positive and direct action by employers in planning and operating programs, not just in relatively passive or easy acceptance of programs that had been planned without input from the private sector.

PSIP succeeded in fostering a variety of different forms of business participation. The forms of employer involvement most often encountered in PSIP were giving advice on the design of programs and the content of the curricula for training programs; providing information about both micro and macro labor market conditions and needs; directly operating PSIP programs as service deliverers under contract to the PIC or Prime Sponsor; and contributing services, equipment, space, or staff to PSIP programs. Occurring less frequently were acting as formal or informal intermediaries to help place trainees graduating from PSIP programs and helping to screen applicants for PSIP programs. There was also a group of idiosyncratic forms of participation found at only one or two sites. Except for the operation of programs, all of these types of participation were volunteered, not provided in exchange for a fee.

Some form of business participation was present in each of the 25 study sites. When present, participation was almost always due to PSIP—in only a few cases did business participation develop independently of PSIP. There was thus a very positive response from the private sector to PSIP's invitation to get involved (Ripley and associates, 1981c:116–130). Nonetheless, not all kinds of participation were equally widespread. In any individual site, a given type of business activity could be absent. No site had all seven kinds of activity; some sites had only one or two. Table 5-3 summarizes the distribution of types of business participation among the 25 Prime Sponsorships studied.

An additional aspect of private sector involvement is the extent of the participation. Table 5-4 shows that business participation was not limited only to employers who were members of the PIC. There was, however, a difference between the types of activity engaged in by PIC members and by employers outside the PIC. Employers who belonged to the PIC were more likely to engage in placement aid and labor-market feedback than the employers who were not PIC members. That latter group was more likely to screen applicants, operate programs, or make in-kind contributions. Both groups of employers were likely to be involved in developing curricula.

To go beyond a discussion of the mere presence or absence of business involvement, we developed a business participation index that included: (1) the importance of the participation (was it systematic or sporadic? did it have any impact on program operations and outcomes?); (2) the magnitude of PSIP-induced change in business participation; and (3) the extent to which the business participation in PSIP had spilled over into non-PSIP parts of the local employment and training system. Even using these more demanding criteria, PSIP's achievements were notable—just under half of the study sites ranked in the High category, while only a fourth were in the Low category (see Ripley and associates, 1981c:127). There was a very strong relationship between the business participation index rankings and

TABLE 5-3: *Business participation in PSIP programs and the effect of the PSIP stimulus, 1979–1981 (Entries are number of sites out of 25 studied)*

TYPES OF PARTICIPATION FOUND	SITES WHERE PARTICIPATION WAS PRESENT AND WAS DUE TO PSIP	EFFECT OF PSIP		SITES WHERE PARTICIPATION WAS PRESENT BUT WAS NOT DUE TO PSIP	SITES WHERE PARTICIPATION WAS ABSENT
		STIMULATED NEW ACTIVITY	MODIFIED A PRIOR ACTIVITY		
Advising on programs and training curricula	16	10	6	3	6
Labor market feedback	13	11	2	3	9
Operating programs	13	8	5	2	10
In-kind contributions	11	7	4	1	13
Assisting placement	9	9	0	0	16
Screening applicants	8	8	0	0	17
Other activity	7	7	0	0	18

TABLE 5-4: *Involvement of PIC and non-PIC employers in PSIP business participation, 1979–1981*

FORM OF PARTICIPATION	NUMBER OF SITES WHERE ACTIVITY WAS PRESENT	NON-PIC EMPLOYERS		PIC EMPLOYERS	
		NUMBER OF SITES[a]	PERCENT	NUMBER OF SITES[a]	PERCENT
Applicant screening	8	8	100%	4	50%
Operating programs	15	13	87%	5	33%
In-kind contributions	12	9	75%	3	25%
Advising on programs and curricula	19	17	89%	15	79%
Other	7	4	57%	7	100%
Labor market feedback	16	10	63%	16	100%
Placement aid	9	4	44%	8	89%

Source: Research data from OSU Mershon Center PSIP Implementation study
[a]These columns add to more than the figure in the first column because both PIC and non-PIC employers could be involved in each activity at individual sites.

institutional development of PICs. Sites with the strongest PICs had the highest scores on the index, while sites with weak PICs tended to have the lowest.

PSIP RESULTS: PERFORMANCE INDICATORS[2]

The short-term program results that implementation research on employment and training programs can address include placements, wages, and cost of operations. We developed a series of performance indicators derived from standard local data reports required by DOL: (1) rate of obtaining jobs for enrollees, (2) percent of placements that were obtained in the private sector, (3) wage gain for previously employed participants who were placed after their PSIP training, (4) hourly wage for enrollees at the time of placement, and (5) the average cost of obtaining jobs for participants. (Appendix D discusses the derivation of the measures and the nature of the data used.)

Data on PSIP performance for all sites in the U.S. during the first two full years of program operation, presented in Table 5-5, show that PSIP did a better job in FY 1981 than in 1980 on most indicators, with the most dramatic improvement occurring in the cost per placement. The comparison of PSIP and the basic CETA training title, Title IIBC, provides information about relative performance; results, however, must be interpreted with restraint. Program performance measured using quantitative indicators should be only one of several elements for assessing the performance and accomplishments of PSIP, and a higher level of PSIP performance on various indicators should not be equated with inherent superiority of PSIP over Title IIBC. The programs operated under Title IIBC were broader in scope, more varied in purpose, and typically served a more disadvantaged population. Higher or lower placement rates or program costs were not automatic indications that one title was "better" than the other (see Smith, 1982:59, and General Accounting Office, 1983). As Table 5-5 shows, the performance of PSIP and Title IIBC was quite similar in FY 1980. The placement rate and the average wage gain were almost equal for both titles. More of PSIP's placements occurred in the private sector, but it is not surprising that the Title IIBC cost per placement was far

2. The discussion in this section is drawn from Franklin and Ripley, 1983.

TABLE 5-5: *Aggregate performance indicators for PSIP and Title IIBC, Fiscal Years 1980 and 1981, U.S. Totals*

	Title VII		Title IIBC	
	FY 1980	FY 1981	FY 1980	FY 1981
Percent of Enrollees Placed	23%	35%	26%	30%
Percent of placements in the private sector	81%	89%	70%	80%
Cost per placement	$7887	$4903	$5134	$5221
Average hourly wage after placement[a]	$4.10	$4.57	$3.76	$4.40
Average wage gain after placement[a]	$.69/hour	$.60/hour	$.65/hour	$.59/hour

[a]Excluding participants with no earnings before program participation.

Source: Department of Labor, Employment and Training Administration, Final Fiscal Year 1980 and Fiscal Year 1981 Reports on Program Status and Financial Summary and Participant Characteristics. Issued April 10, 1981 and April 27, 1982. (Report Numbers OAM 5-81 and 2-82.)

below that of PSIP, since so many PIC programs were just beginning, while IIBC had established smooth operating routines.

By the end of the second full year, PSIP performance had improved, but so also had Title IIBC performance. Although the placement rate for both titles was still similar, PSIP had a slight edge (35 percent versus 30 percent). The cost of achieving placements was also similar, with PSIP having an advantage of abut $300 less per placement. The average wage paid after placement was only incrementally higher for PSIP ($4.57 versus $4.40 per hour), and the wage gain was almost identical (60¢ and 59¢). Both PSIP and Title IIBC slipped from their previous year's performance in obtaining wage gain. Only in private sector placements did PSIP show a distinct advantage over Title IIBC: almost 90 percent of all ·PSIP placements were made in the private sector, compared to 80 percent for Title IIBC.

These figures indicate the PSIP, more than three years after its inception and two years after funds were allocated to localities, had not achieved a distinct performance advantage over Title IIBC. These results may have been disappointing to PSIP supporters, but it is important to keep in mind that Title IIBC was not the failure that many of its critics portrayed it to be; the implementation of PSIP entailed more time-consuming tasks than its planners had anticipated; and Title IIBC relied on work experience to serve a clientele that was younger and less educated than that of Title VII (work experience lowers placement rates).

Because the PSIP data reported in Table 5-5 are national averages, masking the diverse activities and performance that occurred in individual sites, we recorded how the PSIP performance of our 25 study sites compared to the Title IIBC programs in those same 25 sites. A clear majority of the sites (60 percent) had PSIP placement rates that were higher than those for Title IIBC and had a cost per placement that was lower. But only half of the sites (55 percent) had an hourly wage after placement that was at least 15 cents an hour higher than that of Title IIBC. For the other indicators, the performance of PSIP was not so good as that of Title IIBC. Since fewer than half of the sites had average wage gains higher than those for Title IIBC, and barely a quarter of the sites had a larger proportion of placement in the private sector than did the Title IIBC program, it is clear that sites varied widely in the Title VII performance, and that Title IIBC was not a flabby set of programs soon to be shown up by the newer PSIP effort.

OTHER PSIP RESULTS

Additional aspects of PSIP's accomplishments on which we focused included the quality of jobs for which the participants were being trained, the extent of program innovation, the establishment of a local network involving PSIP and economic development, and the extent to which other parts of the local employment and training network had been affected by PSIP programs and practices.

QUALITY OF JOBS. In half of the study sites the jobs for PSIP participants were of high quality. Participants were being trained and placed in moderately to highly skilled occupations, for which there was a demand in the labor market, with wages above the minimum, with advancement potential, and in lower turnover postions. Sites divided evenly on how job quality in PSIP and Title IIBC compared. At half the sites, staff and other involved persons felt that Title VII was superior; at the other half, local implementers felt that Title IIBC and Title VII were comparable in terms of job quality (Ripley and associates, 1981b:36).

PROGRAM INNOVATION. In assessing innovation, programs were compared only to each local employment and training context, not to an arbitrary ideal standard. Innovation is not, of course, synonymous with success or superiority. Many of the innovative programs introduced by PICs also experienced difficulties in implementation and performance.

PSIP offered an opportunity and a challenge to innovate and experiment, to design new programs and new approaches to management. The response of PICs was varied and slow to emerge, but by the end of FY 1981 few of the study sites had not introduced some kind of innovations. In one-third of the sites, innovations were major: that is, at least half of the programs operating in the locality were new and different from previous local programs and practices. In two-fifths of the sites, innovations of a less extensive nature had been implemented, along with a combination of more conventional programs (Ripley and associates, 1981c:62). Innovations that PICs implemented include adding programs that had not been tried before in the locality, such as on-the-job training, job search, self-directed placement, and customized training, as well as new management practices, such as performance-based contracting with service deliverers, simplified contracting with employers offering on-the-job training, and special employer advisory councils responsible for overseeing a single program from start to finish.

ECONOMIC DEVELOPMENT LINKAGES. PSIP spurred some PICs to think in terms of creating new jobs in addition to training for existing jobs. These PICs turned in varying degrees to economic development activities, either on their own or in partnership with CETA and economic development agencies.

A few PICs nationwide immersed themselves completely in economic development. They, and sometimes the rest of the CETA staff, worked in partnership with economic development staff to solicit employer participation in economic development projects. The economic development agencies had development resources for employers (loans, grants, cutting red tape), while PICs and CETA provided manpower expertise (training programs, referral and screening of participants, tax credits) and money for marketing, staff salaries, and special projects or employer incentives. The number of PICs adhering to such a full-blown strategy of economic development was small—about 10 percent in our sample.

In general, economic development agencies were reluctant to become involved in employment and training efforts. Like their clients in the private sector, they were suspicious of CETA in general and dubious of the ability of Prime Sponsors to provide services of value to them. Thus PICs and CETA staff had to win them over by a combination of persistence and competence. Having a pocketful of PSIP money to spend on economic development activities certainly smoothed the initial introductions. In the sites where the partnerships were most fully developed, each partner saw benefits to participation and felt that cooperation served mutual advantages (Van Horn, Ford, and Beauregard, 1983:97–98).

By the end of FY 1981, just over two-fifths of the 25 sites had developed substantial economic development links. Within this group, half had achieved tangible results in the form of new jobs for CETA participants (Ripley and associates, 1981c:76).

CHANGES IN THE CETA SYSTEM. Implicit within PSIP was the assumption that PICs and PSIP programs would have effects beyond just Title VII, and that

> PICs will help reorient CETA to the private sector, either by providing examples of good programming upon which the remainder of the CETA training system can build or by providing a vehicle through which representatives of the business community can influence prime sponsor activities generally to become more relevant and responsive to employer needs (Smith, 1981:1).

By the end of FY 1981, PSIP was responsible for a modest level of change in programs and procedures in the rest of the CETA system. A variety of changes was evident, and no single type of change or spill-over effect was dominant. The extent of change also varied greatly. In half of the 25 study sites, no PSIP-induced change existed; in a third of the sites, four or five different kinds of changes had been incorporated into the local employment and training system as a result of PSIP. Table 5-6 summarizes PSIP's effects on the local employment and training system.

Implementation and Impact:
Additional Observations

Two other PSIP implementation studies were conducted concurrently with the one we directed at Ohio State University's Mershon Center. The Corporation for Public/Private Ventures (P/PV) began tracking PSIP in 34 special demonstration sites when the program was operated on a pilot basis even before the legislation authorizing PSIP was passed. The number of sites in subsequent P/PV field visits in 1979 and later years varied between twelve and seventeen. The P/PV research was broadgauged but focused particularly on the development and roles of PICs, the participation of business, and an assessment of PSIP

TABLE 5-6: *CETA system alterations stemming from PSIP by the end of Fiscal Year 1981*
(Entries are numbers of sites, out of a total of 25 observed)

WAYS PSIP AFFECTED OTHER PARTS OF LOCAL CETA SYSTEMS	NUMBER OF SITES WHERE CHANGE OCCURRED
Changes in the types or identity of *programs* operated in other titles	9
Changes in the *curricula* offered by existing vendors in other titles	8
Changes in the identity of *vendors* in other titles	8
Changes in the *criteria* (and application of those criteria) for selecting programs and vendors in other titles	6
Changes in the *assessment* of CETA applicants	3
Changes in the processes for *monitoring* programs in other titles	2
Changes in the *admission* process	2
Other kinds of changes	5
No changes at all	12

program performance relative to Title IIBC. Funding for P/PV's research came from private foundations (for reports on the research, see Jaffe, 1978; Seessel, 1980; Smith, 1981; and Smith, 1982).

The other major PSIP study was done by MDC, Inc. through a contract with DOL. Like the other two studies, MDC relied on multiple visits to local sites (17 sites were studied), but unlike the others, MDC focused on only one major aspect of PSIP; the planning, implementation, and results of employment generating services (see MDC, 1982a).

It is important to note that the findings of the three major studies were very similar for similar phenomena. None of the studies produced findings contradictory or incompatible with the others. All used unique sets of sample sites. Beyond the overall consistency in results, the P/PV and MDC studies also generated supplementary views that complement the major findings discussed in the previous section; it is those additional findings that we wish to address now.

THE MDC STUDY

The MDC study grouped the myriad individual employment generating services (EGS) projects into five categories (MDC, 1982a:32–57). The first two types addressed broad community needs: economic development projects and linkage mechanisms; and activities directed at other community activities, such as education. The other three types were addressed to narrower needs within the CETA system: marketing and job development; collecting and analyzing labor market information; and activities designed to effect institutional change in local employment and training systems.

MDC explored in some detail the results of the various EGS activities, using multiple criteria for evaluation, such as number of jobs created or retained, favorable publicity generated, number of businesses served, and feedback from businesses served. Tangible indicators of outcome were scarce and hard to verify. In only half of the sites, for example, did EGS projects in economic development lead to measurable employment opportunities [the total number of jobs created in all 17 locations was estimated to be 400 by the end of summer in 1981 (1982a:67)].

Although EGS projects were imaginative, local implementers paid little attention to setting quantitative goals for EGS projects and made little effort to evaluate the results of their projects. Virtually no effort was made to ensure that jobs created by economic development projects went to economically disadvantaged persons.

The role of PICs was inevitably linked to the decisions and outcomes of EGS. MDC found three developmental patterns among PICs: Active Expansionist, Predetermined, and Passive Reactive (1982a:18–21). The Active Expansionist PICs, which were usually separate from the Prime Sponsor structure, set their own agendas and passed through a "time-phased hierarchy" of roles that began with employment and training issues but ultimately transcended them. Predetermined PICs were selected by local elected officials to deal with some pressing local problem such as economic development; their activities were closely allied with the priorities of the local officials who appointed them. Passive PICs, the third development category, responded to priorities set by people other than themselves or their staff; their EGS activities were diffuse and unfocused.

Using quantitative indicators—placement rate, placements in the private sector, dropouts—MDC found some relationship between the functional roles of the PICs and PSIP program performance. Active Expansionist PICs showed dramatic improvement between FY 1980 and 1981; Passive PICs and Predetermined PICs showed no improvement in performance; Passive PICs had much weaker performance overall than the other types of PICs (1982a:92–96).

THE P/PV STUDY

In its final summary report (Smith, 1982:80), P/PV concluded that PICs had made a small but perceptible difference in the study sites. The visibility of their programs was limited in some cases because of a deliberate strategy to avoid a high profile; in other cases the impact was limited because of the relatively small level of funding.

. P/PV used an assessment framework that stressed multiple indicators of outcomes, including quantitative measures of performance such as placement rates, costs, and client characteristics; qualitative aspects of PSIP programs; the extent of private sector involvement; improvements made to CETA programs other than Title VII; and distinctive or innovative PSIP programs.

Three types of impacts emerged from the P/PV sites: broad, systemic changes in employment and training activities in the local manpower system, different approaches to design and management of programs and activities, and changes initiated in Prime Sponsor operations through altered design and management of programs.

P/PV developed a threefold classification of PICs based on their activity and impacts. Those PICs with a system-wide focus looking at all aspects of employment and training programs, not just Title VII programs, were classified as "Change Agents." Their activities were designed basically to produce alterations in the local manpower systems. "Program Operators," on the other hand, were PICs whose central function was the design and operation of classroom training or on-the-job training programs in Title VII. The final category, "Single Purpose" PICs, concentrated on one particular program or type of activity within Title VII and tended to remain separate from other Prime Sponsor activities.

Whatever the role that PICs took, their development was slow and followed unique local patterns in each site. As the Executive Vice President of P/PV noted, councils took a long time to put together coherent agendas, and not all of them were able to do so (Saxon, 1982). In explaining the ability of PICs to evolve into stable institutions, P/PV noted the importance of local context: PICs with the best records built on existing community traditions of prior involvement of the private sector and an emphasis from Prime Sponsors on responding to the needs of the private sector (Smith, 1981:3). Other factors associated with successful PICs included active business involvement, competent professional staff support, and lack of tension or disputes in the local environment. Although business participation was important, P/PV found it took the form of a small, active core group on each PIC rather than being a broad-based phenomenon (Smith, 1982:5, 42).

The results reported by P/PV with respect to the type of

programs operated and the standard measures of program performance were quite similar to our findings. The types of programs did not differ greatly from those operated under Title IIBC. Though there was little "innovative" programming, PICs did introduce a variety of new management techniques, such as performance-based contracting, simplified OJT contracts, and training to meet employer specifications.

P/PV data on the characteristics of persons served in PSIP programs in the study sites suggest that PSIP may appear to have a better performance record than the IIBC programs because the clients that PICs enrolled tended to be easier to serve. The PICs showed a distinct tendency to choose the most "job ready" applicants from among the CETA-eligible pool of applicants; PIC programs were not directed towards the most disadvantaged participants.

P/PV concluded that PICs and PSIP were relatively successful in some localities and less successful in others. Their reports emphasized that local factors and local administrative discretion were most important in explaining program performance.

Conclusions

PSIP (Title VII) was added to CETA as a demonstration program in 1978 in order to increase the participation of private employers in public employment and training programs. Through the Private Industry Councils, which had responsibility for planning for Title VII resources, businesses had a new opportunity for shaping employment and training resources to meet their needs.

The results of PSIP after two and a half years of implementation were mixed. That this should be so is neither discouraging nor surprising. Principal results included the following:

1. Employer participation on and off the PICs was good in most sites. Participation took a variety of forms and represented an increase from pre-PSIP levels.

2. In about two-thirds of the Prime Sponsorships PICs emerged as strong or moderately strong institutions that were important in PSIP decision-making.

3. PSIP did not differ much from Title IIBC in terms of stan-

dard performance indicators. Title VII placement rates were slightly higher, but costs and wage gain for participants were nearly equal. PSIP participants tended to be older and better educated than those enrolled under Title IIBC. PSIP devoted a greater share of its resources to training programs than did Title IIBC.

4. The extent of program innovation was limited in PSIP; viable ties with economic development agencies were emerging in about 40 percent of the Prime Sponsorships. PSIP was also generating extensive changes in the broader CETA system procedures in about one-third of the localities.

The model in Figure 5-1 attempts to show the relationship of the multiple dimensions of performance with other explanatory factors. The environmental features (previous programs, economy) affect implementation decisions, intermediate results, and short-run outcomes. Implementation decisions (organization, recruitment, program choices) affect intermediate results and short-term outcomes. The intermediate results (PIC development, employer participation) affect short-term outcomes and long-term impact on institutions. Short-term outcomes (quantitative indicators and quality of jobs) affect the long-term impacts on clients and feedback into programs and organization choices (implementation choices). Finally, long-term outcomes feed back into organization and program choices, either by altering them or reinforcing them. In theory long-term outcomes can also feed back into the environment and alter the economic conditions, but this did not occur with PSIP because the level of resources was so small and the time so short.

The key factors that facilitated or impeded PSIP achievement, summarized in Table 5-7, are subject to direct control by local program managers. The non-manipulable factors do not determine program outcomes, especially if a strong staff is present, if the program has clearly stated goals, and if the relationship between the PIC and the Prime Sponsor is productive.

In short, a national intervention aimed at changing a basic feature of local CETA systems by inducing more participation of the private sector had some impact. The extent and nature of the impact was still very much a product of local action or inaction, conditioned by local factors. But the efforts at change generated

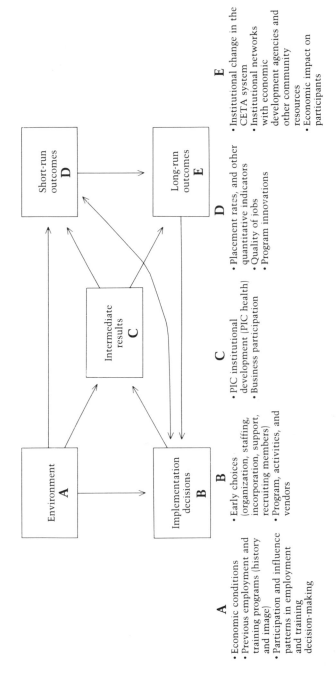

FIGURE 5-1: *A model of PSIP performance*

A
- Economic conditions
- Previous employment and training programs (history and image)
- Participation and influence patterns in employment and training decision-making

B
- Early choices (organization, staffing, incorporation, support, recruiting members)
- Program, activities, and vendors

C
- PIC institutional development (PIC health)
- Business participation

D
- Placement rates, and other quantitative indicators
- Quality of jobs
- Program innovations

E
- Institutional change in the CETA system
- Institutional networks with economic development agencies and other community resources
- Economic impact on participants

TABLE 5-7: *Manipulability of the most important local conditions facilitating and impeding PSIP performance*

Facilitating Conditions

Relatively Manipulable

High quality local staff

PIC members with appropriate value and time commitments

Good working relationships between CETA and PSIP

Relatively Non-Manipulable

Conducive local economic conditions

Impeding Conditions

Relatively Manipulable

Lack of appropriate staff or PIC leadership

Lackluster staff

Hostility between CETA and PSIP

PIC membership with inappropriate commitments or not much time or interest

Relatively Non-Manipulable

Non-conducive local economic conditions

Ingrained hostility on part of local private business people to any government program

by the national amendment were not wasted and had desirable impacts in some localities. Change at the local level is rarely so simple to generate as those at the national level seem to assume; on the other hand, it is far from impossible. But, ultimately, meaningful change depends on the efforts of local implementers to work within the spirit of new national programs.

CHAPTER SIX

★

CETA and Intergovernmental Relations

 CETA WAS DESIGNED TO BE IMPLEMENTED in a federalistic way—that is, with important roles for the federal government, states, and localities. The character of the relations between the territorial levels and the relative influence and content of their actions helped determine what CETA could and could not accomplish. The politics of such intergovernmental relations in CETA is the focus of this chapter.

The essence of federalism is the allocation of responsibilities among levels of government. This chapter begins with a discussion of the main characteristics of American federalism and of how intergovernmental relations in general have shifted over time. It then turns to the relatively distinct phases of intergovernmental relationships in the employment and training area and describes the nature of interactions that characterized the pre-CETA and CETA eras.

The most important part of this chapter is the discussion of the federal role in CETA, which included actions of Congress, the Employment and Training Administration in DOL, and the regional offices of DOL located in ten cities across the country. The national government, both in Washington and in the regional offices, was of primary importance in the intergovernmental partnership because of its hierarchical position, its range of responsibilities, and its position as funding agent.

The federal role, constantly changing, had limited programmatic coherence or consistency. In contrast, the role of local governments in CETA was always clear: they were grant recipients and program implementers. The shifting and gradually encroaching federal role, however, left local governments with limited options for creativity.

The concluding sections in the chapter discuss the restricted participation of state governments in CETA programs and the future of federalism in the post-CETA era, which promises a much greater role to states.

American Federalism and Social Policy

American federalism has undergone a revolution, beginning with the years of Franklin Delano Roosevelt's presidency (see Advisory Commission on Intergovernmental Relations, 1980). Until that time, the conventional view of the proper distribution of responsibilities between the national government in Washington and state and local governments could be generally characterized as "dual federalism" or "layer cake federalism," with separate responsibilities carried out by each level of government and limited interaction among the levels. Under Roosevelt, however, the federal government's initiatives in new policy areas, especially in economic and fiscal policy, challenged traditional views of the proper spheres of activity for the federal government and set in motion a trend of increasing federal responsibility. "Dual federalism," if it ever existed in reality, was replaced by the "marble cake" theory of federalism, also known as "cooperative federalism," in which responsibilities were shared vertically by all levels of government, not divided horizontally (see Grodzins, 1960, and Elazar, 1962).

By the 1960s the momentum of the growing federal presence in the areas of "cooperation" had increased rapidly. As James Sundquist (1969) described it:

In the nineteen-sixties, the American federal system entered a new phase. Through a series of dramatic enactments, the Congress asserted the national interest and authority in a wide range of governmental functions that until then had been the province, exclusively or predominantly, of state and local governments. The new legislation not only established federal-state-local relations in entirely new fields of activity and on a vast scale but it established new patterns of relationships as well.

The government's involvement in vast new areas of domestic social policy came almost exclusively through the proliferation of federal grants-in-aid to states and localities. Grants-in-aid were not themselves a new or different means of transferring funds. What was new was that beginning in the late 1950's, the purposes for which grant money was being spent were being defined by the federal government, not by the recipients. Again, Sundquist (1969:4–5): "Before 1960 the typical federal assistance program did not involve an expressly stated *national* purpose. It was instituted as a means of helping state or local governments accomplish *their* objectives. . . . In the newer model the federal grant is conceived of as a means of enabling the federal govenment to achieve *its* objectives. . . . The motive force is federal, with the state and communities assisting. . . ."

Categorical grants, the type that Sundquist refers to, are ones in which program purposes are defined by Congress and implementation is carried out by state and local agencies according to narrowly defined federal guidelines. Though intergovernmental in implementation, this type of grant retains a strong national presence in planning and oversight; little is left to the discretion of recipients. The profusion of categorical grants in the 1960's was accompanied by a growing awareness of problems involving implementation, ranging from lack of coordination to redundancy, competition, and confusion.

Partly in response to this situation, President Nixon in the late 1960's proposed "block grants," which would consolidate categorical grants in related functional areas, such as manpower programs or education. Administrators in states and localities would decide on the precise combination of programs, depending on local conditions though following broad national directives. As part of his New Federalism, which proposed to return discretion and decision-making to subnational governments, President Nixon also introduced the concept of General Revenue Sharing, in which federal tax receipts would be returned to local jurisdictions to be spent as local needs determined with no federal guidelines. Nixon's controversial New Federalism proposals were not welcomed by the web of interconnected interests and actors that surrounded and protected individual categorical grants. But General Revenue Sharing, which passed and went into effect in 1972, proved to be enormously popular with recipients. By 1973, President Nixon's first block grant or "special revenue sharing program" was also inaugurated—in the field of employment and training programs. CETA was followed by block grants in community development (CDBG) and Title XX of Social Security, but these alternative modes of federal assistance did not displace categorical grants as the primary means of providing aid to states and localities. In 1981 almost 80 percent of the federal grants to states and localities was for categorical grants (Patterson, Davidson, and Ripley, 1982:483).

In the 1980s President Reagan introduced his version of New Federalism. Like the Republican presidents that preceded him, he decried the growth of the federal government and its intrusion into the policy agendas of subnational governments, and he proposed a reduction of federal responsibilities. His plan included a dramatic consolidation of categorical programs into block grants, coupled with large cuts in federal funding and a major federal-state swap of responsibility for medicaid and welfare programs. Most of Reagan's proposals were stymied as of late 1983 because the recipient states and localities did not like the terms—increased responsibility with decreased funding. The Job Training Partnership Act (JTPA), passed in 1982, represents the largest block grant thus far that generally follows the guidelines of Reagan's New Federalism.

The data in Table 6-1 summarize grants-in-aid spending from 1950 with a projection through 1986. Growth in absolute dollars continues into the 1980s, but a gradual reduction is evident in the percent of total Federal outlays and the percent of gross national product (GNP) accounted for by grants-in-aid. The number of discrete grant programs is also declining from a high of over 550 in the mid 1970s. The fiscal dependence of states and local governments is beginning to decline slightly: in FY 1982 the figure was 22.1 percent (no projections for 1985 or 1986 were available).

Figure 6-1 portrays the complexities of administering the profusion of grants. Any combination of administrative levels diagrammed there could be involved in implementing indi-

TABLE 6-1: *Federal grants-in-aid to state and local governments, selected years, 1950–1986*

FISCAL YEARS	TOTAL GRANTS-IN-AID ($ MILLIONS)	PORTION REPRESENTED BY FEDERAL GRANTS (PERCENT)		
		TOTAL BUDGET OUTLAYS	STATE AND LOCAL EXPENDITURES	GROSS NATIONAL PRODUCT
1950	2,253	5.3	10.4	0.9
1955	3,207	4.7	10.1	0.8
1960	7,020	7.6	14.7	1.4
1965	10,904	9.2	15.3	1.7
1970	24,014	12.3	19.2	2.3
1975	49,834	15.4	23.0	3.3
1980	91,472	15.9	26.2	3.6
1985 (estimate)	99,162	10.8	NA	2.6
1986 (estimate)	102,468	10.4	NA	2.5

NA = Not available

Source: Adapted from *Special Analyses, Budget of the United States. Fiscal Year 1984*, Table H-6, p. H-16.

158

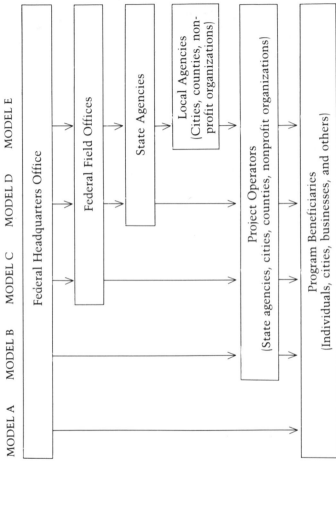

FIGURE 6-1: *Models of administrative organization for providing assistance to program beneficiaries in various federal grant programs*

MODEL A   MODEL B   MODEL C   MODEL D   MODEL E

Federal Headquarters Office

Federal Field Offices

State Agencies

Local Agencies
(Cities, counties, nonprofit organizations)

Project Operators
(State agencies, cities, counties, nonprofit organizations)

Program Beneficiaries
(Individuals, cities, businesses, and others)

Source: Adapted from U.S. General Accounting Office, 1978, *The Federal Government Should But Doesn't Know the Cost of Administering its Assistance Programs*, p. 3.

vidual grant programs. CETA approximated the most complicated model (Model E).

A review of American federalism recorded some of the administrative implications of the growth in federal grants-in-aid (see Mosher, 1980:546): an increasing reliance by the federal government on nonfederal employees (including state and local government bureaucrats, private for-profit and nonprofit organizations) to implement Federal programs; an increase in the amount of political pressure and in the number of access points for bringing that pressure to bear; an increase in the activity and influence of interest groups; greater difficulty in achieving coordination among programs; a decline in direct accountability as the number of actors and the levels of government involved increases; and changes in federal administrators' clout and techniques reflecting a shift from command and control to negotiation and bargaining. Although derived from a review of all grant programs, these issues were relevant to CETA and complicated implementation of it.

Intergovernmental Relations in Employment and Training

THE PRE-CETA PERIOD

In the pre-CETA era (1962–1974), the principal feature of intergovernmental relations in employment and training policy was the dominance of the federal government and the absence of involvement by local and state government agencies and officials. The programs operating under the authority of MDTA, EOA, and other legislation were designed, funded, and managed by Congress and federal agencies. The federal government interacted directly with service deliverers for the various programs—Neighborhood Youth Corps, Operation Mainstream, MDTA classroom training, and on-the-job training. DOL wrote and oversaw more than 10,000 contracts with service deliverers operating programs at the local level (Mirengoff and Rindler, 1976:1). Local and state governments were not involved in the relationship except in the infrequent role of service deliverer (Franklin, 1977:269).

Programs manufactured and dispersed so readily from the

national level created a genuine programmatic tangle at the local level. By the end of the MDTA era, there were 17 separate categorical programs operating with separate legislative and organizational bases in Washington (these were summarized earlier in Table 1-1; see also Advisory Commission on Intergovernmental Relations, 1977:17). Program planning and operational guidelines detailing how much of what could be done by whom and for whom and when emanated from Washington to local program operators. In administering the various categorical programs, the Department of Labor interacted with:

> individual school districts in the Neighborhood Youth Corps In-School program; with City Halls and independent Community Action Agencies in the Neighborhood Youth Corps programs; with rural county governments or agencies in the Operation Mainstream program; State Employment Services and Vocational Education agencies in the MDTA-Institutional program; the Employment Service and Welfare departments with regard to the Work Incentive Program; and with individual employers and unions for MDTA-OJT, pre-apprenticeship and JOBS programs. (Shultz, 1970:85)

The need for coordination was obvious. Efforts at the federal level to promote coordination were made, but with limited results. The principal obstacles, fragmentation and territorialism among federal agencies at the national level, proved to be virtually insurmountable, as a vivid description of the most serious pre-CETA coordination effort, the Concentrated Employment Program (CEP), makes clear (Williams, 1971:43–49; see also Williams, 1980:33; and Ruttenberg and Gutchess, 1970:64–71). DOL had responsibility for implementing CEP but lacked the authority and resources to force a reallocation of roles and responsibilities among community action agencies and Employment Service offices. The coordination of equals by an equal yielded only superficial changes.

There was uniform agreement in Congress and among Johnson Administration officials that the MDTA version of federalism was flawed, to put it mildly. Fragmentation, lack of coordination, duplication, and gaps in manpower services required redressing. CEP was the Johnson Administration's last attempt to try to correct the problems: President Johnson turned down a proposal to implement a decentralized manpower block grant. President Nixon would not rely on attempts to coordinate from the national level; for him, the block grant was the answer.

FEDERALISM IN THE CETA ERA

The Nixon Administration perceived all of the problems of categorical employment and training programs that were evident to the Johnson Administration and Congress, which had created the programs. But the Nixonians were not wedded to the ideals of social reform that motivated the Great Society programs, and their ideological and party preferences fueled their determination to reform not just manpower programs but the shape of federalism. The Nixon officials criticized—and justly—the proliferation of employment and training programs and the paucity of positive results from them. They also attacked overregulation and excessive supervision by the federal government and lack of participation by local governments. Decategorization and decentralization were viewed as the means to achieve the goals of disengaging the federal bureaucracy from program operations and channelling authority to local elected officials (Williams, 1971:34–36).

Because of the nature of the compromises made to obtain passage and approval of the legislation (see Ch. 1), there could be no certainty about the "proper" relationship among federal, state, and local governments as CETA implementation began. The pursuit of multiple objectives and the inclusion of vague and imprecise statutory language concerning the extent of the Secretary of Labor's authority relative to Prime Sponsors contributed to multiple views about what could be expected and what "should" happen as DOL and Prime Sponsors hammered out working relationships (Advisory Commission on Intergovernmental Relationships, 1977:18). In the law, the regulations, and internal DOL documents such as handbooks and field memos, there was much ambiguity about what the federal role would be in specific terms.

Broad outlines of the revised relationships were apparent. CETA redistributed responsibilities for program planning, operations, and evaluation. Local Prime Sponsors were to assess local manpower needs and client groups, plan programs to meet local needs using mandated councils for advice, select service deliverers, write contracts, and oversee program operations.

Categorical employment and training programs were for the most part abolished and the federal government was no longer involved in program contracting. It retained responsibility for program oversight, data collection, approval of Prime Sponsor plans, and providing technical assistance to Prime Sponsors to enable them to assume their new duties.

New actors were introduced into the implementation of this hybrid block grant program and old actors were placed in new relationships. New to the employment and training arena were mayors and county commissioners, Prime Sponsor bureaucrats administering CETA, and manpower planning councils (citizen bodies with an advisory role mandated by the law). Old actors placed in new relationships included service providers and DOL, who had previously dealt directly with one another. Service deliverers now dealt with local Prime Sponsors and were dependent on them for funding rather than DOL. DOL employees were placed into new roles as generalists, expected to be knowledgeable about all aspects of Prime Sponsor service delivery, when previously they had been program specialists dealing with a single program such as work experience or on-the-job training.

In contrast to the pre-CETA period when the federal government was without question the dominant governmental actor in manpower program implementation, decentralization at the outset of CETA seemed to have given local governments an undisputed degree of authority and discretion to shape manpower programs to meet local needs, with the federal government playing a supportive and relatively subordinate role. As the implementation of CETA proceeded, however, this allocation of power was gradually eroded (in the eyes of at least one observer, the erosion was inevitable—see McPherson, 1976:20). In one sense, the federal role in CETA did decrease compared to the pre-CETA period (Hargrove and Dean, 1980:137). There was a diminution of federal responsibility for direct program choices and program administration. But there was also a great increase in federal emphasis on procedural rather than substantive matters. DOL's policy stances were inconsistent from one time to another as well as from region to region. Moreover, the degree and quality of leadership from DOL varied depending on the issue. DOL cared much more about expenditure rates for public service employment programs than about patterns of service to clients, for example, and hence harassed Prime Sponsors far more over the former than the latter (see Van Horn, 1979:74). The amount of federal intervention in the operations of Prime Sponsors began to increase after the first year of implementation (see Bailis, 1975), but the quality and extent of technical assistance to Prime Sponsors failed to improve and was generally regarded as weak at best (Van Horn, 1978:163–64).

The place of state governments on the intergovernmental scene was enhanced slightly with the advent of CETA. States were given two new roles in the legislation: to coordinate all manpower services operating in the state and to administer programs as a Prime Sponsor for the "Balance of State"—that portion not included in city and county Prime Sponsor jurisdictions. As Balance of State Prime Sponsors, however, states enjoyed no advantages over other Prime Sponsors in dealing with DOL. And as coordinators of statewide manpower services, most states had limited interest in doing more than simply collecting their share of the grant and funding a variety of projects that did not encroach on the turf of local Prime Sponsors. Even in states where coordination was viewed with interest by state administrators, there were limited resources and minimal leverage over the local Prime Sponsors who avidly resisted suggestions of closer coordination, utilizing state agencies as service deliverers, or anything else that further limited their already limited flexibility.

Through increased reporting requirements, tightening and expanding regulations, proliferating directives to the field, and increasing numbers of categorical programs, DOL reclaimed a strong managerial role for itself by the end of the period of CETA's first authorization, 1974 to 1978, thereby limiting the latitude of Prime Sponsors for comprehensive planning and innovative programming. DOL intrusiveness increased during the period of the second CETA authorization, 1978 to 1982.

The Nature and Impact of the Federal Role in CETA

The actions of Congress and the national and regional offices of DOL were responsible for the changing complexion of intergovernmental relations with state and local Prime Sponsors. In this section, we want to describe the major areas of federal activity and inactivity and the political and substantive impacts of those activities. We cannot cover every aspect of involvement, but we have tried to select the areas in which the substantive impacts were greatest. Some of the roles and impacts discussed below were formal and others were informal; some were initiated deliberately and others emerged unintentionally.

The behavior of Congress and DOL in administering CETA appears, when viewed in the aggregate and with the advantage of hindsight, to have been inconsistent and to have lacked continuity. Congress frequently altered its own legislative priorities—from categorical to decentralized, decategorized programs; from comprehensive programs to recategorized programs—and DOL of necessity followed suit. DOL's actions were inconsistent because the legislation had multiple and conflicting goals and because both DOL and Congress emphasized different goals at different times. In part this was in response to changing economic conditions, in part due to changing political conditions (change in the party of the President, change in the coalitions within Congress supporting employment and training legislation), and in part because of discretion left to administrative managers within DOL.

Our discussion of the nature of the federal role is divided into three parts: DOL's activity in promoting achievement of statutory CETA goals, DOL's administrative priorities (which were not directly linked to promoting goal achievement), and other federal activities. An assessment of the impact of the federal role on intergovernmental relationship forms the concluding part of the section.

THE NATURE OF FEDERAL INVOLVEMENT:
PROMOTING STATUTORY GOALS[1]

CETA legislation in 1973 and 1978 embraced at least five broad goals: decentralization, decategorization, citizen participation, service to economically disadvantaged participants, and private sector participation (the last not added until the 1978 amendments). Our judgments about the extent of federal

1. We happily acknowledge the large debt we owe our colleague, Carl Van Horn, in this section. We have adapted his approach for assessing federal performance relative to national CETA goals (see Van Horn, 1978).

concern and activity in promoting these goals during CETA's life are summarized in Table 6-2 and discussed in the sections that follow.

DECENTRALIZATION. Responsibility was transferred on paper from the federal government to states and localities when the legislation was passed at the end of 1973. The immediate effect of the new law was the creation of hundreds of new local bureaucracies to implement the new program at the local level.

The real test of decentralization came when implementation actually began on July 1, 1974. That test involved DOL's ability to relinquish control and to assist the fledgling Prime Sponsors to plan and develop programs by providing technical assistance that was timely, substantive, and useful.

Relinquishing control was partially a matter of attitudes. The bureaucrats in the national and regional offices had been shaped by the preceding twelve years of experience as program specialists: they had effectively ruled the intergovernmental roost. The transition was a difficult one for them to make because they not only gave up control over what was familiar but they also

TABLE 6-2: *DOL promotion of national CETA goals*

GOAL	PERIOD		COMMENTS
	1974–1978	1978–1982	
Decentralization	Medium initially, low by 1978	Low to none	Attention declined as DOL recentralized control
Decategorization	Medium initially, low by 1978	Low	Attention declined as emphasis shifted to recategorized programs
Pattern of service to participants	Low	Medium	Attention increased due to 1978 amendments
Citizen participation	Low	Low	Not a priority
Private sector involvement	Very low	Medium	Attention stimulated by 1978 amendments

assumed nominally subservient positions in a new environment with which they were unfamiliar. Resentment and scorn for inexperienced Prime Sponsor staffs were not uncommon in regional offices at the outset of the implementation. Prime Sponsors were viewed as upstarts.

The technical assistance role for DOL employees was also new, requiring them to provide practical advice and guidance for the new Prime Sponsors. This was often beyond their capacity to offer, especially in the first year of CETA. Regional office staff rarely knew more and usually knew less than the Prime Sponsor staff implementing the program. Prime Sponsors often got better information more quickly from public interest groups such as the National Association of Counties or the U.S. Conference of Mayors than they received from DOL. The attitudes of Prime Sponsor staff toward the federal technical assistance effort were generally negative during the entire CETA period. That "TA" effort was criticized for being too little, too late, too focused on paperwork and green eyeshade management, and not directed toward substantive issues or questions of political management (see Mirengoff and associates, 1980:41). Prime Sponsor staff were plagued by frequent rotation of the individuals from the regional offices ("Fed reps") who embodied the federal presence, provided much of the technical assistance, and who also did the program monitoring.

Essentially, the regional offices were placed in an untenable situation. They had to re-educate their own staff about CETA and try to produce a generalist mentality to replace the previous specialist outlook. Moreover, the quality of staff that were assigned as federal representatives was often less than sterling: they were frequently responsible for guiding Prime Sponsors in programmatic areas of which they themselves were ignorant (see Levitan and Mangum, 1981:63). The regional offices had to respond to changing policy signals from Washington by providing guidance to Prime Sponsors before deadlines had elapsed. Rarely was there time for them to prepare useful technical assistance for Prime Sponsor staff in the face of rapidly changing directives and schedules. Contributing to the woes of the regional offices was the inherent conflict between the parallel roles DOL was assigned: the role of monitoring Prime Sponsor compliance with CETA requirements was incompatible with that of providing technical assistance to help build a local institutional capability for administration. The technical assistance role suffered in the evolution of CETA. The relationship between the regional offices and Prime Sponsor staff often deteriorated to an adversarial one.

Van Horn (1978:163) concludes that "DOL did not constructively foster the process of decentralization by contributing to the development of local control over programs or expertise about manpower." Williams (1980:68) offers a concurring opinion: "Little real help was given to the prime sponsors in terms of substantive technical assistance or capacity building." These judgments, based on relatively early performance, were still accurate at the end of CETA, even though DOL took steps to centralize technical assistance in the national office and to improve its quality. The head of ETA's Office of Comprehensive Employment and Training was candid in his assessment of DOL's execution of this responsibility during CETA's existence when he said that technical assistance is "one of the things we have done least well" (Roberts Jones, quoted in *Employment and Training Reporter*, 4/20/83:969).

DECATEGORIZATION. All of DOL's pre-CETA administrative experience had been with categorical programs like the Neighborhood Youth Corps and MDTA OJT. There was a strong tendency for federal representatives to promote categorical types of programs with the less experienced new Prime Sponsors because that was what they knew and because the more naive among Prime Sponsor staff were vulnerable to being guided in this fashion at the outset of CETA (see Williams, 1980:67).

At the beginning of CETA the staff in DOL had no conception about or capability to plan a comprehensive manpower system for individual Prime Sponsors. Technical assistance guides developed by the national office did not deal with local planning for comprehensive programs, and the regional offices could give no guidance in this area (Van Horn, 1978:166). Even when some individual federal representatives ventured to give advice about how to build a local service delivery system that was both comprehensive and decategorized, there was strong local pressure from entrenched pre-CETA service deliverers to continue the status quo. In short, even at the outset of CETA, DOL had no capacity to promote comprehensive manpower services with Prime Sponsors because the concept was alien.

The concept was largely ignored except in rhetoric as Congress and DOL proceeded during CETA's middle years to impose a new series of categorical programs upon Prime Sponsors' operational agendas. The push began midway in the first year of implementing CETA with a new PSE title and picked up great momentum in 1977 with a huge infusion of PSE money as well as an array of youth programs, a veterans program, and a new skills training program. In 1978 the private sector program was added. The notion of decategorized, comprehensive manpower programs designed at the local level was forgotten except by wistful Prime Sponsor staff (see Wurzburg, 1980; and Ripley and associates, 1979c, for detailed discussions of the impacts that the fragmented youth and veterans programs had at the local level).

PATTERNS OF SERVICE TO PARTICIPANTS. CETA was intended to improve employability of economically disadvantaged citizens. Although the legislation contained eligibility criteria for Prime Sponsors to use in recruiting participants, it simultaneously enlarged the pool of persons eligible for manpower assistance beyond its pre-CETA size by including the unemployed and underemployed as well as those of low income. DOL simply did not emphasize service to the most disadvantaged as an important goal, even though the law specified that "to the maximum extent feasible, manpower services . . . will be provided to those most in need of them" (Section 105 of the original statute). Indeed, other DOL activities encouraged less service to the disadvantaged, as Van Horn has noted (1978:165). The emphasis in the mid-1970s on the buildup of PSE enrollments and on the rapid expenditure of PSE and youth funds led Prime Sponsors to enroll less disadvantaged persons, a practice the law permitted in PSE until FY 1979. In non-PSE titles, Prime Sponsor staff found it impossible to focus programs on the most disadvantaged clients partly because of pressure from DOL to increase placements, decrease costs, and serve more people.

National attention to patterns of service to participants was raised during the 1978 reauthorization debate. Amendments redirected the eligibility for PSE titles toward a more disadvantaged clientele, and DOL monitoring was subsequently more attentive to this issue. Prime Sponsor plans were altered to show how planned levels of service to various significant segments compared to the actual occurrence of those groups in the local eligible population. Written justification for over-serving or under-serving these groups was required.

The percentage of disadvantaged persons served in all CETA titles increased as a result of the 1978 amendments (see Mirengoff and associates, 1982:6), but except for intermittent bursts of attention, patterns of service to participants were never more than a secondary concern of DOL's monitoring and policy activity. Other goals and administrative priorities took precedence.

DOL did, from time to time, insist on increased service or special attention at the local level to what the law and regulations designated as "significant segments" in the local population. The "significant segments"—special groups identified from time to time for special emphasis—included women, veterans, ex-offenders, handicapped, various minorities, and so on. Such changing federal emphasis produced three major kinds of problems, no matter how well motivated the federal insistence was in each individual case.

First, the federal government did, in fact, treat the emphasis on each individual group separately. Thus, for example, if veterans' groups in Washington put pressure on DOL to stress veterans—and especially if the push from the interest groups was reinforced by members of Congress seeking veterans' votes or even a Secretary of Labor or White House staff seeking to aid the re-election prospects of an incumbent President—veterans would be stressed. Then, six months later, a new set of interests might generate pressure resulting in a new DOL push for handicapped persons. In short, there was never any systematic attention to the full array of "significant segments." Instead, at one time or another, every segment with some political clout was stressed. The result invalidated whatever logic might have motivated emphasis on significant segments: if everyone is special, no one is special.

Second, the constantly shifting federal emphasis on different segments gave various local interest groups licenses to seek the scalps of local political officials and CETA staff members when they felt that they were being "underserved" and wished to demand a larger share of resources. The local allocation of resources was, by definition, zero-sum at any given time. Resources were fixed, and if veterans got more then some other segment would automatically receive less. The pie did not grow. The federal government just encouraged local interests to ask for bigger slices of pie. And of course, not all groups could get larger slices simultaneously. This federal intrusion helped upset whatever planning local implementers were able to undertake.

Third, there was no agreed-on national method for measuring concepts such as "significance" or "under-service." The definitions themselves were both incredibly loose and intuitive and, also, simultaneously, totally political in content.

CITIZEN PARTICIPATION. Manpower planning councils were created in the original legislation to allow citizens to be involved in the debate on local needs and program design. The law specified in general terms the composition of the councils and their role but limited their power. Councils were only advisory: they did not have decision-making authority, and they were clearly subordinate to Prime Sponsors. Because of their community-wide representation, the councils possessed a potential for ensuring accountability of the actions of Prime Sponsors and for checking tendencies of CETA programs to under-serve minorities and the most disadvantaged. But DOL did not devote attention to promoting effective councils. Like participant service patterns, citizen participation was a secondary goal that was pushed aside by other priorities. DOL technical assistance to council members was virtually nonexistent, and guidance to Prime Sponsor staffs on how best to use councils was limited. DOL's annual program performance assessments of Prime Sponsors' operations addressed planning councils, but only superficially (whether the council existed, met, and included the required representatives). DOL assessments did not venture into questions about council effectiveness or utilization of council recommendations, even though it knew through the reports of federal representatives that many councils were inactive or rubber stamps. Thus, although federal actions imposed an additional structure on the administering bureaucracy (in later years, the Youth council and the Private Industry Council were also added), DOL did not actively help these councils reach full potential in their localities. To have done so would have meant, in many cases, challenging Prime Sponsors that did not want active councils. Given the press of other business, citizen participation was relegated to a place of lesser importance by DOL.

PRIVATE SECTOR PARTICIPATION. The 1978 CETA reauthorization debate was the occasion of a shift in thinking and policy actions by Congress, DOL, and nongovernmental actors regarding involvement of the private sector in employment and training projects. This shift resulted in the addition of Title VII of CETA, the Private Sector Initiative Program (PSIP), and the creation of Private Industry Councils (PICs) in all Prime Sponsor jurisdictions.

Prior to PSIP, private sector participation in CETA programs was quite limited in both scope and magnitude (see Ripley and Franklin, 1981, 1983). After 1978, DOL monitoring was redirected to include PSIP implementation, but once again DOL was in an awkward and uneasy position. In terms of DOL interaction with local Prime Sponsor staff, the early years of PSIP implementation were a rerun of the first years of CETA implementation. Regional office staff knew little more and often less about the new programs than the Prime Sponsor staff. Technical assistance sessions for local staff on how to attract private sector participation once PICs were formed simply did not exist. Instead, DOL's attention was riveted on simply getting the PICs created, not on questions of how PICs were used. DOL voluntarily minimized its role in helping Prime Sponsors implement PSIP when it gave the National Alliance of Business, a national business intermediary organization with local offices, a large contract to provide technical assistance and conduct nationwide marketing for the program. DOL's rationale in delegating to NAB was that a business organization would be more effective than DOL in setting up a new program for the private sector.

But this assumption turned out to be invalid because NAB lacked credibility with both most Prime Sponsors and many businesses.

DOL's role in encouraging private sector participation was thus limited to administrative tinkering: it altered required reports so that Prime Sponsors had to show the number of placements in the private sector, and it gave favorable publicity to Prime Sponsors with good private sector ties, although sometimes the regional offices' nominations of sites were based on erroneous perceptions. DOL's impact was limited in promoting this goal with local Prime Sponsors because it lacked concrete technical expertise.

CONCLUSIONS. DOL was not effective in promoting the achievement of national goals by Prime Sponsors during CETA's existence. DOL's effectiveness was impeded by numerous factors. It shifted from goal to goal, rarely concentrating on one for very long. Congress, too, changed its emphases, causing DOL to alter its priorities. Furthermore, within DOL there was confusion and uncertainty about how to achieve certain goals, especially decategorization and private sector participation. There was inherent competition and inconsistency among different goals, with the result that actions taken to promote one would impede achievement of another (see Mirengoff and associates, 1980:5; see also Hill and Marks, 1982:102, for a good discussion of the effect that goal confusion has on federal implementation strategies). DOL lacked enough well-qualified, trained staff to carry out its role properly through its regional offices. It generally found itself in a self-made trap of being so caught up in daily implementation issues that it lost sight of the broad substantive goals toward which implementation activity was presumably directed.

THE NATURE OF FEDERAL INVOLVEMENT: ADMINISTRATIVE ACTIVITY

The general administrative environment in which Prime Sponsors operated was largely a creation of Congress and the national office of DOL. It was characterized by complex and frequently changing administrative rules, delays and changes in funding, uncertainty over pending reauthorizations, and additions, modifications, and deletions of programs. DOL was unable to push Prime Sponsors toward national goal achievement, but it very nearly pushed them into administrative gridlock by proliferating administrative requirements.

CETA rules and regulations required Prime Sponsors to prepare and submit reams of paperwork for each program that they operated. A partial list includes annual plans (with very detailed subsections and tables); plan modifications (for additions, changes, or alterations in funding levels); quarterly reports on programs, participants, and finances; and annual reports on program status and participants. The DOL handbook explaining how to fill out these required reports for FY 1981 was over an inch thick. These reports were supplemented by additional requirements for recordkeeping on finances and participants. The volume of paperwork increased as new programs were added over the years and constituted an enormous burden on Prime Sponsors.

DOL's administrative intrusions increased in frequency after the 1978 reauthorization, which resulted in numerous changes to improve management and to reduce opportunities for fraud and abuse in local programs (see Mirengoff and associates, 1982, for a good review of the reauthorization changes).

DOL's monitoring activity occurred over an annual cycle. First came the review and approval of the Prime Sponsors' annual plans. Approval was not automatic, although regional offices typically focused on trivial aspects and avoided substantive areas of program choices. The next phase in the monitoring cycle was the review of quarterly reports on program status, financial status, and characteristics of participants served. The review compared actual performance to planned performance for the quarter, and if a deviation of more than 15 percent was present, a corrective action plan had to be submitted to DOL. Onsite visits by the federal representative and annual performance assessments completed the monitoring activities.

Before the 1978 amendments, DOL's monitoring was preoccupied with numbers, and it skirted questions of quality. DOL emphasized things like rate of expenditures and levels of enrollments during the first year of CETA's implementation, the PSE buildup in the mid 1970s, the HIRE program, and many others. The driving concern was to get the money out and spent. Program content and quality were ignored.

After the 1978 reauthorization, DOL monitoring was oriented towards compliance and audit. Focused on processes to insure that fraud and abuse would not occur, it included attention to matters such as checking the Prime Sponsors' newly created Independent Monitoring Units, certifying their newly required participant eligibility verification systems, and increasing the number of program audits.

The first DOL annual performance assessment was a disaster (see Snedeker and Snedeker, 1978:45–46). Instead of developing uniform national procedures, each regional office designed its own assessment. There were wide variations in the tone and emphasis of the assessments, although they all focused on rate of expenditures. In subsequent years, uniformity of the assessment document increased, as did the scope and complexity of issues addressed. After the 1978 amendments, the focus shifted to legal compliance, management systems, and measurable program outcomes.

The annual assessments by DOL typically identified only a tiny fraction of Prime Sponsors with "serious problems" (the most deficient category), another slightly larger group with "some problems," and a vast majority with "no problems" (that is, they had achieved—or reported as achievement—the numerical goals in their plans and were in compliance with the legislation). The number of Prime Sponsors with serious problems was never a large segment. For example, in FY 1978, before the reauthorization, eleven percent had serious problems; in FY 1982, only two percent.

The "serious problem" rating served as a warning but did not result in loss of funds for the next fiscal year. DOL funding would be continued for Prime Sponsors with serious problems if corrective action plans were developed jointly between the Prime Sponsor staff and regional office staff. In the whole history of CETA, only one Prime Sponsor ever lost funding for problems beyond the ability of DOL to resolve or ignore.

Prime Sponsor staff did not view the performance assessment as a helpful exercise. In their eyes it was makework, an additional hoop to go through to get refunded. It ignored substantive issues of program content, and was directed at identifying problems, not at identifying or rewarding good performance.

The main effect of DOL's administrative activity in implementing CETA was to harass Prime Sponsor staffs and to reduce local flexibility in managing programs. There certainly was a need for a federal administrative role in CETA, but DOL focused on process over substance, numbers over quality, and punishing bad performance rather than encouraging good performance. The recentralization of administration evident after the 1978 amendments reduced the potential for fraud and abuse, but at the cost of the flexibility implied by decentralization (Mirengoff and associates, 1982:72–74).

THE NATURE OF FEDERAL INVOLVEMENT: OTHER ACTIVITIES

NURTURING INTEREST GROUPS. Theodore Lowi (1979) has written that government has clothed interest groups with the powers of government by delegating many of its responsibilities to them. In the CETA arena Congress and DOL unequivocally accepted the legitimacy of interest group access and participation in governmental decision-making and implementation. Indeed, an operational principle emerged, *de facto:* all groups could be induced to support CETA if all of them were given a concrete stake in it through creating pieces of the program designated as their various preserves. As a result:

★ National community-based organizations (CBOs) were given a variety of national contracts and favorable notice in statutes. Title III national funding increased fourfold between 1976 and 1980, and the "big three" of employment and training CBOs became the "big 15."

★ The Human Resource Development Institute of the AFL-CIO was funded, and union participation and concurrence was protected, encouraged, and occasionally required in various parts of the statutes and regulations.

★ The National Alliance of Business and other business organizations received contracts, and there were exhortations in the regulations to coordinate with them.

★ The interest groups representing local units of government all received contracts for various purposes, and their interests were considered in at least some provisions in the regulations and statutes.

★ The influence of groups representing veterans, the handicapped, displaced homemakers, and others was evident throughout the regulations and statutes, as well as in decisions made by DOL concerning the allocation of discretionary funds.

The understandable instincts of Congress and DOL to respond to all interest groups have their costs, notably the resulting difficulty with producing an integrated policy at the national level. In this case, the national placation of competing interest groups often created very difficult situations for Prime Sponsors politically and even legally. The creation of categorical programs produced fragmented programs, disintegrated local planning, and decreased local flexibility to allocate resources. National identification of numerous "significant segments" for local attention created local political tensions at minimum and occasioned some lawsuits against Prime Sponsors. Furthermore, programs viewed locally as national categorical intrusions attracted little positive local support during implementation.

PERFORMANCE STANDARDS. The question of measuring program performance was actively debated throughout the life of CETA. The debate continues under CETA's replacement, JTPA. Prime Sponsors resisted simplistic and unidimensional indicators of performance, and DOL rejected reliance on idiosyncratic measures for each individual Prime Sponsor. In the first four years of CETA, performance measurement was largely a paper activity, limited to simple data on program status and participant characteristics collected from Prime Sponsor plans and quarterly reports. Despite some statistical manipulation of these data within DOL, no real use was made of them in terms of affecting decisions. Since the data were both suspect and based on very limited conceptualization, the failure to use these primitive "standards" was probably a good outcome.

In the 1978 reauthorization, Congress instructed DOL to develop performance standards for CETA. Subsequently a Technical Workgroup was formed, headed by national office staff and involving Prime Sponsor and regional office staff. The Workgroup labored for months to develop a formula that would avoid arbitrariness. They kept the familiar performance indicators already used by DOL but allowed each Prime Sponsor to calculate its own unique expected range of variation for each indicator based on weightings of various local conditions (see *Employment and Training Reporter*,4/1/81:853).

The final draft version of the performance standards was not completed until early in 1981, and implementation of the standards was caught up in the 1982 reauthorization process. The first implementation was done on a trial basis in FY 1982 with no rewards or sanctions attached. The standards drifted into nonexistence during the year, however, and were lost entirely in the shuffle of DOL staff cuts, closing CETA, and making the transition to JTPA during FY 1983. Performance benchmarks were used on an optional and unofficial basis by regional offices in the FY 1983 grant review process. The idea of variable ranges of performance for Prime Sponsors depending on local conditions was a good one, but it came too late to have any effect in the CETA context.

The JTPA legislation retains the interest in performance standards. Section 106 of the law outlines the general results that Congress expects from the new program: increased employment and earnings and decreased welfare dependency. Actual criteria must be developed by the staff of DOL and are to be implemented in FY 1984, although 1985 or 1986 is much more likely to witness movement in this area—if there is ever any implementation of performance standards.

IMPACTS OF THE FEDERAL ROLE ON CETA

The various interventions of Congress and DOL during the life of CETA were structural, procedural, and substantive in character and impact. The principal structural impact of the original law was the creation of new bureaucratic entities, the Prime Sponsorships, to implement the CETA program at the local level. Subsequent amendments introduced additional structural features to the shape of the Prime Sponsor bureaucracy, primarily in the form of new councils and an Independent Monitoring Unit. The procedural impacts of detailing requirements for planning, participants, reporting, monitoring, and coordination with other agencies set numerous limitations on how the Prime Sponsor bureaucracy would operate. The substantive impacts came in the form of programmatic specifications; the recategorization of programs between 1974 and 1978 sharply curtailed programmatic flexibility at the local level. (For a somewhat different assessment of federal impacts, see Dalton and Fitzpatrick, 1983.)

The impacts affected all local implementers in a variety of ways. Administrative complexity increased as requirements and regulations mushroomed and extensive changes in local management systems were imposed on Prime Sponsors. Funds for administration did not increase, however. Local flexibility, both managerial and programmatic, decreased as options were constrained by nationally imposed limits and mandates. Increasing local fiscal liability helped reduce incentives to innovate. Morale of staff plummeted and frustration soared due to the aggregate effect of the federal interventions, the assumption of guilt implicit in the changes made in the 1978 reauthorization, and the spiraling staff layoffs between 1979 and 1983 as first PSE and then all of CETA were phased out.

In sum, the federal impact on CETA was negative. Quickly reneging on the original 1974 concept of decentralization and flexibility, the federal government through its activities created an adversarial relationship with state and local implementers. After 1978, the federal government was unquestionably dominant. From the local perspective, the CETA experiment had promised much but delivered little save headaches. Intergovernmental relations had soured.

The Role of the States in CETA

CETA legislation and regulations seemed to give states a good deal of responsibility for planning and coordinating statewide delivery of manpower services and for monitoring local Prime Sponsors' CETA programs. In practice, however, most of the states were unimportant. Functioning as Prime Sponsors for state areas that were not included in the jurisdictions of local Prime Sponsors and serving as conduits for disbursing discretionary and earmarked funds to local Prime Sponsors and other applicants, they lacked resources and leverage to achieve statewide coordination or to have any impact on programs of local Prime Sponsors (see Mirengoff and Rindler, 1976:80; Snedeker and Snedeker, 1978:57; and Dement, 1981).

STATES AS PRIME SPONSORS

In the law states were offered two roles: a relatively well defined one as administrator of manpower programs for the Balance of State area and a vaguer opportunity to oversee program operations of local Prime Sponsors and to coordinate statewide programs. Although states did not make a formal choice between these two roles, in practice they concentrated their energies on organizing and operating as Balance of State Prime Sponsors and avoided the more slippery issues of coordination and oversight. The uncertainties and difficulties of trying to develop and implement statewide coordination were easily set aside as states grappled with the same administrative problems that confronted local Prime Sponsors.

Balance of State operations received no special consideration or extra services from the DOL despite their extra burdens of size and geographic spread. An experienced observer described the complexities confronting the Balance of State (BOS) Prime Sponsor (Dement, 1981:263):

CETA may have asked too much, too soon, of a BOS system poorly prepared to handle the responsibilities thrust upon it. Thus far, management capacity has been inadequate to the demands of a ponderous system in which problems faced by local CETA sponsors are exacerbated by the scale and scope of the BOS service area, the plethora of program operators rendering CETA services, excessive federal expectations, and the administrative layering inherent in state government operations. Rather than being in a position to articulate program policies, refine decision-making procedures, and promote training quality, the BOS staff has struggled simply to function as grants broker and funding conduit for contractors numbering in the hundreds, and projects in the thousands.

STATE MANPOWER SERVICES

By law each state had to create a State Manpower Services Council (SMSC), composed of citizens and representatives of community groups, state agencies, and local government. The role of these councils was to review the annual plans of local Prime Sponsors, to monitor program operations, and to make recommendations for improving coordination between Prime

Sponsors and state agencies. This role existed primarily on paper. With very few exceptions, state councils rarely had any influence on plans or programs of local Prime Sponsors (Mirengoff and Rindler, 1976:79) or on state coordination (Snedeker and Snedeker, 1978:64). Instead, SMSCs helped distribute the so-called four-percent funds, also known as the governors' discretionary funds. This pot of money (which cynics referred to as a buyoff of the governors' lobby for passing CETA legislation) was spent primarily to fund state agency manpower projects and to serve special participant groups (such as women, minorities, youth, handicapped). Virtually none of the states used the discretionary money to effect statewide coordination.

CETA legislation provided an additional pot of buyoff money, this one for the vocational education lobby. Six percent of the amount of the basic training title (five percent in the first CETA authorization) went to the governors to be channeled to Prime Sponsors for vocational education purposes. State Departments of Education and SMSCs were involved to varying degrees in setting guidelines for how Prime Sponsors were to use this money, but the funds were never regarded by Prime Sponsor staff as anything more than an automatic addition to their resources. The funds had no effect on the nature of the linkage between Prime Sponsors and local education agencies.

CONCLUSIONS ABOUT THE ROLE OF STATES

Despite the rhetoric of the law, states lacked any serious opportunity to influence local Prime Sponsor programs, planning, and coordination. First, and most important, a state was itself just another Prime Sponsor, and operating a Balance of State Prime Sponsorship occupied nearly all of the attention of state manpower staffs. In addition, the state staff was always less experienced in manpower affairs than the staff of the local Prime Sponsors. States had limited fiscal and other resources available to induce desired behavior among Prime Sponsors, even when the state was so inclined. Finally, the law gave states an insufficient statutory base for intervening in the affairs of local Prime Sponsors and other state agencies. Coordination would have required a vast expenditure of effort, particularly in enormous bureaucratic fights with the education and employment service agencies as well as with Prime Sponsors. It is no wonder that states concentrated on trying to run their Prime Sponsorships and downplayed coordination and oversight.

The Shape of Federalism after CETA

The issues of decategorization and decentralization surfaced again with passage of the Job Training Partnership Act (JTPA) which replaced CETA. The new law eliminated the array of categorical programs that had operated under CETA. The primary training title, Title II, authorized localities to operate year-round programs for adults and youth as well as a summer youth program. The states were authorized to operate a program for displaced workers under Title III of the act. Title IV outlines programs and activities operated by the federal government (the Job Corps, programs for veterans and native Americans, research, and labor market information). Titles I and V outline administrative provisions.

Roles and responsibilities of all levels of government have been significantly altered by JTPA. The role of the federal government is sharply reduced, while that of the states is greatly expanded. Local governments remain responsible for service delivery but will share power with newly constituted or reconstituted Private Industry Councils, which have been made partners for program planning and operations. Local governments must now deal with governors on matters that DOL once handled—plan approval, funding, monitoring, and performance standards, for example.

Policy statements issued early in the transition to JTPA showed that the federal government was intent on maintaining a low profile. The following excerpts from policy guidance issued by the Assistant Secretary of the Employment and Training Administration to the regional offices show the philosophical back-pedalling that had occurred at DOL (see Angrisani, 1982):

★ . . . the delivery system will reflect the block grant features of the New Federalism . . .
★ . . . the states will be given the maximum degree of authority and discretion permitted under the law . . .
★ . . . the Federal role in the new job training program will be narrowly defined . . .

★ . . .the Federal role will emphasize oversight rather than
program management . . .

★ . . . the private sector shall have a decisive role in planning and implementing local training programs . . .

★ . . . reporting requirements and paperwork will be kept to
an absolute minimum . . . .

During the transition activities, the DOL staff were extraordi-
narily faithful to the creed of noninterference. Despite frequent
and impassioned pleas for more guidance, especially in substantive areas, from the states, local governments, and interest
groups, DOL limited its activities to writing barebones regulations, prescribing recordkeeping and minimum reporting
standards, and serving as a broker to help states provide technical
assistance to each other. DOL also funded the National Governors Association and the National Alliance of Business to
provide training and technical assistance to states and localities.
But the change from a federal stance characterized by meddling
and directiveness to a hands-off posture was so abrupt that
states had to make major psychological as well as behavioral
adjustments.

States were by far the weakest link in the implementation
chain of CETA, but under JTPA, they became responsible for a
host of implementation activities: designating service delivery
areas (SDAs, the new term replacing Prime Sponsor), certifying
local PICs, approving SDA plans (with the advice of newly
organized State Job Training Coordinating Councils), and monitoring SDA performance. Perhaps most important, states became responsible for providing technical assistance to SDAs,
because DOL stepped out of this activity. After years of being
told what to do and how to do it by DOL, many states were
paralyzed by their lack of organizational capacity and staff expertise when confronted with the flexibility in the new act.

A study of state JTPA implementation activities near the end
of 1982 showed that many states had barely begun to prepare for
the new act (MDC, 1982b). Little activity had been directed
toward developing statewide goals and coordination or to promoting participation of the private sector. The overriding concerns influenced other decisions. DOL's own tracking of how
the states implemented JTPA showed that SDAs had been estab-

lished in six states by the end of March 1983, six months after the enactment of JTPA, and that progress in other areas was also slow (*Employment and Training Reporter*, 3/30/83:873).

JTPA has completely juggled the distribution of involvement and influence among levels of government. It is too early to say how well the new scheme will function or how long it will last before it is modified. Historically, the temptation for Congress and DOL to reinsert themselves through administrative intervention and program recategorization has been irresistible. Through the summer of 1983 DOL shrugged off pleas from states and complaints from localities and interest groups that it was not providing enough specific guidance during the transition to JTPA. Maybe this time the federal government will actually stay on the sidelines and let the states run a decentralized program.

Conclusions

The essence of intergovernmental relations is the relative influence of different levels of government in reacting to and implementing national policy. The principal characteristic of intergovernmental relations is change, and the source of change is the national government.

The primary trends of federalism in the employment and training arena over the last twenty or so years have included a vacillating role at the federal level and a growing role for subnational governments. A very strong federal presence characterized manpower programs in the 1960s. In the 1970s local governments obtained a significant new role. The federal role shifted from substance to procedure, but remained strong. The 1980s at present are characterized by a greatly diminished federal role coupled with a very strong state role.

The shape of the next iteration in federalism in unclear, but there certainly will be a change, and it would not be at all surprising if it included a resurgent federal presence. The incentives and characteristics of the policy-making process push Congress, government agencies, and interest groups to create private preserves. The Reagan Administration's bold plan for a New Federalism failed to flower as originally conceived (most of the plan failed even to germinate). JTPA is presently the only major implemented element in the plan. Whether the federal government, particularly Congress and the Department of Labor, can withstand the temptation to meddle in this newly decentralized program is doubtful. The odds favor resumed meddling.

CHAPTER SEVEN

★

CETA: *A Summary of Its Life and Legacy*

CETA WAS A LARGE, COMPLICATED, AND DYNA-
MIC PROGRAM occupying a signficant place in the
domestic policy of the United States between 1974 and
1983. We have analyzed major parts of CETA thoroughly
(although we have not looked at every title and program within
CETA), with our major goal being to explain what we observed
in terms of political factors. Having weighed a broadly political
explanation of CETA results against competing explanations,
we remain convinced that the political factors are the most
important. We think this kind of political analysis can advance
the general cause of expanding knowledge about major aspects
of domestic policymaking, program implementation, and policy and program impact in the United States.

In this final chapter we want to undertake three principal
tasks. We will summarize the major themes contained in the
specific findings presented in the previous chapters. We will
also summarize and expand our assessment of CETA's accomplishments during its lifetime. Then we will relate what we
have found specifically about CETA to some findings about a
few other recent, comparable programs, and, most importantly,
to broader tendencies in American politics generally.

A Portrait of CETA:
The Most Important General Observations

The picture of CETA we have presented in the preceding chapters on the basis of careful empirical study includes the following general features that are of greatest importance:

* Since policy about CETA was constantly evolving, there was little consistency and stability in the program and the policies guiding it. Not only did the program and policies change, but there were, inevitably, areas of murkiness.

* The sources of most of the changes in policies and, therefore, in program details were political. Political pressures formed the principal framework for most major decisions regardless of whether those decisions were made formally by local bureaucrats, state bureaucrats, national bureaucrats, Congress, or local, state, or national political officials. And many, though not all, of the political pressures inhibited maximum programmatic service to the most disadvantaged part of the eligible population.

* Within the context of change and political pressure, local professional employment and training staff—especially the staff director—had the most consistent influence. But this does not mean they could always do what they wanted. In fact, the great variety of local management styles arose partially because of different patterns of local political interests and pressures. These local conditions were primary, as were local actors. But both the confusion and the guidelines coming from the federal level could alter the constraints faced by all local professional staff. The need, for example, to build up a local PSE program rapidly would inevitably change the character of the whole local program no matter where it was and who was in charge.

* Despite various constraints, local managers had considerable latitude in shaping their actions. What they did and how they did it made a difference in the results the programs produced. Programmatic outcomes and re-

sults were not predetermined by forces that could not be changed or manipulated, at least in part, by skillful local managers.

★ Particular local attention to a specific form of planning (considerably different from most textbook models of planning) helped local program productivity. This form of local planning demanded that the staff possess political sensitivity and management skills.

★ Privatization of employment and training programs in any sweeping or simple-minded form had little to commend it. The role of the private sector in CETA was enhanced by statute in 1978, with mixed results, including some increased program productivity. But beyond a certain point, the local private sector was neither able nor willing to assume programmatic responsibilities. And even the strongest programs took years to develop because they first had to build an institutional infrastructure in order to achieve even modest incremental gains in program results. In short, if employment and training programs are to have any reasonable hope of desired results, they must continue to have a central role for public agencies and officials.

★ General advisory councils that presumably broadened non-governmental participation in employment and training programs generally had only marginal impacts, and even those were achievable only when local staff and political officials wanted them. Both general advisory councils and PICs provided useful window-dressing rather than concrete results. But a few councils, supported by local staff and at least not opposed by political officials, did help push program results in a positive direction.

★ Despite some rhetoric to the contrary, the federal government's instinct—in both Congress and DOL—was to centralize programs and meddle with local programs. Efforts to arrive at the most productive delegation of authority to local levels probably always face an uphill fight. At the same time, in CETA, the federal government chose to meddle with relatively secondary mat-

ters and ignored the primary redistributive question
involving who received services most of the time.
★ All of the constraints and problems nothwithstanding, in
many ways the central training title of CETA resulted in
generally productive programs for participants. But the
training effort was dwarfed by the mammoth PSE part of
CETA, and their reputations suffered together.

An Assessment of CETA's Accomplishments, 1974–1983

In this section we will present a brief cumulative assessment
of CETA's accomplishments based on the studies we conducted
ourselves and reported in the previous chapters and also on the
findings of several other major studies (these include Levitan
and Mangum, 1981; Taggart, 1981; Mangum, 1981; Mirengoff
and associates; 1982; and General Accounting Office, 1982a).
Our primary focus in this section, as it has been throughout this
book, is on the core training title of CETA. However, we also
address PSE because of its magnitude and implications for management of the core training title.

In asking what CETA achieved, it is important to keep in
mind that no single measure of performance can adequately
gauge performance and impact. CETA was a diverse set of programs, with diverse objectives and diverse locations. Judgments
about success must acknowledge that diversity.

MULTIPLE CRITERIA FOR SUCCESS

CETA was a complex set of programs that changed during
its years of operation. Its complexity prevents us from using
a single measure of performance as the basis for judging
CETA's success. From its creation and during its numerous
program accretions and occasional program deletions, CETA
had many different objectives, impacts, and institutional and
process outcomes. We use these objectives to identify dimensions of performance and discuss CETA's accomplishments in
terms of them.

Among CETA's process objectives were development of local
institutional capability and mechanisms for citizen participation, consolidation of service delivery systems at the local level,
coordination of CETA and non-CETA agencies and programs,

and participation of the private sector in program planning and operations.

Among CETA's ultimate objectives were serving the economically disadvantaged, placing program participants in unsubsidized employment, achieving a positive economic impact on participants, and achieving positive societal benefits. Only for the last item, gauging CETA's societal impact (which would include things such as impact on welfare dependency, crime rate, taxpaying, and job creation) is evidence too sketchy to allow us to discuss CETA's performance (for a related economic analysis of the Job Corps' impacts, see Mathematica Policy Research, 1978 and 1980).

As a preface to the discussion that follows, we must emphasize the perhaps obvious but still very important point that different Prime Sponsors had different implementation experiences and produced different results. On any single indicator of accomplishments, performance of Prime Sponsors was scattered along a continuum from very good to quite poor. If the indicators are combined in the search for a judgment of how CETA did overall, a similar mixed bag of results emerges, with only a modestly small group of Prime Sponsors doing well on all or most of the indicators. There is a large group in the middle and another cluster at the bottom. Given the diversity of the almost 500 Prime Sponsors responsible for implementing CETA, there is no reason to expect that performance would be uniform. CETA, like most social programs, produced mixed results. It could not have done otherwise in the context of national regulations and economic conditions in which it operated.

INSTITUTIONAL DEVELOPMENT

Perhaps the most visible of CETA's accomplishments was the creation of a decentralized bureaucracy for the delivery of federally funded employment and training programs. By the time CETA ended there were almost 500 Prime Sponsorships administering CETA programs. The manpower staff in the Prime Sponsorships grew into their roles at different rates and with varying levels of competence. But overall they were successful in developing and implementing management strategies and skills for administering their service delivery systems. Their accomplishments extended beyond purely technical aspects of personnel and budget management to include political management strategies, conflict resolution, public planning processes, and responsiveness to unpredictable directives from the national and regional offices of DOL. The staffs that were most successful in developing local institutional capability by and large did so in spite of, not because of, assistance from DOL.

CITIZEN PARTICIPATION

CETA provided two principal vehicles for obtaining participation from a variety of groups in planning employment and training programs, the manpower advisory councils (MACs) and the Private Industry Councils (PICs). These councils did not serve the purpose of citizen participation if that purpose is interpreted narrowly to mean that the general public, disinterested citizens, or representatives of "the common good" became involved in manpower planning. The councils did, however, successfully broaden the circle of actors involved in CETA planning and allocation decisions beyond just the staff to include community-based organizations, service deliverers, local government agencies, and education, labor, and business representatives. Though staff were still the most important actors, MACs and PICs permitted a range of special interest groups to have access to the process.

Access was not the same as influence, however. The degree of council influence was negotiated locally in each site. The extent to which councils were used in substantive ways and given real work to do depended on the attitude of staff and elected officials. By law, PICs were slightly more influential over Title VII than MACs were over planning for other titles, but the nature of the roles and influence of PICs, no less than that of MACs, was dependent on the partnership between the staff, councils, and elected officials. On the average, about one-third of the MACs and PICs were strong local institutions with active members and a well-defined role in local decision-making. Given the inherent limits of volunteer councils and the special constraints on CETA councils, this is a very respectable achievement. The remaining councils were either intermittently involved or dormant and passive. (We will elaborate on the limits of volunteer councils later in the chapter.)

SERVICE DELIVERY STRUCTURE

CETA, despite the "comprehensive" in its name, did not, except in a very small number of Prime Sponsorships, produce integrated program delivery at the local level. Although CETA certainly reduced the fragmentation of service delivery that characterized programs operated in the MDTA era, Congress did not place all manpower programs under the CETA umbrella, and not all of the programs subsumed by CETA were decategorized. In its first year, just 42 percent of all CETA appropriations were for Title I, the only decategorized title. By FY 1977, Title I received only 23 percent of the total funds (Mirengoff and Rindler, 1976:45). The remaining funds were earmarked for programs dealing, for example, with subsidized employment and youth unemployment.

All of the directives and pressures from Washington to Prime Sponsors assumed that separate programs should and would be operated for each CETA title. Pooling resources, transferring clients between programs, providing services on an areawide basis, and coordinating services available under different titles taxed the management skills of Prime Sponsor staff who wished to resist the national pressures and operate a locally comprehensive set of programs. Only a fraction were successful in implementing a system that was fully, or even in significant part, comprehensive.

COORDINATION

Achieving linkages between CETA programs and other public and private programs remained only an aspiration in most Prime Sponsorships by the time CETA ended. Despite exhortations from DOL to Prime Sponsors to coordinate with a variety of organizations including the Employment Service as well as education and economic development agencies, the extent of actual linkages was limited. Exhortations were easy to produce; statutory changes and money to alter agency priorities were rare. In the absence of mandated cooperation, forging real linkages depended on local actors' attitudes, commitments, and politicial skills.

Local education agencies received an automatic 22 percent of the Prime Sponsors' youth allocations, and state education agencies received 6 percent of the state CETA allocation. But these funds, usually treated by recipients as incontestable "rights," did little to generate useful coordination between the Prime Sponsor and programs in the schools.

Employment Service offices and Prime Sponsors cooperated in a number of localities through both financial and nonfinancial agreements, but the Employment Service's position as a service deliverer gradually eroded. The Employment Service was regarded by many Prime Sponsor staff, even those that cooperated with them, as insensitive to CETA participants and overwhelmed by its own agenda.

Prime Sponsors and PICs began to explore coordination with economic development agencies, but the latter were slow to lose their distrust and skepticism of CETA programs and clients. The general economic climate in most parts of the nation in 1979 to 1983 cramped opportunities for nascent ties to grow, and Prime Sponsors received no extra funds from DOL to implement economic development linkages. The Employment Initiatives program announced during President Carter's Administration died on the vine for lack of funds to implement it. Some PICs established working relationships with economic development agencies by using PSIP funds. In about one-fifth of the PICs we studied, these linkages were producing concrete results by the end of FY 1981.

BUSINESS PARTICIPATION

Until PSIP was implemented, CETA programs had directed little attention toward involving private sector employers in employment and training programs. Expenditures for OJT accounted for only 11 percent of the total spent in Title I and involved businesses only on the receiving end of CETA services, not in planning or operating programs. PSIP was clearly successful in generating business involvement in decision-making for Title VII funds (a relatively small amount compared to Title I funds).

About one-third of all Prime Sponsorships had strong PICs with active members from the private sector and a variety of forms of business participation. In another third, business participation was present but at much more modest levels. And in the remainder, PSIP failed to generate the involvement of employers. These results, though encouraging, should be examined in context. PICs generally were making decisions only for Title VII; they did not seek to become involved in other local CETA programs. And although some forms of business participation did spill over to affect other CETA programs, this effect was limited. It is also important to remember that the link between participation of the private sector and program results has not yet been clearly demonstrated empirically. Involvement of the private sector does not guarantee better program performance (see Franklin and Ripley, 1983; and General Accounting Office, 1983).

PATTERNS OF SERVICE TO PARTICIPANTS

Services to clients under the basic CETA training title show three significant features. First, the number of participants decreased. Second, the proportion of participants who were economically disadvantaged increased, following an initial drop, compared to pre-CETA enrollment levels. And finally, although the participants enrolled were economically disadvantaged, those most in need of services were being screened out. Fewer youths and persons without high school degrees were enrolled as time passed, and this tendency was even more exaggerated in PSIP.

Table 7-1 shows that pre-CETA enrollment figures stood at just over half million persons. In its early years, CETA Title I enrolled well over a million clients annually. But by FY 1982, budget cuts had forced a reduction in service levels until about 300,000 fewer were being assisted.

The participants served by Title I were less disadvantaged in the early years of CETA than pre-CETA participants. And persons enrolled in the PSE titles were much more likely to be male, white, and better educated than Title I enrollees. By the end of FY 1982, however, these patterns had shifted, because of the effect of amendments introduced in 1976 and 1978. Economically disadvantaged participants had increased to 99 percent of the total in the basic training title (Table 7-1). Enrollment in PSE was increasingly drawn from the disadvantaged (see Mirengoff and associates, 1982: Ch. 4).

The increasing emphasis on the economically disadvantaged

TABLE 7-1: *Characteristics of persons enrolled in training programs, selected years, 1974–1982*

PROGRAM (YEAR)	TOTAL PARTICIPANTS (THOUSANDS)	DEMOGRAPHIC GROUPS ENROLLED (PERCENT)					
		FEMALE	YOUTH (UNDER 22)	HIGH SCHOOL EDUCATION	WELFARE RECIPIENT	ECONOMICALLY DISADVANTAGED	NONWHITE
Pre-CETA[a] (FY 1974)	550	42	63	34	23	87	45
Title I (FY 1975)	1,130	46	62	39	27	77	45
Title I (FY 1977)	1,140	48	51	50	26	78	43
Title II BC (FY 1982)	830	51	41	58	30	99	49
Title VII (FY 1982)	125	46	33	68	24	97	47

[a]Includes programs comparable to CETA operated under Manpower Development and Training Act and Economic Opportunity Act.
Source: Adapted from data furnished by the Employment and Training Administration, U.S. Department of Labor.

was counterbalanced by two other trends: declining enrollment of young people and growing enrollment of participants with at least 12 years of formal education. These changes are clearly indicated in Table 7-1. The PSIP program (Title VII) was even more selective in enrolling participants. PICs recruited a higher proportion of adults and high school graduates than did Title IIBC programs. This tendency of the private sector to concentrate on the best participants raises a concern for the future implementation of CETA's successor. If the trend continues, what will happen to those individuals who are left out?

PLACEMENT

It was not until the last few years of CETA that DOL began to emphasize placement in the private sector as the primary objective of employment and training programs. The Reagan Administration phased out all PSE programs and pressured Prime Sponsors to improve placement rates.

The longitudinal trend in CETA placements for all Prime Sponsors, charted in Table 7-2, is quite clear. Placements reached a highwater mark in FY 1978, before the reauthorization amendments intended to improve performance went into effect and before the Reagan "revolution." Placements declined thereafter partially because funding shrank and local resources had to be spread farther at the same time that the nation was suffering from a recession. The trend is also partially due to the reactions of Prime Sponsor staff and delivery systems to program cuts, funding reductions, more restrictive administrative requirements, and repudiation by the Reagan Administration. All the signals from the national level were negative after 1978, and productivity did not rise under such conditions.

Whether the basic CETA program embodied in Title I/IIBC could have placed more people is problematic. The PSIP program had a slightly higher placement rate, but it also served a more advantaged clientele and operated fewer work-experience programs (see General Accounting Office, 1982a). Although almost 60 percent of all Title I/IIBC programs were for classroom training or OJT, the training was short term, lasting less that 52 weeks. Longer-term training would have had greater impact on participants' earnings but would also have reduced

TABLE 7-2: *Nationwide placement rates for Title I/IIBC, Fiscal Years 1975–1982*

FISCAL YEAR	PLACEMENT RATE[a] (percent)
1975	16
1976	22
1977	29
1978	34
1979	32
1980	26
1981	30
1982	33

[a]Placement rate is computed as the percent of persons employed from among all persons enrolled.

the number of participants served (see Levitan and Mangum, 1981).

Certainly it is important to examine the ability of employment and training programs to obtain employment for participants, but placement rates are not the only valid measure of performance. Placement rates indicate nothing about the quality of jobs or the duration of employment obtained. Providing work experience for youth and obtaining other positive outcomes (e.g., enrollees joining the military or returning to school) are also important for the disadvantaged clientele CETA was serving.

Although placement rates after training comprise a short-term measure of performance, their relationship to the ultimate measure of CETA performance, economic impact on participants, is not clear. There is serious concern among experts about whether the placement rate is a valid indicator of economic benefits derived by participants from involvement in CETA programs (see, for example, General Accounting Office 1982a; Borus, 1978; Gay and Borus, 1980; Finifter, 1980; and Westat, 1981). This uncertainty lends weight to our argument that program assessment must be broad-gauged and include many more indicators of performance than just placement.

ECONOMIC IMPACT ON PARTICIPANTS

Finding out what happens to CETA participants after they leave the program requires research and resources beyond the ability of individual Prime Sponsors to provide. Some Prime Sponsor staffs did local followup surveys of previous participants, but the only systematic national study was DOL's Continuous Longitudinal Manpower Survey (CLMS) conducted by Westat, Inc.

CLMS maintained data on social and demographic characteristics of each year's new CETA enrollees, as well as a comparison group of non-participants. Records on earnings for both groups were also collected. CLMS was designed to allow researchers to determine the amount of change in earnings due entirely to CETA program participation. But the lengthy time necessary to manipulate the data sets was a serious drawback to the utility of the study. As CETA was winding down in 1983, the most current CLMS information available described wage gains of 1976 enrollees who had been out of the program for two years. These data (reported in Westat, 1982, and *Employment and Training Reporter*, 11/17/82 and 11/24/82) provide an array of information about impacts on participation.

★ After two years, the average annual positive impact on wages for all participants who had left the program was $300, which was about 6 percent more than for the comparison group of non-participants.

★ Wage gains for OJT participants were about $600 in 1978, 11 percent more than for the comparison group. On average, OJT and PSE terminees were employed more and had higher earnings than terminees from other programs.

★ Women showed greater economic gains than men, and minority women received the greatest income boost of all subgroups ($700, which was 26 percent more than for the comparison group).

★ In every program activity, participants who were hired after program completion registered very large employment gains, 33 percent in the first year and 24 percent in the second year, compared to the nonparticipants.

★ Length of time in the program made a difference in subsequent earnings. Persons who were enrolled at least 20 weeks showed greater economic gains than those enrolled for shorter periods of time.

★ Average annual earnings were $5750 in the second post-CETA year, which was 250 percent of the average pre-CETA level. The average percent of time employed was 72 percent in the second year.

★ Welfare dependency dropped. The percentage of participants receiving public assistance fell from 39 percent in the pre-CETA year to 25 percent during the second post-CETA year.

CONCLUSIONS

What this array of information about CETA's accomplishments means is simply that CETA participation had positive and lasting economic benefits for participants. Taggart (1981:283) summarizes data that showed CETA also had a favorable return on public investment from a societal point of view: every dollar invested in classroom training, for example, produced a return of $1.38. The return for on-the-job training ranged between $1.21 and $8.28.

In spite of the good performance documented by this data, the positive message was not available in time nor was it of sufficient influence to affect the political calculus that decided CETA's fate in 1981 and 1982. CETA had many positive accomplishments. But they were not dramatic, nor were they effectively communicated. Most importantly, comprehensive data were not available in time to affect decisions about CETA's future. In many ways, CETA was generally or significantly successful in achieving a variety of program results. But as Mangum (1981) noted, CETA failed to sell itself and its accomplishments politically.

That CETA's accomplishments were not widely recognized or that its achievements were not more numerous is understandable when one considers the national implementation context in which CETA was set. Local program managers had wide discretion, but the nature of relations between the supposed "partners" in the federal system imposed limits on what could be done.

These relations between 1973 and 1983 were erratic. Roles and responsibilities in the employment and training arena shifted among levels of government, and lengthy learning curves were hardly completed before new changes occurred. Congress and DOL recentralized and recategorized much of CETA after 1974 so that there was never a true test of comprehensive decategorized local program planning and delivery. Rising unemployment and swelling PSE enrollments were the kiss of death for CETA's original intentions, and ultimately for CETA itself.

CETA managers were beset with changing signals from the national government. Leadership and direction from DOL were inconsistent and erratic. Policy emphases shifted from training and comprehensive programs to PSE to youth unemployment to the participation of the private sector back to training and finally to placement (the policy goal of the Reagan Administration since 1981). CETA goals were multiple and often represented incompatible packages. PSE enrollment and expenditures crowded out attention to Title I planning. Emphasis on serving the most disadvantaged conflicted with high placements. Long term training conflicted with cost efficiency and spreading out benefits to a large number of participants. The conflict among goals meant that Prime Sponsors could choose to emphasize what they preferred.

Within this patchwork context, Prime Sponsor managers still had to implement local programs. Despite the disruptions and administrative difficulties caused by the national government, some local managers were able to generate good performance in relation to the variety of objectives we have described above. In general, as the analyses reported in Chapters 2 through 6 showed, the factors most important in explaining progress and positive performance were subject to control by local actors. Non-manipulable factors such as economic conditions, demographics, and program history set outer limits but did not dictate outcomes. And the nonmanipulable factors were less important in explaining performance results than the manipulable ones.

Manipulable factors important to promoting good performance included attitudes (such as commitment to placement as an objective and willingness to cooperate with other agencies) and management practices such as cultivating good staff (through training, experience, and rewards), high-quality monitoring and evaluation of programs and service deliverers, a public planning process with an active role for the advisory council, and appropriate networking and conflict resolution strategies. Political skills were important in balancing demands from interest groups against the needs of the eligible population and the employer community. The sites that did the best job in maintaining steady performances according to a variety of measures developed a balance of technical and political skills and used these to achieve clearly defined local goals.

CETA in the American Political Tradition

An analysis of CETA both illustrates and reinforces some of the general characteristics of American politics in dealing with the broad category of social welfare policy. Although this book is a longitudinal analysis of one large, complicated federal social program over its entire life, in fact that program is not idosyncratic nor is it markedly different from the way other social programs are handled by American institutions. Studies by political scientists of other programs similar to CETA (for example, block grants dealing with health care, social services, law enforcement, and housing and community development) have produced findings consistent with ours.

To illustrate how the CETA case typifies the politics of domestic social programs, we will present a series of seven general propositions about the character of American politics in the sphere of domestic social programs. Then we will discuss the propositions, drawing on findings from other programs and suggesting how the CETA experience fits the general patterns.

In comparing CETA to other programs during the same era we have relied most heavily on conclusions presented in seven studies (Advisory Commission on Intergovernmental Relations, 1978; Dommel and associates, 1982; General Accounting Office, 1982b; Hale and Palley, 1981; Kettl, 1980; Van Horn, 1979; and Williams, 1980). Together these offer a full picture of programs comparable to CETA.

Obviously, in discussing these propositions about American politics, we are not testing them in a rigorous sense. But we believe our analysis of CETA will augment the empirical basis for understanding American politics. The propositions follow.

★ Domestic programs are rarely completely unique in design. Rather, they tend to emerge in clusters with some important common characteristics.

★ There are a number of pressures to define policies and programs, including those in the social arena, as distributive (that is, involving subsidy).

★ Interest groups penetrate both the policy formation and policy implementation processees at all points. This does not mean they control all decisions, but they certainly finfluence them constantly.

★ Organizations in the private sector (including citizen groups or councils) cannot replace full-time government agencies in implementing domestic social programs without producing significant confusion and inefficiency.

★ Federalism in action creates both confusion and opportunities in the implementation process.

★ Governmental actors, particularly those in Congress and the top levels of the executive branch, demand quick, positive results from programs. They begin searching for alternative programs if such results are not forthcoming.

★ Political considerations almost always outweigh technical considerations when policy and program decisions are made in the domestic social arena.

PROGRAM CLUSTERS

Domestic programs are rarely completely unique in design. Rather, they tend to emerge in clusters with some important common characteristics.

Programs emerge in clusters or, put analytically, employ a common strategy (Rivlin, 1974). Social insurance policies have, for example, represented a continuing cluster since the successful adoption of Social Security in 1935. CETA represents one of a number of so-called block grant or special revenue sharing programs adopted in the late Johnson years or the Nixon-Ford years (not to be confused with the block grants of the Reagan years, which are different in design). This means that political patterns should also be similar when several programs covering roughly the same time period using roughly the same strategy or set of explicit or implicit design features are considered.

Thus it comes as no surprise that CETA's implementation experience was not unique among the five major federal block grants created between 1966 and 1975. In addition to CETA these were the Partnership for Health Act of 1966 (PHA); the Omnibus Crime and Safe Streets Act of 1968, which created the Law Enforcement Assistance Administration (LEAA); the Housing and Community Development Act of 1974, which created community development block grants (CDBG); and Title X (social services) of the Social Security Act, which was added in 1975 (T. XX).

Central common characteristics of block grant implementation included the following. All applied to CETA.

1. Other block grants were created as hybrids (that is, they were neither fully revenue sharing nor categorical grants). They did not completely decategorize the programs they were embracing (CDBG, LEAA, PHA). The block grants did not cover all federally aided activities in their functional areas, and thus the fragmentation of the grant system was not improved (CDBG, PHA).

2. The grants were subject to creeping recategorization as Congress, interest groups, and federal administrators sought to promote various priorities and assure funding for particular programs or groups at different times. Recategorization of course limited the flexibility of grant recipients (PHA, CDBG, LEAA).

3. The block grants created new planning, advisory, and decision-making mechanisms at the state, local, and substate levels. The modes and extent of citizen participation varied, and the influence of advisory councils was mixed (CDBG, LEAA, T. XX).

4. The balance between the flexibility for grant recipients implied by decentralization and the need for accountability to the federal government for the expenditure of taxpayers' money usually tilted toward accountability. Federal requirements for planning, reporting, and auditing increased to maintain federal oversight ability (CDBG, T. XX, LEAA).

5. Conflicting goals in block grants resulted in shifting program directions and confusion over program purposes (especially in CDBG and PHA).

6. The role of the state government was downgraded at the expense of a direct federal-local relationship (except in PHA and LEAA).

7. Benefits were distributed widely rather than concentrated on a narrow target group or location (all programs).

8. The personal involvement of elected officials was limited. They deferred to program specialists for administration, except in CDBG, where they were involved in allocation decisions about distributing benefits to neighborhoods.

CDBG came closest to mirroring CETA's implementation experience, but all block grants demonstrated similarities in various aspects of implementation. In short, block grants have been beset with ambiguity of purpose, multiple goals, recurrent federal interventions, and decreasing local flexibility. Under the Reagan Administration, at least some of these operating maxims may change. Seven small block grants were authorized in 1981, and JTPA was passed in 1982. The new recipe for block grants includes a decreased federal role, increased state government responsibility, and an emphasis on accountability without reducing flexibility of grant recipients.

THE LURE OF DISTRIBUTIVE POLICY

There are a number of pressures to define policies and programs as distributive.

Distributive policies and programs are aimed at promoting private activities that supporters think are desirable and beneficial to society as a whole and which, in theory, would not be undertaken without governmental support in the form of assistance (subsidy). Other domestic programs have other purposes. Some, with *competitive regulatory* purposes, limit the provision of specific goods and services to only one or a few designated deliverers chosen from a large number of potential or actual deliverers. Those with *protective regulatory* purposes are designed to protect the public by setting the conditions under which various private activities can occur. Finally, the policies and programs with *redistributive* purposes seek to readjust the allocation of wealth, property, rights, or some other value among social classes or racial/ethnic/gender groups in society.

Typically, in the United States, only policies seeking to redistribute in favor of the relatively disadvantaged classes or racial/ethnic/gender groups are considered to be redistributive. Policies that actually favor the already advantaged are not considered in that light (for extended discussion of these policy types and many examples of both policy formation and program implementation, see Ripley and Franklin, 1984, 1982).

The natural dynamics of American policy—both at the stage of policy formation (formal legislation) and in the myriad of implementation activities—push most policy toward being defined as distributive. Subsidy is easier to deal with politically, since everybody can appear to win without threatening anybody else. The more people and groups that are given resources, the more people and groups that have a concrete reason for some contentment. The more people and groups perceive themselves to be losing resources in favor of someone else (either through redistribution or in some competitive and protective regulatory situations), the more conflict will result. Politicians—both elected and unelected (for bureaucrats in the United States are also politicians)—try to avoid conflict where they can.

Those opposed to redistributive policy can seek to mute its social impact and convert it into something desirable by redefining its details as distributive.

CETA—like other programs from the 1960s and 1970s such as CDBG, model cities, income tax revision, aid to education, and housing assistance—underwent considerable transformation from redistributive to distributive as it was handled in the political processes of both formation and implementation (see Kettl, 1980, and Dommel and associates, 1982, on CDBG; see Ripley and Franklin, 1984, ch. 6, on the other examples mentioned). As the preceding chapters have made clear, the emphasis on helping the most disadvantaged (a redistributive end) came and went. Federal attention and energy applied to this goal was sporadic; local attention, with few exceptions, tended to be focused on other matters.

Not only was the major redistributive end of the program given only sporadic and half-hearted attention, but more clearly distributive parts of the program were stressed:

* The growth and design of PSE represented pure distribution to states and localities. Everybody got something and could be happy. Local politicians were particularly pleased.
* Participant eligibility was broadened in the period from 1974 through 1978. An apparent consequence was that the benefits (enrollment in training programs, placement in jobs, and so on) could go to a much broader range of citizens than originally envisioned in a redistributive definition of CETA.
* Additional categorical programs demanded by vocal national and local interest groups were added for specific target populations.
* A broad spectrum of national interest groups received direct funding from DOL.

CETA, then, became highly distributive. It enjoyed political support during the mid-1970s. But by the late 1970s and certainly when Ronald Reagan became President, two things happened that left it in a very weak position. First, publicity about some local abuses of PSE money soured perceptions among both the public and important officials. Second, the Reagan Administration emphasized domestic budget cuts as a major part of their economic program to reduce federal spending and deficits. CETA, especially PSE, was highly vulnerable and received large reductions. For at least several years public support was behind these Reagan objectives and the Democrats were either decimated or in disarray or in sympathy with them.

It was not only Washington that felt distributive pressures. The same pressures—leading to the same "spread the goodies" results—were also felt in virtually all Prime Sponsorships across the country. Not all succumbed to the pressures, but a number did. Thus the initial redistributive impact of CETA was diluted in Congress, at both the national and regional levels of DOL, and at most local levels. These dilutions were interactive and cumulative.

THE PENTRATION OF INTEREST GROUPS

Interest groups penetrate both the policy formation and policy implementation processes at all points.

Interest groups are unbiquitous in the American policy process. Analysis of CETA shows them to be important throughout all the processes from formation to implementation. Some new interest groups came into being because CETA made resources available for them. Once in being (and often partially funded with public money either directly by DOL or through Prime Sponsors or both), these groups pressed for continuing redefinition of the program, inevitably in the direction of recategorization and increased fragmentation of purposes and control. Even though they were not in control of the processes and did not get all they wanted, in many instances interest groups and officials did not disagree on the way in which policy should be formulated or programs implemented. Furthermore, they agreed much of the time and cooperated in recategorization, emphasis on subsidy, and ultimate fragmentation of the entire enterprise. A few officials resisted, but more did not. Many national and local level interest groups also became service delivery agencies (a development paralleled in CDBG, which led Kettl [1981b] to write about "the fourth face of federalism").

The lesson from CETA is not that interest groups are monolithic in their views (they most assuredly are not) nor that they control public officials by political weight (they do not). Rather, the lesson is that they have constant access and that, at least during the life of CETA, public officials for the most part believed in a high degree of cooperation with and support for a broad range of interest groups, including incorporating them as delivery agencies of various kinds.

This instinct on the part of public officials was, of course, tied to the instinct in favor of the political benefits of programs defined as subsidy. In their view the more recipients who benefitted the better and the more groups who benefitted the better because the spreading of benefits reduced conflicts and tensions. Wholesale distribution of benefits was much easier to do at the national level in the 1970s when, for all practical purposes, the concern about the ultimate limits on the budget resources was miniscule. It was much more costly, even in the 1970s, at the local level where the resources were limited and fixed (because they came in the form of federal grants with specific dollar amounts) and were sufficient to serve only about one in ten of legitimate claimants (those defined by law and regulation as being in the eligible population). Not all of those who did not get served made claims either personally or through organized local groups for more service. But, even with the "silent eligibles" removed from the local allocation context, the "noisy eligibles," whose noise was magnified by local interest groups, certainly far exceeded the number who could be served in virtually every one of the 400 to 500 Prime Sponsorships in the United States during the life of CETA.

PRIVATE SECTOR AND CITIZEN COUNCIL IMPLEMENTATION

Organizations in the private sector (including citizen groups or councils) cannot replace full-time government agencies in implementing domestic social programs without producing significant confusion and inefficiency.

"Privatization" has become a fashionable word in the rhetoric of American public policy in the last few years. It has become similarly fashionable in Thatcherite Britain. It proponents seem to use it indiscriminately to apply to such diverse activities as garbage collection (where, indeed, it may work reasonably well), education (where there are many points to debate), the weather service, and various social programs including employment and training. The necessities of these different activities are also different and need to be examined individually or at least in clusters that make sense.

Throughout this book we have sought to inspect carefully the role of both citizen groups (in the form of mandated councils in CETA) and the private business sector (in our careful examination of the antecedents of PSIP and PSIP itself) in the area of employment and training. The results of our analysis present a mixed picture. Most advisory councils appear to have only minimal impact. And in no sense can they be expected to replace publicly employed staff in the implementation process. Even councils with mandated concurrence power—such as PICs had for the expenditure of Title VII funds—rarely were effective implementation agents. Most PICs had the wisdom not to seek a central role as direct program operators. Rather they sought a policy role and left program operation to publicly employed staff. The few PICs that sought to be active implementers of a program tended to bog down, leaving it incomplete.

But what about the private sector? How far can it go in implementing the purposes of public employment and training programs? Before programs emerged that were specifically targeted at the private sector (for example, STIP and PSIP), the evidence suggests that the private sector had very little interest in getting involved. The evidence from STIP and PSIP—which in some localities were well planned and focused attempts to involve the private sector—presents a more mixed picture. In some localities, considerable new private sector involvement emerged, although this involvement could still not be said to replace public agency implementation, nor was it expected to.

In short, we conclude that results of carefully crafted local efforts to get the private sector involved in local employment and training programs can only supplement public implementation, not supplant it. Evidence gleaned from prior programs suggests that expectations more grandiose than that for "privatization" in this area seem bound to fail. Fortunately, few in the private sector itself—no matter how interested in employment and training they may be—have unreasonable expectations about "privatization" of any complete sort in this area.

The broader lesson about both councils and the private sector is that concrete, explicit efforts have to be made to get them to participate in any meaningful way. There is no set of inherent motivations or dynamics that will lead to such participation without some leadership by public officials, including above all, staff.

FEDERALISM

Federalism in action creates both confusion and opportunities in the implementation process.

As an entire chapter was devoted to the federalistic aspect of CETA, it is sufficient here simply to note that in CETA, as in many programs including the other block grants from the 1960s and 1970s, federalism had mixed impact. In CETA the federal government produced mainly confusion in the system. But, on the other hand, some of the local operations were skillful, efficient, and effective. Some were awful. And many were so-so, with aspects of quality and aspects of waste or ineffectiveness. But the virtue of a decentralized approach to employment and training was that, in principle, the local operations with strong staff and a good programmatic vision (and—perhaps—some luck) were free to experiment and to fit their programs to needs that were locally perceived and locally determined. Overall, CETA produced more benefits in the training area than its predecessors. It could have produced even more if both Congress and DOL had proceeded more intelligently and consistently and with focused concerns rather than seemingly universal concerns. But the federal urge to regulate and centralize could not be restrained (for an analysis of some parallel developments in CDBG see Kettl, 1981a).

The characteristics of the best local programs need not all be repeated here. By way of summary, it should be emphasized that those localities that proceeded on the basis of clear goals and that consciously built networks of supporters, processes, and programs in pursuit of those goals did best. Architectonic program implementation at the local level (including, without fail, local political considerations as part of the raw material requiring architectonic skills) paid off.

IMPATIENCE FOR RESULTS

Governmental actors, particularly those in Congress and the top levels of the executive branch, demand quick, positive results from programs. They begin searching for alternative programs if such results are not forthcoming.

Programmatic tastes in the United States are often fickle, particularly in relation to programs that are either wholly or partially redistributive or that fly in the face of what at any given time is taken to be conventional economic, social, and political wisdom. Always at least partially redistributive, CETA was made more so in the training titles by the 1978 reauthorization. Simultaneously, it became conventional wisdom by the late 1970s that PSE was wasteful.

CETA, like virtually all programs in the U.S., also suffered from the general expectation of quick successes. Congress and the executive branch generate programs and almost immediately begin demanding results, even though it is not reasonable to expect results with such celerity. As we have tried to show throughout this book, local programs are built in stages. And the stages of institution-building, planning, and creating operational programs all necessarily had to precede any hope of achieving desired impacts. This took years of hard, skillful work. And yet Congress and the executive branch remained ready to shift courses, juggle resources, pronounce failure, and look for alternatives (including forgetting the entire area of employment and training) constantly, on short notice, in a short time frame, and with no particular evidence except anecdotes and political considerations.

Most American social programs are in constant flux. There is rarely political patience with them that will allow them adequate time for implementation and testing before decisions about the future are made. The future is always now in the view of national policy-makers. Thus policy and programs remain highly volatile and anything resembling long-term planning is not only a rarity but a luxury.

Partially because of this demand for instant results, the coalitions in Congress, the executive branch, and the interest groups in Washington supporting different versions of employment and training operations shifted constantly throughout the life of CETA. The constant amendments of both law and regulations coming from Washington reflected the impatience and the instability of the coalitions and the accepted and predominant programmatic views in any given month or year. CETA implementers at the local level can take slight comfort in the fact that they were not the victims of discrimination but were simply being treated in standard fashion for domestic social programs.

The constant thrashing about in terms of substance, funding, and emphases that characterized CETA is, in part, normal behavior for a set of national institutions perpetually engaged in the quest for a "quick fix" for whatever problems are perceived to beset the polity or parts of it. Policy fads abound. But when they do not prove to be overnight wonders they are quickly abandoned for new fads.

POLITICS AND ADMINISTRATION

Political considerations almost always outweigh technical

considerations when policy and program decisions are made in the domestic social arena.

Politics and "administration" were once, in the dim recesses of time in the study of American politics, thought to be separate phenomena. M re recently, the two were discovered to be intermingled. Then it was discovered that in many policy areas "technical" considerations, often linked with professional administration and technical expertise, played some role along with political considerations (see, for example, Jones, 1975, on air pollution implementation).

However, if "administration" includes "technical considerations"—and we are stipulating that it does for purposes of making our comments—then it appears that most CETA decisions at both the national and the local level were made primarily on the basis of political considerations. A few incremental decisions were made on the basis of more "technical" concerns. A few actually assessed the rich variety of empirical findings that were generated during the 1970s. But most decisions were made on the basis of intuition, anecdote, and political advantage.

We do not argue that "technical" considerations, especially the use of systematic social science research, should dominate decision-making on employment and training or any other social program. However, some sort of blend of administrative/technical considerations with political considerations seems appropriate, particularly where there is good systematic analysis available. In the case of CETA, the political considerations were almost exclusively dominant at the national level and usually almost exclusively dominant at the local level. The notable exceptions were a few Prime Sponsorships in which evidence and the "technical" decisions supported by the evidence were taken seriously and acted on, within, of course, the realm of the politically feasible.

We have no quarrel with a major role for political considerations or political feasibility in program decision-making. But the political concerns should not be the only ones. Recognition of the degree to which CETA was politicized helps explain some of its problems as well as some of the problems endemic to a broad range of domestic programs in the United States.

Appendices

The appendices contain technical material related to Chapters 2 through 5. Appendix A is composed of tables. Appendix B presents the criteria used to select the 15 Prime Sponsorships for the management study. Appendix C outlines the variables and calculations used to measure program outcomes for the management study. Appendix D summarizes the performance indicators used in the PSIP study.

Appendix A: Supplementary Tables

TABLE A 2-1: *Prime Sponsorship and labor force characteristics,
Ohio, Fiscal Year 1976*

LOCATION	TOTAL POPULATION, 1970	BLACKS IN POPULATION, 1970 (PERCENT)	HIGH SCHOOL EDUCATION OR ABOVE, 1970 (PERCENT)
State of Ohio (total)	10,651,841	9.1	36.7
Akron	761,956	7.2	38.5
Allen	111,144	8.3	35.3
Butler	226,207	4.9	35.9
Canton	459,333	5.0	36.2
Cincinnati	452,550	27.6	34.0
Clark	156,946	8.4	35.0
Cleveland	1,981,477	16.7	37.8
Columbus	833,249	12.5	42.6
Greene	124,422	6.7	41.9
Hamilton	471,468	4.3	36.9
Licking/Delaware	150,707	1.9	39.0
Lorain	256,843	6.4	34.2
Miami Valley	638,947	13.0	37.9
Northeast	742,550	7.4	35.6
Southwest	254,976	1.3	28.0
Toledo	574,092	9.6	37.8
Balance of State	2,818,546	2.3	33.9

Families below poverty level, 1970 (percent)	Families on public assistance or welfare, 1970 (percent)	Unemployment rate, 1974 (percent)	Unemploy ment rate, May 1976 (percent)	Size of labor force, May 1976
7.1	3.8	4.8	6.9	4,707,450
5.4	3.5	4.4	7.7	323,999
6.2	1.9	5.5	7.8	51,257
6.3	3.3	6.3	8.3	102,736
5.5	2.7	4.3	7.4	210,388
12.2	8.3	5.4[a]	7.1[a]	409,678[a]
6.9	3.7	4.8	7.9	66,907
6.6	4.1	4.3	6.1	845,888
7.1	4.5	3.7	6.3	416,931
4.9	1.4	4.2	5.5	48,890
3.7	1.9	5.4[a]	7.1[a]	409,678[a]
6.9	2.2	4.5	7.6	67,699
5.6	3.3	5.0	6.1	117,361
5.7	2.1	4.8	6.3	271,089
6.3	3.9	5.0	8.4	325,326
9.6	2.3	5.7	7.3	109,357
6.2	4.5	5.4	6.2	257,471
8.9	3.4	5.1	7.0	1,082,473

[a]Figures are for the totality of Hamilton County, which encompasses both the Cincinnati and balance of Hamilton County Prime Sponsorships. Disaggregated data were not available.

Sources: 1970 Census and Ohio Bureau of Employment Services.

TABLE A 2-2: *Base CETA allocations, Fiscal Year 1976, and type of Prime Sponsorship, Ohio*

	BASE ALLOCATIONS[a] ($ THOUSANDS)		
LOCATION	TITLE I	TITLE II	TITLE VI
Akron	4,070	1,314	4,920
Allen	506	332	1,356
Butler	954	601	2,445
Canton	1,820	792	2,914
Cincinnati	5,220	997	3,902
Clark	644	230	823
Clermont	1,599	494	1,915
Cleveland	14,960	2,875	10,377
Columbus	4,735	986	4,334
Greene	368	128	544
Hamilton	1,033	238	1,676
Licking/Delaware	714	254	937
Lorain	992	485	1,848
Miami Valley	4,621	1,028	3,782
Northeast	4,194	1,590	6,216
Toledo	3,416	1,324	5,214
Balance of State	12,780	5,045	19,613

Type of Prime Sponsorship	Comments
Consortium	Central city (275,000), its county, and two adjoining counties
County	Single county with small central city (54,000)
County	Single county with two small central cities (68,000 and 49,000)
Consortium	Central city (110,000), its county, and one adjoining county
City	Central city (453,000)
County	Single county with small central city (82,000)
Consortium	Five counties—two largely commuter suburban and three rural; no cities over 10,000
Consortium	Central city (751,000), its county (including a suburb of 100,000), and two adjoining counties
Consortium	Central city (540,000) and its county
County	Single county with small county seat (25,000); largely rural and commuter suburban
County	Balance of county for Cincinnati; suburban but with considerable industrial base of its own
Consortium	Two county consortium adjoining Columbus; one with small central city (42,000); rural and commuter suburban
County	Single industrial county with two small central cities (78,000 and 53,000)
Consortium	Central city (244,000), its county, and adjoining rural county
Consortium	Central city (141,000), its county, and three other counties (two over 100,000)
Consortium	Central city (384,000), its county, and one adjoining county
Balance of State	58 counties, mostly rural and small town; only one county over 100,000

[a]These figures do not include the transition quarter. The Title I figures do include the consortium incentives. Source: *Federal Register*, Dec. 18, 1975.

TABLE A 2-3: *Data from interviews and meetings, September 15, 1974–July 15, 1976, Ohio study*

LOCATION AND ACTIVITY	OPEN-ENDED INTERVIEWS AND MEETINGS OBSERVED	CLOSED-ENDED[a] INTERVIEWS AND QUESTIONNAIRES
Prime Sponsorships		
Interviews		
Professional staff	207	115
Political figures	41	38
Service deliverers	113	89
Chairpersons of manpower planning councils	18	NA
Members of manpower planning councils	NA	194
Meetings observed		
Advisory councils	133	NA
Others (e.g., committees, staff, consortium boards)	36	NA
State of Ohio		
Interviews	28	NA
Meetings observed (manpower services council, other statewide meetings)	19	NA
Regional office, Department of Labor		
Interviews		
Federal representatives	27	13
Other officials	10	NA

[a]Note that in analyses reported in the text in Chapter 2 the number of responses for any given question will sometimes be slightly less than the total number conducted because some respondents chose not to answer some questions.
NA = Not applicable.

TABLE A 2-4: *Characteristics of participants in national employment and training programs, Fiscal Years 1974 and 1976*

PROGRAM (YEAR)	TOTAL PARTICIPANTS	FEMALE	YOUTH (UNDER 22)	HIGH SCHOOL EDUCATION	WELFARE RECIPIENT	ECONOMICALLY DISADVANTAGED	NONWHITE
				DISTRIBUTION OF PARTICIPANTS (PERCENT)			
Categorical programs[a] (FY 1974)	549,700	42	63	34	23	87	45
PEP (FY 1974)	66,200	34	23	77	10	34	31
CETA Title I (FY 1976)	1,731,500	46	57	45	26	76	45
CETA Title II (FY 1976)	255,700	36	22	74	15	46	39
CETA Title VI (FY 1976)	495,200	35	22	74	13	44	32

[a]Includes MDTA-Institutional, JOP/OJT, NYC in-school, NYC out-of-school, Operation Mainstream, JOBS, and CEP.
Source: Office of Administration and Management, Employment and Training Administration, U.S. Department of Labor

TABLE A 3-1: *Region, size of program, and type of Prime Sponsorship, management study sites*

NAME	FEDERAL REGION	SIZE OF PROGRAM ($ MILLIONS)	
		TITLE I[a]	PSE[b]
Connecticut Balance of State	I	8.9	12.9
Lowell Consortium, Mass.	I	2.0	2.7
Cumberland County, N.J.	II	1.2	1.6
Yonkers, New York	II	1.3	1.6
Wilmington, Delaware	III	1.1	0.9
Luzerne County, Pennsylvania	III	3.0	3.4
Birmingham Area Manpower Corsortium, Alabama	IV	4.7	3.7
Cumberland County, N.C.	IV	1.1	0.8
Duluth, Minnesota	V	1.4	0.9
Arkansas Balance of State	VI	12.5	9.7
Dallas County Consortium, Texas	VI	2.0	1.1
Central Iowa Regional Assn. of Local Governments	VII	3.0	2.0
Denver, Colorado	VIII	3.9	3.8
Sacramento-Yolo Consortium, Cal.	IX	5.2	6.1
King-Snohomish Manpower Consortium, Washington	X	11.1	11.9

Type of Prime Sponsorship	Comments
BOS[c]	Rural, suburban, small town areas.
Consortium	Central small city of Lowell (94,000) and eight surrounding towns.
County	Rural and small town areas.
City	Moderate sized city next to New York City.
City	Small city.
County	Small city (58,000) in a heavily populated and industrialized county.
Consortium	City of Birmingham (301,000) and surrounding county.
County	Small city (53,000) and its county.
City	Small city.
BOS[c]	Rural and small town areas.
Consortium	Balance of suburban county surrounding Dallas city.
Consortium	The city of Des Moines (201,000), its county, and seven other counties.
City	Moderately large city (city and county are coterminous and are a single government).
Consortium	Moderate sized city (257,000), its county, and neighboring suburban and rural county.
Consortium	Moderately large city of Seattle (531,000), its county, and neighboring county.

[a]This figure is the Title I base allocation for FY 77 announced on 10/22/76.
[b]This figure combines the base Title II allocation announced on 11/22/76 and the base Title VI allocation announced on 12/17/76.
[c]BOS = Balance of state
Source for allocations: Office of Information, U.S. Department of Labor.

TABLE A 3-2: *Population and unemployment, management study sites*

	TOTAL POPULATION, 1970[a]	ECONOMICALLY DISADVANTAGED FAMILIES, 1970[a] (PERCENT)	NONWHITE, 1970[a] (PERCENT)
Connecticut	1,719,941	4.0	2
Lowell	182,731	6.1	1
Cumberland, N.J.	121,374	9.2	14
Yonkers	204,297	5.6	7
Wilmington	80,386	16.0	44
Luzerne	342,301	8.9	1
Birmingham	644,991	14.5	33
Cumberland, N.C.	212,042	17.1	26
Duluth	100,578	7.4	2
Arkansas	1,497,599	20.1	19
Dallas	881,547	8.1	25
Central Iowa	502,206	7.0	3
Denver	514,678	6.8	11
Sacramento-Yolo	723,286	8.9	10
King-Snohomish	1,421,869	5.2	6

Spanish-speaking, 1970[a] (percent)	Unemployed[b] (percent)		
	April–June, 1975	April–June, 1976	Oct.–Nov. 1976
1	9.2	9.4	8.2
1	12.7	8.5	6.2
6	14.5	10.9	9.4
4	8.4	8.5	7.9
2	13.2	11.3	10.9
*	11.3	9.9	10.3
*	6.6	7.1	6.0
3	6.1	6.7	7.6
*	8.5	8.1	6.3
4	9.4	6.2	5.6
9	4.8	4.3	3.7
1	5.1	4.9	3.8
15	8.0	7.4	7.6
8	8.7	9.5	8.8
2	8.9	8.6	7.5

[a]Source: 1970 Census. Disadvantaged families are those below the poverty level.
[b]Source: U.S. Department of Labor. Figures are averages of the monthly figures for the months indicated
* = less than 0.5%.

TABLE A 3-3: *Distribution of interviews conducted at 15 management sites and 10 regional offices, 1976–1977*

CATEGORY OF INDIVIDUALS INTERVIEWED	NUMBER OF INTERVIEWS
Prime Sponsor professional staff	320
Political figures	50
Service deliverers	173
Members of Manpower Advisory Councils	62
Federal regional office officials	60
Total	665

TABLE A 4-1: *Profile of 12 Prime Sponsorships in planning study*

NAME OF PRIME SPONSORSHIP	FEDERAL REGION	TYPE OF PRIME SPONSORSHIP	FY 1978 TITLE I ALLOCATION[a] ($ MILLIONS)	JUNE 1977 UNEMPLOYMENT RATE[b] (percent)
Penobscot Consortium, Maine	I	Consortium	1.2	7.6
Syracuse, New York	II	City	1.7	8.0
Bergen County, New Jersey	II	County	5.6	7.9
Baltimore Consortium, Maryland	III	Consortium	13.8	6.8
Atlanta, Georgia	IV	City	5.3	8.0
Heartland Consortium, Florida	IV	Consortium	2.9	8.8
Gulf Coast Consortium, Texas	VI	Consortium	2.2	4.8
Albuquerque Consortium, New Mexico	VI	Consortium	2.8	8.4
Omaha Consortium, Nebraska	VII	Consortium	3.0	3.9
Denver, Colorado	VIII	City	3.7	6.9
San Francisco, California	IX	City	7.8	9.6
King-Snohomish Consortium, Washington	X	Consortium	11.0	6.7

[a]Figures exclude consortium bonuses.
[b]National average = 7.5%.

TABLE A 4-2: *Relation of management decisions to models of planning*

MODEL TYPE AND SITE	QUALITY OF KEY STAFF	DISCONTINUITY IN KEY STAFF OR ADMINISTRATION	SUBSTANTIVE AREAS OF INFLUENCE (MAXIMUM IS FOUR)	
			SERVICE DELIVERERS	ADVISORY COMMITTEES
Future Oriented				
Baltimore	H	C	1	N
Penobscot	H	C	N	1
Syracuse	H	C	N	3
Operations Management				
Albuquerque	MH	D	4	3
Atlanta	MH	C	4	3
Bergen	H	C	3	3
Gulf Coast	MH	C	3	N
Heartland	MH	C	1	3
King-Snohomish	MH	D	4	3
Omaha	H	C	N	N
San Francisco	H	C	4	3
Crisis Management				
Denver	MH	D	4	1

Involvement of Business	Support of Political Officials	Extent and Quality of Monitoring	Optional Program Activity
H	Above average	H/H	S/YI
H	Above average	H/H	S
H	Above average	H/H	S/YII
N	Above average	H/M	S/YII
L	Above average	H/MH	S
L	Average	H/H	S
N	Average	ML/M	N
N	Above average	ML/ML	N
L	Average	H/M	YI
M	Above average	H/H	N
L	Average	H/H	S
M	Above average	L/L	S/YI

Key to abbreviations:
H = High   D = Discontinuity   S = STIP
M = Medium   C = Continuity   YI = YIEPP Tier I
L = Low   YII — YIEPP Tier II
N = None

TABLE A 5-1: *Prime Sponsorships in Ohio State PSIP study*

Prime Sponsorship	Federal Region	Type of Prime Sponsorship	PSIP FY 1981 Funds ($ thousands)	PSIP share of all FY 1981 Funds (percent)	PSIP share of training funds, FY 1981 (IIBC & VII) (percent)
Adams Co., CO	VIII	County	255	6.8	15.6
Alamo Csrt., TX	VI	Consortium	1548	6.6	16.1
Clark Co., OH	V	County	200	6.2	14.5
Dayton, OH	V	City	475	5.0	14.1
Erie Csrt., NY	II	Consortium	1196	6.5	16.5
Hartford Csrt., CN	I	Consortium	583	6.3	14.5
Houston, TX	VI	City	1255	3.6	14.4
Kansas City Csrt., MO	VII	Consortium	767	5.1	11.7
Louisville/Jefferson Csrt., KY	IV	Consortium	785	5.9	14.3
Memphis Csrt., TN	IV	Consortium	910	6.5	14.7
Milwaukee Co., WI	V	County	814	4.4	11.1
Minneapolis, MN	V	City	375	5.5	12.0
Morris Co., NJ	II	County	321	6.5	16.5
Penobscot/Hancock Csrt., ME	I	Consortium	249	4.5	11.5

Pittsburgh, PA	III	City	838	5.9	15.7
Portland, OR	X	City	694	6.7	16.1
Sacramento Csrt., CA	IX	Consortium	1250	6.1	14.8
St. Louis, MO	VII	City	899	4.0	12.2
San Diego RETC, CA	IX	Consortium	2356	5.5	13.6
San Francisco, CA	IX	City	1315	5.9	14.5
Santa Clara Csrt., CA	IX	Consortium	1444	6.3	15.1
Southern Alleghenies Csrt., PA	III	Consortium	1000	5.2	14.2
Syracuse, NY	II	City	270	5.1	12.6
Tampa, FL	IV	City	431	6.0	14.6
Wayne Co., MI	V	County	1360	5.0	13.8

Appendix B: Criteria for Selecting Management Study Sites

THE STUDY summarized in Chapter 3 examined 15 Prime Sponsorships throughout the United States. The criteria for selecting these sites are discussed below.

1. *Geographical spread.* We wanted at least one Prime Sponsorship in every federal region and no more than two in any region.

2. *Size of program.* We eliminated about one-third of all Prime Sponsors on the grounds that they were simply too small. We used an arbitrary limit of $1 million for a base Title I allocation as our cutting point. We also decided not to attempt any of the very largest Prime Sponsorships in the country. Within the eligible range we sought to choose sites with substantial variation.

3. *Type of Prime Sponsorship.* We wanted at least several examples each of consortia, cities, counties, and balances of state.

4. *General economic conditions.* We inspected unemployment figures so that we would have a range of Prime Sponsorships in terms of general economic health.

5. *Ethnic composition of population.* We inspected figures on percent of non-white population and percent of Spanish-speaking population so that we would have a mix of different ethnic characteristics.

6. *Non-duplication of other intensive field studies.* We decided to avoid using sites already used by the National Academy of Sciences study (28 sites) and the Employment and Training Administration (ETA) in-house study (66 sites). We also eliminated all Ohio Prime Sponsorships since we had already studied them.

7. *Reputation for "general success."* We did not want Prime Sponsorships that were so badly managed that all we could report was a lack of management decisions that were consciously aimed at affecting program performance. On the other hand, we did not want only the "best" prime sponsorships in the country. We wanted a broad variation in general management style,

competence, and effectiveness above a low minimum level. We also wanted a broad variation in program performance measured in a number of ways.

To help us screen out unacceptably unmanaged Prime Sponsorships we used three pieces of evidence: those rated "significant underperformers" by the Department of Labor field assessment in the spring of 1975 were eliminated; those rated "marginal" or "unsatisfactory" in the 1976 spring field assessment were eliminated (this left over 260 rated "satisfactory"); and a few with special problems identified by national ETA officials were eliminated.

We used judgmental information we solicited to get "positive" nominations. First, we talked with appropriate ETA officials to get their impressionistic nominations. Second, a Field Memorandum (180–76, May 26, 1976) was sent to all Regional Administrators that first described the project briefly and then asked each of them to nominate five or six of the "most generally successful" prime sponsorships in the region for study.

8. *Willingness to cooperate at the local level.* Given the nature of the research we needed to undertake, it would have been pointless to choose Prime Sponsorships in which the professional staff would not cooperate. Thus we selected our 15 preferred sites on the basis of the above seven criteria and then made extended phone calls (preceded by written descriptions of what we wanted to do) to the CETA Director at each site. On the basis of those phone calls we judged that there would be a high level of cooperation at 13 of the sites but that we ought to replace two of our first choices with alternates, which we did.

Table A 3-1 presents summary information on region, size of program, and type of Prime Sponsorship for the 15 sites. Table A 3-2 presents summary information on the population and unemployment rates in the sites.

DATA FOR THE MANAGEMENT STUDY

The data on the 15 sites came from such sources as the 1970 Census; quarterly reports filed by the sites with the Department of Labor from September 1974, through December 1976 (although the quality of the September 1974, reports were so mixed we did not use them in the analysis); Employment Service Automated Reporting System (ESARS); Employment Service data on unemployment; a variety of documents and files (annual plans, MAC minutes and minutes of other relevant meetings, newspaper clippings, memoranda and letters, internal reports, Regional Office field assessments and backup materials); almost 700 personal interviews with professional staff, political officials, key MAC members, service deliverers, and a range of individuals at the appropriate Regional Office (the Regional Administrator or his Deputy, the relevant Associate Regional Administrator and his Deputy, and one or more Federal Representatives who were or had been assigned to the specific sites); 174 completed questionnaires from MAC members; and observation of MAC meetings and other relevant meetings such as Executive Boards.

Table A 3-3 summarizes the interviews that produced much of the information for the study. Table A 3-4 summarizes the computation of standard indicators of program performance that were used in the statistical analyses.

233

Appendix C: Calculation of Standard Indicators Used to Measure Program Outcomes

Five indicators of termination were used in Chapter 3: placement efficiency, CETA placement rate, indirect placement rate, entered employment rate, and nonpositive termination rate. To assess program costs, three indicators were used: cost per placement, cost per indirect placement, and cost per enrollee.

Placement efficiency is a measure of the overall effectiveness of CETA as a mechanism for getting people into unsubsidized employment. It is calculated as the number of people entering employment divided by the number of all persons enrolled. The measure indicates what proportion of people who are enrolled end up with a job. This indicator is a crucial test of how well CETA is working in terms of getting people employed.

CETA placement rate is a similar kind of measure, but it narrows the focus even more by indicating what proportion of all enrollees get a job after receiving CETA services other than assessment and referral. It is calculated as the number of indirect placements divided by the number of people enrolled.

Indirect placement rate is calculated as the number of indirect placements divided by the number of people entering employment. This measure indicates what proportion of the people who got jobs had received some CETA services other than assessment and referral. This was one of the national indicators used by DOL during FY 1976.

The *entered employment rate* indicates what percentage of the people who leave a CETA program do so because they got a job. It is computed by dividing the number of people entering employment by the total number of terminations. This was also a DOL standard indicator in FY 1976.

Nonpositive termination rate is the number of nonpositive terminations divided by the total number of terminations. It indicates the proportion of people who are leaving a CETA program for reasons other than getting a job, going back to school, joining the military, or other "positive" reasons. This was a standard indicator used by DOL in FY 1976.

Cost per placement indicates how much it cost the Prime Sponsor to put a CETA participant into a job. It is computed by dividing the total accrued expenditures by the number of people entering employment.

Cost per indirect placement is computed by dividing total accrued expenditures by the number of indirect placements. It indicates the cost for each person who was placed after receiving CETA services other than assessment and referral, and was another one of the DOL standard indicators in FY 1976.

Cost per enrollee indicates how much it costs the Prime Sponsor to serve each participant enrolled. It is computed by dividing accrued expenditures by number of enrollees.

Appendix D: Performance Indicators Used in the OSU PSIP Study

THE *percent of enrollees placed* measures the percentage of enrollees who got jobs. It is computed as A divided by B, where A is the number of persons entering unsubsidized employment and B is the total number of persons enrolled in the program.

This indicator is calculated differently from the Department of Labor's traditional measure of placement rate, in which the value of B became the total number of persons terminating from the program. We developed the stricter and narrower measure because it produces a less inflated percentage rate than the DOL method.

The *percent of placements in the private sector* measures the percentage of jobs obtained in the private sector. It is computed as C divided by A, where C is the number of persons entering employment in a private sector job, and A is the total number of persons placed.

The *average hourly wage after placement* indicates the average hourly wage paid at the time of placement to CETA "graduates." It is computed by Prime Sponsors or PICs by averaging the starting wages paid to participants who got jobs after PSIP. It is reported for both participants with no earnings prior to enrolling in PSIP and for participants who had earned some wage previously. In this study, we used the average hourly wage figure for participants *with a pre-PSIP wage.*

The *average wage gain after placement* indicates the difference in wages earned by participants before and after their PSIP experience. It is calculated as E minus D, where E is the average wage paid at the time of placement, and D is the average wage earned before participation. We calculated this measure only for persons who were employed before enrolling in PSIP. Including persons with no previous wage skewed the before and after results.

The *cost per placement* indicates the average cost of obtaining a job. It is computed as F divided by A, where F is the total money spent and A is the number of persons who entered unsubsidized employment.

NATURE OF THE DATA

The data for calculating performance indicators comes from three standard reports that PICs and Prime Sponsors provided to the Department of Labor. These are called the Quarterly Summary of Participant Characteristics, the Program Status Summary, and the Financial Status Review. These data have many shortcomings. They are often incomplete and inaccurate, sometimes accidentally, sometimes deliberately. They are self-reported by PICs and Prime Sponsors and there is no mechanism other than self-regulation to verify results reported. The reports aggregate statistics for all programs operated under a title, so that variations in individual programs or types of programs cannot be tracked. These data are all that exists for purposes of evaluation, and so they must be used, although we do so with caution. They serve as a guide to rather than an absolute judgment of performance.

References

Advisory Commission on Intergovernmental Relations. 1977. *The Comprehensive Employment and Training Act: Early Readings from a Hybrid Block Grant.* Report A-58. Washington, D.C.: ACIR (June).
———. 1980. *The Federal Role in the Federal System: The Dynamics of Growth—A Crisis of Confidence and Competence.* Report A-77. Washington, D.C.: ACIR (July).
Angrisani, A. 1982. Department of Labor policy directive reprinted in *Employment and Training Reporter* (Oct. 27):224.
Bailis, L.N. 1975. "Manpower Revenue Sharing: Rhetoric, Roles, and Results," paper prepared for delivery to American Political Science Association meeting (Sept.).
Baumer, D.C., and C.E. Van Horn. 1984. *The Politics of Unemployment.* Washington, D.C.: Congressional Quarterly Press.
Baumer, D.C., C.E. Van Horn, and M.K. Marvel. 1979. "Explaining Benefit Distribution in CETA Programs," *Journal of Human Resources* 14 (Spring):171–96.
Blalock, H.M. 1972. *Social Statistics.* New York: McGraw-Hill.
Borus, M.E. 1978. "Indicators of CETA Peformance," *Industrial and Labor Relations Review* 32:3–14.
Clague, E., and L. Kramer. 1976. *Manpower Policies and Programs: A Review: 1935–1975.* Kalamazoo, Mich.: Upjohn Institute.
Cohn, J. 1971. *The Conscience of the Corporations: Business and Urban Affairs, 1967–1970.* Baltimore: Johns Hopkins Univ. Press
Committee for Economic Development Research and Policy Committee. 1978. *Jobs for the Hard-to-Employ: New Directions for a Public-Private Partnership.* New York: CED (Jan.).

Congressional Quarterly, Inc. 1965. *Congress and the Nation*, vol. 1. Washington, D.C.: CQ.
————. 1966. *Congressional Quarterly Almanac, 1965*. Washington D.C.: CQ.
————. 1969. *Congress and the Nation*, vol. 2. Washington, D.C.: CQ.
————. 1974. *Congressional Quarterly Almanac, 1973*. Washington, D.C.: CQ.
Dalton, T.C., and L.C. Fitzpatrick. 1983. "The Effects of Federal Policy on State and Local Governance Processes," paper prepared for delivery to Western Political Science Association meeting (March).
Davidson, R.H. 1972. *The Politics of Comprehensive Manpower Legislation*. Baltimore: Johns Hopkins Univ. Press.
Davies, D.G. 1971. "The Efficiency of Public vs. Private Firms: The Case of Australia's Two Airlines," *Journal of Law and Economics* (April).
Davis, O.A., M.A.H. Dempster, and A. Wildavsky. 1966. "A Theory of the Budgetary Process," *American Political Science Review* 60 (Sept.): 529–47.
deLone, R.H. 1978. "Youth Employment and the Private Sector," in National Commission for Manpower Policy, *Increasing Job Opportunities in the Private Sector: A Conference Report*. Washington, D.C.: NCMP (Nov.).
Dement, E.F. 1981. "North Carolina Balance-of-State: Decentralization and Discontinuity," in S.A. Levitan and G.L. Mangum, eds., *The T in CETA*. Kalamazoo, Mich.: Upjohn Institute.
Dommel, P.R., and associates. 1982. *Decentralizing Urban Policy: Case Studies in Community Development*. Washington, D.C.: Brookings Institution.
Elazar, D.J. 1962. *The American Partnership*. Chicago: Univ. of Chicago Press.
Employment and Training Reporter. A weekly journal of developments in employment and training policy. Washington, D.C.: Bureau of National Affairs. Specific dates are cited in the text.
Finifter, D.H. 1980. *An Analysis of Two-Year Post-Program Earnings Paths of CETA Participants Using Early CLMS Cohorts* (Jan. 1975–June 1975 Entry). Washington, D.C.: U.S. Department of Labor, Employment and Training Administration, Office of Program Evaluation (Dec.).

Fiorina, M.P. 1977. *Congress: Keystone of the Washington Establishment.* New Haven: Yale Univ. Press.

Franklin, G.A. 1977. "Federalism in Action: Manpower Revenue Sharing," in R.B. Ripley and G.A. Franklin, eds., *National Government and Policy in the United States.* Itasca, Ill.: Peacock.

Franklin, G.A., and R.B. Ripley. 1983. "An Evaluation of the Public-Private Partnerships in the Private Sector Initiative Program," *Journal of Health and Human Resources Administration* 6 (Summer): 185–208.

Gay, R.S., and M.E. Borus. 1980. "Validating Performance Indicators for Employment and Training Programs," *Journal of Human Resources* 15:29–48.

Gist, J.R. 1974. "Mandatory Expenditures and the Defense Sector: Theory of Budget Incrementalism," *Sage Professional Papers in American Politics,* no. 20.

Goodman, M.R. 1982. "Programmatic Conflict in Public/Private Programs: The Case of the Private Sector Initiative Program," Ph.D. Dissertation, Ohio State Univ.

Government Accounting Office. 1982a. CETA *Programs for Disadvantaged Adults—What Do We Know about Their Enrollees, Services, and Effectiveness?* Report GAO/IPE-82-2. Washington, D.C.

———. 1982b. *Lessons Learned from Past Block Grants: Implications for Congressional Oversight.* Report GAO/IPE-82-8. Washington, D.C.

———. 1983. *Federal Job Training: A Comparison of Public and Private Sector Performance.* Report GAO/IPE-83-5. Washington, D.C.

Grodzins, M. 1960. "The Federal System," in *A Report of the President's Commission on National Goals:* ch. 12. Prentice-Hall: Englewood Cliffs, N.J.

Hale, G.E., and M.L. Palley. 1981. *The Politics of Federal Grants.* Washington, D.C.: Congressional Quarterly.

Hargrove, E.C., and G. Dean. 1980. "Federal Authority and Grass Roots Accountability: The Case of CETA," *Policy Analysis* 6 (Spring):127–150.

Hill, P.T., and E.L. Marks. 1982. *Federal Influence over State and Local Government: The Case of Nondiscrimination in Education.* Report prepared for the National Institute of Education (no. R-2868-NIEO). Santa Monica, Calif.: Rand Publications (Dec.).

240 CETA: *Politics and Policy, 1973-1982*

Jaffe, N. 1978. *Private Industry Council Development.* Philadelphia: Corporation for Public/Private Ventures (Oct.).

Jones, C.O. 1975. *Clean Air: The Policies and Politics of Pollution Control.* Pittsburgh: Univ. of Pittsburgh Press.

Kettl, D.F. 1980. *Managing Community Development in the New Federalism.* New York: Praeger.

————. 1981a. "The Fourth Face of Federalism," *Public Administration Review* 41 (May/June):366–371.

————. 1981b. "Regulating the Cities," *Publius* 11 (Spring): 111–125.

Levitan, S.A. 1973. *Programs in Aid of the Poor for the 1970s,* rev. ed. Baltimore: John Hopkins Univ. Press.

Levitan, S.A. and G.L. Mangum, eds. 1981. *The T in CETA: Local and National Perspectives.* Kalamazoo, Mich.: Upjohn Institute.

Levitan, S.A., G.L. Mangum, and R. Marshall. 1976. *Human Resources and Labor Markets,* 2nd ed. New York: Harper and Row.

Levitan, S.A., G.L. Mangum, and R. Taggart III. 1970. *Economic Opportunity in the Ghetto: The Partnership of Government and Business.* Baltimore: Johns Hopkins Univ. Press.

Levitan, S.A., and J.K. Zickler. 1974. *The Quest for a Workable Manpower Partnership.* Cambridge, Mass.: Harvard Univ. Press.

Lindblom, C.E. 1959. "The 'Science' of Muddling Through," *Public Administration Review* 19 (Spring):79–88.

Lowi, T.J. 1979. *The End of Liberalism,* 2nd ed. New York: W.W. Norton.

Mangum, G.L. 1981. "Twenty Years of Employment and Training Programs: Whatever Happened to the Consensus?", in G.L. Mangum, ed., *CETA Results and Redesign.* Washington, D.C.: National Council on Employment Policy (June).

Mangum, G.L., and D. Snedeker. 1974. *Manpower Planning for Local Labor Markets.* Salt Lake City: Olympus.

Mangum, G.L., and J. Walsh. 1973. *A Decade of Manpower Development and Training.* Salt Lake City: Olympus.

Mathematica Policy Research, Inc. 1978. *Evaluation of the Economic Impact of the Job Corps Program—First Followup Report* (MEL 79-04). Washington D.C.: U.S. Department of Labor, Employment and Training Administration, Office of Program Evaluation (Dec.).

————. 1980. *Evaluation of the Economic Impact of the Job Corps Program—Second Followup Report* (MEL 80-07).

Washington, D.C.: U.S. Department of Labor, Employment and Training Administration, Office of Program Evaluation (April).

McPherson, R. 1976. "CETA: The Basic Assumptions and Future Prospects," in National Commission for Manpower Policy, *A Collection of Policy Papers Prepared for Three Regional Conferences*, special report no. 14:195–214. Washington: NCMP (Dec.).

MDC, Inc. 1982a. *PIC Roles and Employment Generating Services: Types, Outcomes and Policies, Final Report.* Chapel Hill, N.C.: MDC, Inc. (March).

———. 1982b. *Tracking the Transition: Early State Level Preparations for JTPA Implementation.* Report prepared for National Commission for Employment Policy. Chapel Hill, N.C.: MDC, Inc. (Dec.).

Mirengoff, W., and L. Rindler. 1976. *The Comprehensive Employment and Training Act.* Washington, D.C.: National Academy of Sciences.

———. 1978. *CETA Manpower Programs Under Local Control.* Washington, D.C.: National Academy of Sciences.

Mirengoff, W., and associates. 1980. *The New CETA: Effect on Public Service Employment Programs, Final Report.* Washington, D.C.: National Academy Press.

———. 1982. *CETA: Accomplishments, Problems, and Solutions.* Kalamazoo, Mich. Upjohn Institute.

Mosher, F.C. 1980. "The Changing Responsibilities and Tactics of the Federal Government," *Public Administration Review* 40 (Nov./Dec.):541–547.

Natchez, P.B., and I.C. Bupp. 1973. "Policy and Priority in the Budgetary Process," *American Political Science Review* 67 (Sept.):951–963.

Nathan, R.P., A.D. Manvel, S.E. Calkins, and associates. 1975. *Monitoring Revenue Sharing.* Washington, D.C.: Brookings.

Nathan, R.P., C.F. Adams, Jr., and associates. 1977. *Revenue Sharing: The Second Round.* Washington, D.C.: Brookings.

National Commission for Manpower Policy. 1978. *An Enlarged Role for the Private Sector in Federal Employment and Training Programs.* Fourth Annual Report. Washington, D.C.: NCMP (Dec.).

Patterson, S.C., R.H. Davidson, and R.B. Ripley. 1982. *A More Perfect Union*, rev. ed. Homewood, Ill.: Dorsey Press.

Perry, C.R., et al. 1975. *The Impact of Government Manpower Programs.* Philadelphia: Univ. of Pennsylvania Press.

Ripley, R.B. 1981. "Management of the CETA System," in G.L. Mangum, ed., *CETA Results and Redesign.* Washington: National Council on Employment Policy (June).

Ripley, R.B., and G.A. Franklin, eds. 1975. *Policy-Making in the Federal Executive Branch.* New York: Free Press.

―――. 1981. *Private Sector Involvement in Employment and Training Programs.* Paper prepared for the National Commission on Employment Policy. Washington: NCMP (Dec.).

―――. 1982. *Bureaucracy and Policy Implementation.* Homewood, Ill.: Dorsey Press.

―――. 1983. "The Private Sector in Public Employment and Training Programs," *Policy Studies Review* 2 (May):695–714.

―――. 1984. *Congress, the Bureaucracy, and Public Policy,* 3rd ed. Homewood, Ill.: Dorsey Press.

Ripley, R.B., and associates. 1977. *The Implementation of CETA in Ohio.* R&D Monograph #44, U.S. Department of Labor, Employment and Training Administration. Washington, D.C.: USGPO.

―――. 1978. *CETA Prime Sponsor Management Decisions and Program Goal Achievement.* R&D Monograph #56. U.S. Department of Labor, Employment and Training Administration. Washington, D.C.: USGPO.

―――. 1979a. *A Formative Evaluation of the Private Sector Initiative Program: First Interim Report.* Washington, D.C.: U.S. Department of Labor, Employment and Training Administration, Office of Program Evaluation, MEL 79-14 (May).

―――. 1979b. *A Formative Evaluation of the Private Sector Initiative Program: Second Interim Report.* Washington, D.C.: U.S. Department of Labor, Employment and Training Administration, Office of Program Evaluation, MEL 79-21 (Oct.).

―――. 1979c. *The Implementation of HIRE II: Final Report.* Washington, D.C.: U.S. Department of Labor, Employment and Training Administration, Office of Program Evaluation, MEL 79-17 (July).

―――. 1979d. *Areawide Planning in CETA.* R&D Monograph #74, U.S. Department of Labor, Employment and Training Administration. Washington, D.C.: USGPO.

―――. 1980a. *A Formative Evaluation of the Private Sector Initiative Program: Third Interim Report.* Washington, D.C.: U.S. Department of Labor, Employment and Training Administration, Office of Program Evaluation, MEL 80-02 (Jan.)

―――. 1980b. *A Formative Evaluation of the Private Sector*

Initiative Program: Fourth Interim Report. Washington, D.C.: U.S. Department of Labor, Employment and Training Administration, Office of Program Evaluation, MEL 80-12 (Aug.).

———. 1981a. *A Formative Evaluation of the Private Sector Initiative Program: Fifth Interim Report.* Washington, D.C.: U.S. Department of Labor, Employment and Training Administration, Office of Program Evaluation, MEL 81-02 (Jan.)

———. 1981b. *A Formative Evaluation of the Private Sector Initiative Program: Sixth Interim Report.* Washington, D.C.: U.S. Department of Labor, Employment and Training Administration, Office of Program Evaluation, MEL 81-10 (May).

———. 1981c. *A Formative Evaluation of the Private Sector Initiative Program: Final Report.* Washington, D.C.: U.S. Department of Labor, Employment and Training Administration, Office of Program Evaluation, MEL 81-13 (Nov.).

Rivlin, A.M. 1974. "Social Policy: Alternate Strategies for the Federal Government," Brookings Institution General Series Reprint 288.

Robison, D. 1978. "The Attitudes of Employers and Business Professionals toward Government Manpower Programs," in National Commission for Manpower Policy, *Increasing Job Opportunities in the Private Sector: A Conference Report.* Washington, D.C.: NCMP (Nov.).

Ruttenberg, S.H., and J. Gutchess. 1970. *Manpower Challenge of the 1970s: Institutions and Social Change.* Baltimore: Johns Hopkins Univ. Press.

Savas, E.S. 1978. "Policy Analysis for Local Governments: Public vs. Private Refuse Collection," in H.F. Freeman, ed., *Policy Studies Annual Review,* vol. 2. Beverly Hills, Calif.: Sage.

Sawhill, I.V. 1978. Remarks at the Conference on the Business Role in Employment Policy, sponsored by the National Commission for Manpower Policy. NCMP Special Report 31: 67–74. Washington, D.C.: NCMP (Nov.).

Sawyer, J.W. 1974. *Crucial Elements in Manpower Planning.* Salt Lake City: Univ. of Utah Human Resources Institue.

Saxon, W. 1982. "Strong U.S. Job Training Role Urged," *New York Times* (May 5).

Seessel, T.V. 1980. *Making the Connections: Private Industry Councils, A New Direction for CETA.* Philadelphia: Public/Private Ventures (Feb.).

Shultz, G. 1970. Testimony at hearings of the Subcommittee on Employment, Manpower, and Poverty, U.S. Seante Committee on Labor and Public Welfare, *Manpower Development and Training Legislation, 1970.* Part I. Washington, D.C.: USGPO.

Smith, T.J. 1981. *Private Sector Initiative Program: CETA Title VII Implementation in 17 Study Sites: Third Interim Report.* Philadelphia: Public/Private Ventures (May).

——. 1982. *Private Sector Initiative Program: Documentation and Assessment of CETA Title VII Implementation, Final Report.* Philadelphia: Public/Private Ventures (April).

Snedeker, B.B., and D.M. Snedeker. 1978. *CETA: Decentralization on Trial.* Salt Lake City: Olympus.

Spann, R.M. 1977. "Public vs. Private Provision of Government Services," in T.E. Borcherding, ed. *Budgets and Bureaucrats: The Source of Government Growth.* Durham, N.C.: Duke Univ. Press.

Sundquist, J.L. 1969. *Making Federalism Work.* Washington, D.C.: Brookings.

Taggart, R. 1981. *A Fisherman's Guide: An Assessment of Training and Remediation Strategies.* Kalamazoo, Mich. Upjohn Institute.

U.S. Department of Labor, Employment and Training Administration. 1975. "Number of Service Deliverers Increased Under CETA," *ETA Interchange* (Oct. 1).

U.S. Executive Office of the President. 1983. *The Budget of the United States, 1984.* Washington, D.C.: USGPO.

Van Horn, C.E. 1978. "Implementing CETA: The Federal Role," *Policy Analysis* 4 (Spring):159–183.

——. 1979. *Policy Implementation in the Federal System.* Lexington, Mass.: Lexington Books.

Van Horn, C.E., D. Ford, and R. Beauregard. 1983. *A Comparative Analysis of the Targeted Jobs Demonstration Program Sites.* Report for the Department of Housing and Urban Development. New Brunswick, N.J.: Rutgers Univ.

Westat, Inc. 1981. *Continuous Longitudinal Manpower Survey. Net Impact Report No. 1: Impact on 1977 Earnings of New FY 76 Enrollees in Selected Program Activities.* Washington, D.C.: U.S. Department of Labor, Employment and Training Administration, Office of Program Evaluation (March).

Westat, Inc. 1982. *Continuous Longitudinal Manpower Survey. Net Impact Report No. 1 (Supplement No. 1): 1978 Earnings Gains of Participants Enrolled July 1975 to June 1976.* Washington, D.C.: U.S. Department of Labor, Employment and Training Administration, Office of Program Evaluation (Nov.).

Williams, W. 1971. *Social Policy Research and Analysis: The Experience in the Federal Social Agencies.* New York: American Elsevier.

————. 1980. *Government by Agency: Lessons from the Social Program Grants-in-Aid Experience.* New York: Academic Press.

Wurzburg, G. 1980. *Youth and the Local Employment Agenda: An Analysis of Prime Sponsor Experience Implementing the Youth Employment and Demonstration Projects Act: Overview and Summaries.* Washington, D.C.: National Council on Employment Policy (Jan.).

Index

CETA: *Politics and Policy, 1973–1982* has been composed into type on a Linotron 202N digital phototypesetter in ten point Trump Medieval with two points of spacing between the lines. The book was designed by Frank O. Williams, typeset by Williams of Chattanooga, printed offset by Thomson-Shore, Inc., and bound by John H. Dekker & Sons. The paper on which the book is printed carries acid-free characteristics formulated for an effective shelf life of at least three hundred years.

THE UNIVERSITY OF TENNESSEE PRESS : KNOXVILLE